ArtScroll Judaica Classics®

Rabbi Nosson Scherman / Rabbi Meir Zlotowitz

General Editors

Darash

VOLUME II

translated by
Rabbi Eliezer Eisenberg
and Rabbi Yisroel Weiss

Prepared for Publication by
Rabbi Yosaif Asher Weiss

דרש משה

Moshe

A selection of
RABBI MOSHE FEINSTEIN'S
choice comments on the Torah

Published by

Mesorah Publications, ltd

FIRST EDITION
First Impression . . . February 1998

Published and Distributed by
MESORAH PUBLICATIONS, Ltd.
4401 Second Avenue
Brooklyn, New York 11232

Distributed in Europe by
J. LEHMANN HEBREW BOOKSELLERS
20 Cambridge Terrace
Gateshead, Tyne and Wear
England NE8 1RP

Distributed in Israel by
SIFRIATI / A. GITLER — BOOKS
10 Hashomer Street
Bnei Brak 51361

Distributed in Australia & New Zealand by
GOLDS BOOK & GIFT CO.
36 William Street
Balaclava 3183, Vic., Australia

Distributed in South Africa by
KOLLEL BOOKSHOP
Shop 8A Norwood Hypermarket
Norwood 2196, Johannesburg, South Africa

ARTSCROLL JUDAICA CLASSICS®
DARASH MOSHE ON THE TORAH — VOL. II
© Copyright 1998, by MESORAH PUBLICATIONS, Ltd.
4401 Second Avenue / Brooklyn, N.Y. 11232 / (718) 921-9000

ISBN
1-57819-158-0 (hard cover)
1-57819-159-9 (paperback)

Typography by Compuscribe at ArtScroll Studios, Ltd.

Printed in the United States of America by Noble Book Press
Bound by Sefercraft, Quality Bookbinders, Ltd. Brooklyn, N.Y.

Dedicated to the memory
of our beloved father

ר׳ שלום יעקב ב״ר צבי ז״ל

נפטר א׳ טבת, תשי״ט

תנצב״ה

He came to these shores as a young man
in the early part of this century
and fought the battle for Torah and *Yiddishkeit*
against the overwhelming assimilationist trends
of his day.

His *tzedakah,* kindness and *chesed*
towards family and community
were his hallmark.

May the *tzedakah* given
to enable publication and distribution
of this important volume be
an uplifting for his *neshamah.*

יחיאל מיכל ועטרה דזשייקאב ומשפחתם

Marvin and Atara Jacob and Family

לזכר נשמת

הרב שמעון הירש בן יוסף שאול ז״ל
יב׳ טבת תשנ״ה

וזוגתו האשה אסתר רבקה בת הרב אהרן יצחק ע״ה
ו׳ מר חשון תשנ״ה

Rabbi Henry and Esther Soille, ע״ה

A generous contribution was given to the

Kollel Beth Medrash L'Torah V'Horoah

in their memory

תשורת שי לזכות זכרון נפשות

רפאל יצחק בן אפרים ליפר ז״ל
נפ׳ כ״ז טבת תש״ן

ורעיתו מלכה בת אריה ליב ע״ה
נפ׳ כ״ה תשרי תשנ״ז

ישראל מנחם בן הלל גערשאן ז״ל
נפ׳ טז כסלו תשל״ג

ורעיתו שרה רבקה בת אליעזר הכהן ע״ה
נפ׳ ל׳ סיון תשנ״ז

אנחנו משתתפים להפיץ ספר זה
לשם הרבצת התורה

מאת בניהם
אפרים ורעיתו חיה פעשא שיחיו ליפר
ונכדידם
אריה ורעיתו חנה אסתר ליפר
ובניהם
תמר עטרה, עליזה רחל, ואברהם דוד חיים שיחיו

אברהם חיים ורעיתו יעל דפנה ליפר
ובתם
תליה נחמה שיחיו
צבי דוד ורעיתו טובה קרעמער
ובנם
ישראל רפאל יצחק שיחיו

מצבת זכרון

ר׳ אליהו ב״ר אליעזר ז״ל
נפטר כ״ח שבט

וזוגתו יעטע בת ר׳ משה הכהן ע״ה
נפטרה יו״ד כסלו

❧❧❧

ר׳ יוסף ב״ר שמעון ז״ל
נפטר י״ג מנחם אב

וזוגתו בילא בת ר׳ גדליה ע״ה
נפטרה ח׳ אדר

❧❧❧

הילד אליהו ב״ר יוסף שמעון ע״ה
נפטר י״ב מנחם אב

תנצב״ה

נר זכרון

לע"נ ידיד נאמן של מרן ראש הישיבה שליט"א

וידיד מסור לישיבתינו הקדושה

חכם רפאל ע"ה

בן חכם רבי חייא זצ"ל

ומלכה בת ר' אליהו זצ"ל

בן בנו של הדיין המצויין המפורסם

לשם ותהילה חה"ש מאור הגולה

הרב הדיין חכם רפאל אריה ס"ט זצוק"ל מקשאן-פרס.

נלב"ע במוצאי שבת קודש ד' שבט התשנ"ז

תנצב"ה

עד אשר יקיצו וירננו שוכני עפר

יהיה זכרו ברוך

הונצח ע"י

מתיבתא תפארת ירושלים

לעילוי נשמת

האשה החשובה והצנועה

מרת גאלדא רייזל בת ר׳ נפתלי ביוביץ ע״ה

נלב״ע ח׳ מר חשון תשנ״ח

תנצב״ה

ונתתי להם בביתי ובחומתי יד ושם

נר לזכרון

לעילוי נשמת

הגה״צ הרב מרדכי אשר בר׳ דוד הלוי זצ״ל

ט׳ כסלו תשנ״ח

ורעיתו

הרבנית הצדקנית רבקה רויזא בת ר׳ אברהם ע״ה

ט״ו מר חשון תשנ״ה

למשפחת ספרנגער

הונצח ע״י משפחתם

לזכרון נצח

In loving memory of our dear parents

Joseph and Bess Wasserman ז"ל

יוסף בן דוב בער ע"ה

ט' טבת תש"מ

בילא בת יעקב ע"ה

י"ב סיון תשמ"ב

Sascha and Regina (Czaczkes) Charles ז"ל

שמריהו בן משה ע"ה

י"ח אלול תשל"ב

רבקה בת הרב יוסף הכהן ע"ה

ט"ו תמוז תשכ"ז

They were our inspiration in life
and their memory continues to light our way —
their mesiras nefesh for family,
community and Jewish children;
their endless quest for learning,
and their love of Klal Yisrael were the bridge
from a rich past to an unfolding future.

Dedicated by

Stanley and Ellen Wasserman

Dedicated in Memory of

my beloved wife

Gertrude Greenfield, ע״ה

by

Dr. Samuel Greenfield

Dedicated by

Mr. and Mrs. Hermann Merkin

לזכר נשמת

האשה מינדל בת ר׳ משולם ע״ה

Kate Ettlinger Goldner

and in honor of

Mr. Charles Goldner

and

Mr. and Mrs. Isadore Gibber

Dedicated by their children

Debbie and Elliot Gibber

לעילוי נשמת – בשערי תורה

ר׳ ישראל אריה ב״ר שמואל הכהן ע״ה

נפ׳ כ״א כסלו תשל״ח

יהי זכרו ברוך

❧❦❧

Dedicated to the Memory of

צירל בת יעקב

Irene Weisel

דוד בן אברהם

David Weisel

אהרון ליב בן משה הלוי

Aaron Louis Gononsky

**Arthur, Susan, Jeffrey and Debbie
Gononsky**

In memory of our dear parents
Victor and Pessy Pesso
Irving and Adele Markowitz

Dedicated by their children
Mr. and Mrs. Jack Pesso

In memory of
Adele Klein

Dedicated by
Loretta and Herb Mehl

Mesiftha Tifereth Jerusalem

thanks all those who

made dedications in this sefer

but wished to remain anonymous

❧ Table of Contents

ספר בראשית ❧

Sefer Bereishis

פרשת בראשית
Parashas Bereishis

וְהָאָרֶץ הָיְתָה תֹהוּ וָבֹהוּ וְחֹשֶׁךְ עַל־פְּנֵי תְהוֹם וְרוּחַ אֱלֹקִים מְרַחֶפֶת עַל־פְּנֵי הַמָּיִם — *When the earth was bewilderment and void, with the darkness over the surface of the deep, and the breath of God was hovering upon the surface of the waters (1:2).*

W hat was the source of the bewilderment spoken of in this verse? *Rashi* attempts to explain this by telling us that conditions prior to the Creation were such that "a person is astonished and baffled over the void within it." This is quite difficult to understand. What was astonishing, baffling, or bewildering about the lack of creation? One would think that the opposite should be true. It is the presence of Hashem's Creation that one should find astonishing. For as David Hamelech says, *"The heavens declare the glory of God, and the firmament tells of his handiwork"* (Tehillim 19:2). The Creation is so great and wondrous that it itself, by virtue of its very existence, declares the existence of a Divine creator. Furthermore, since prior to Hashem's Creation there was no person nor any other type of creation in existence to experience this feeling of astonishment, what is the purpose of this description?

There is indeed a great lesson to learn from this verse. When Hashem imbues a person with the potential to learn His Torah and to accomplish great things, and that person does not make use of his God-given abilities, that is something that we must find astonishing. We should be bewildered by the laziness and other factors that would prevent a person from doing the great things that Hashem has made him capable of. It is this concept that the verse wished to introduce to us prior to recording the Creation. Since Hashem had the ability to create the universe and had not yet done so, the lack of creation was a source of bewilderment.

❧ ❧ ❧

וַיִּקְרָא אֱלֹקִים לָרָקִיעַ שָׁמָיִם — *God called the firmament: "Heavens"* (1:8).

Rashi comments that the word שָׁמַיִם is actually a contraction of the words אֵשׁ, *fire*, and מַיִם, *water*. *Rashi* goes on to explain that Hashem joined fire and water — two things that physically cannot coexist — and from the combination created the heavens. It is for this reason that in our *tefillos* we praise Hashem as *He who makes peace in His heights* (*Iyov* 25:2). Why did Hashem choose to utilize the combination of two items that can only mix as the result of a miracle?

Hashem wished to teach us that the fusing of opposites is a necessary part of our everyday life. When we develop our character traits, it is not enough to cleanse ourselves of traits that we deem negative, while strengthening those that are positive. We must strive to force the two to work together. For example, a person may put tremendous effort into acquiring the trait of humility, learning to always be forgiving of any slights to his honor. Yet, he must always retain an understanding of the attribute of haughtiness — lest he fail to accord his fellow man the honor he deserves. The same lesson applies to the way in which someone treats money. While it is commendable to be generous when giving of one's own monetary resources to worthwhile causes, a person must be stingy in regard to someone else's money. Should a healthy lack of regard for money extend to a disregard of other's money, the road is paved for a lifetime of thievery.

Hashem made peace between the opposites above us. It is our task to make peace between the attributes buried inside us. Only when all of our attributes have been fused together — complimenting each other to serve Hashem — will we be considered ourselves to be at peace. (See also *Darash Moshe* vol. I to *Bamidbar* 19:1.)

❧ ❧ ❧

וַיִּיצֶר ה' אֱלֹקִים אֶת־הָאָדָם עָפָר מִן־הָאֲדָמָה וַיִּפַּח בְּאַפָּיו
נִשְׁמַת חַיִּים וַיְהִי הָאָדָם לְנֶפֶשׁ חַיָּה — *And Hashem*
God formed the man of soil from the earth, and
blew into his nostrils the soul of life; and man
became a living soul (2:7).

R ashi comments: "Animal and beast too were called 'living soul,'
but this soul of man is the most alive of them all, for there was
added to it the faculties of reasoning and speech." (*Targum*
Onkelos refers to the living soul as a "speaking soul," without
mentioning the human's power of reasoning. *Rashi* apparently felt that
the power of speech unaccompanied by the ability to reason would not
be worthy of mention.) While we see from *Rashi* that the living soul of
man is somehow more alive than that of other beings, the purpose of this
living soul is the same in all living creatures. It is this living soul that all
beings utilize for all of their material pursuits. Eating, drinking, and all
other physical needs that are shared by all life on this earth are the
domain of this living soul.

There is, though, a major difference between man and all other life —
and it is portrayed in the above verse. When Hashem created man, He
first *"blew into his nostrils the soul of life,"* and only then did man
become "a living soul." Hashem first imbued man with a *neshamah*, a
spiritual soul with a higher calling, and only then equipped him with the
living soul necessary for his physical needs. This is what makes man
different than any other life form. While our needs may be similar, our
purposes are not. The physical domain of our "living soul" is secondary,
it is only there as a tool to be utilized by our *neshamah* in our pursuit of
Torah and *mitzvos*.

This is something that a person would do well to think about. If not for
our *neshamah*, the part of us that is equipped to become closer to
Hashem through the study of His Torah and adherence to His *mitzvos*,
we would have never received the "living soul" that is our physical life —
because we simply would have had no purpose at all.

❧ ❧ ❧

פרשת נח
Parashas Noach

אֵלֶּה תּוֹלְדֹת נֹחַ נֹחַ אִישׁ צַדִּיק — *These are the offspring of Noach — Noach was a righteous man* (6:9).

R*ashi* comments: From this verse we learn that the main offspring of the righteous are their good deeds. The Talmud (*Moed Katan* 27b) tells us that the verse (*Yirmeyahu* 22:10) which states, *weep rather for the one who went away,* is a reference to one who passed on without leaving behind any children. We may infer from the above *Rashi* that this was not stated regarding people who have good deeds, for these people are considered to have offspring.

In light of this we can also understand the verses in *Yeshayahu* (55:5-6). Hashem comforts those who are barren by telling them that if they keep the commandment not to desecrate the Shabbos, and they follow the will of Hashem, they will have something *better* than children. After seeing *Rashi's* comment here, we can explain that the good deeds amassed by the keeping of the commandments are themselves the equivalent of having children. Indeed, Hashem says that they are better than children — for it is better to have good deeds without children than to have children while being barren of good deeds.

❧ ❧ ❧

While it is true that the main offspring of the righteous are their good deeds, this would hardly seem to apply to Noach. With regard to Noach it would seem that his main offspring were his physical offspring — i.e., his children. After all, Noach's children were the key to beginning new life in the world after the Flood. This was certainly an objective as important to Hashem as the Creation itself. As such, how is it possible to say that Noach's deeds were more beloved than his children — the progenitors of all future human life? If the verse desired to teach us this lesson, it should have been taught someplace else, at a time where the children involved were not imperative to the survival of life. Then we would be able to see that although children are beloved, good deeds are even more beloved before Hashem.

It appears that this verse is coming to teach us that while sustaining life in the world is certainly of great import to Hashem, it is only a means to a desired end. If not for the good deeds of the righteous people (Noach and his family) that He placed in the world to continue life, Hashem would not find sustaining the world worthwhile. Hashem has no desire to perpetuate the raising of evil generations that are bereft of any good deeds. For this reason, the verse chooses Noach as the example to teach us that the main offspring of a person is his good deeds. For while it is true that his physical offspring were vital for the continuation of life, it was only his spiritual offspring — his good deeds — that gave value to such a continuation.

In light of this explanation, we can also understand another comment of *Rashi*. The verse writes concerning the birth of Noach: *Lemech lived one hundred and eighty-two years, and he begot a son (Bereishis 5:28).* The language used in this verse is a departure from the similar verses that precede it. The other verses mention the name of the son that was born, while this verse first states *he begot a son,* and only in the next verse introduces the name of the son (Noach). *Rashi* explains that the verse wished to use the Hebrew word for *son (bein),* because it is linguistically related to the Hebrew word meaning to build (*boneh*); the intent of the verse is to hint that Noach was destined to be the one to rebuild the world. However, a difficulty can be raised: Why was this distinction bestowed upon Noach alone? As Noach's father, Lemech too was the father of all future humanity! In light of the previous explanation, however, we can explain that it is not Noach's position as progenitor of mankind that *Rashi* is addressing. Rather, *Rashi* is saying that the verse wishes to point out that only Noach, whom the verse calls a righteous, perfect man, was fit to be the rebuilder of the world.

We find this concept portrayed in another *Rashi* as well. *Rashi* tells us that the Tanna Reb Yehoshua said: "While Hashem knew that the destiny of the generation of the Flood was to sin and suffer destruction, he still did not refrain from creating them, for the sake of the righteous destined to arise from among them." From this *Rashi* it can be seen that the generation of the Flood, a generation of evil people deserving of destruction, would have been worthless in Hashem's eyes if not for the righteous people destined to descend from them.

❧ ❧ ❧

We may advance another reason why it is most appropriate for the verse to teach us this lesson through the family of Noach. With Noach we see a direct correlation between his good deeds and his children. Unlike the others of his generation, who bore children at a much earlier age, Noach did not have children until the age of 500. When Noach eventually did have children, he only had three — Shem, Cham, and Yafes. *Rashi* comments that Noach did not have children in his earlier years because Hashem "suppressed his fount," causing him to be infertile until his later years. Why was Noach destined to have only three children?

The answer is that Hashem did not wish Noach to have children that might be influenced by the evils of their generation — thus becoming liable to perish along with the rest of mankind. Hashem therefore granted Noach three children — the exact amount that Hashem in His wisdom knew Noach would be able to influence and imbue with his own positive traits. Thus "the main offspring of the righteous are their good deeds," for it is the good deeds of the righteous that will determine the number of offspring that they will be able to have.

This rule does not apply only to Noach. The blessing of offspring is not one granted haphazardly. Hashem analyzes each righteous individual, determining how many sons and daughters they will be able to influence properly. Hashem then grants children to each person according to his abilities.

❧ ❧ ❧

וַיַּעַשׂ נֹחַ כְּכֹל אֲשֶׁר־צִוָּהוּ ה' — *And Noach did according to everything that Hashem had commanded him* (7:5).

Rashi comments that this verse refers to Noach's actual entry into the Ark. Accordingly, the verse would seem to be telling us that Noach entered the Ark solely as a result of Hashem's command. This, however, would seem to be in direct contradiction to a later *Rashi*.

Two verses later, the verse states that Noach and his family came to the Ark *because of the waters of the Flood. Rashi* comments over there that Noach did not enter the Ark "until the waters compelled him to." This *Rashi* would seem to indicate that Noach entered the Ark under the duress of the oncoming waters, and not solely as a result of Hashem's command, as indicated by the earlier *Rashi.*

We can explain that both of *Rashi's* comments are indeed true. The Talmud tells us (*Sanhedrin* 108b) that life in the Ark was not luxurious by any means. The amount of work necessary to care for all of the various species of animals that were aboard was immense. If not for Hashem's commandment to enter the Ark, Noach would have waited, faithfully, believing that Hashem would save him in a different, easier fashion. For this reason, *Rashi* comments that Noach entered the Ark because of Hashem's command. However, while it is true that Noach lovingly accepted the decree of Hashem that his salvation was to come in the form that it did, it is also true that when the waters actually came and Noach entered the Ark, his intention was not so much to heed the word of Hashem as it was to save the lives of himself and his family. It is for this reason that *Rashi* later comments that Noach did not enter the Ark until the waters compelled him to.

We find that after the Flood Noach rose to a higher level. Eager as he must have been to leave the Ark, he did not do so until he was commanded to by Hashem, as attested to in the verse which records Hashem's explicit commandment to Noach: *Go forth from the Ark* (8:15).

❧ ❧ ❧

וַיָּחֶל עוֹד שִׁבְעַת יָמִים אֲחֵרִים — *And he made himself wait again another seven days* (8:12).

I n this verse and in verse ten (two verses earlier), the Torah uses two slightly different words to tell us that Noach waited. *Rashi* explains that in the earlier verse the word means simply that Noach waited. However, in our verse, the later of the two, the Torah tells us that Noach had to *make himself* wait.

The Torah is showing us just how anxious Noach was to leave the Ark at last. Just as a person waiting for some special moment to arrive can find no rest and counts the very seconds until the time comes, so too Noach counted the moments while waiting to exit the Ark. We can see this from Noach's actions. Noach had just sent out the dove, which returned bearing in its mouth an olive branch — evidence that the waters had receded from the earth. Noach knew that to send out the dove again immediately would be a meaningless gesture. [Obviously, the water had yet to recede sufficiently.] Yet, the Torah tells us that Noach found this waiting difficult. As our verse says, he had to *make himself* wait.

Why does the Torah seek to stress this point? In order to show us the extreme righteousness of Noach. Despite the fact that he so desperately desired to leave the Ark, he realized that Hashem in His infinite wisdom wished him to remain inside for a predetermined amount of time. Noach understood that the Ark was more then a mere method of salvation for him and his family. Hashem could have chosen to save them in other ways. Therefore, realizing that Hashem willed him to be in the Ark, Noach did not leave until Hashem expressly commanded him to.

❄   ❄   ❄

פרשת לך לך
Parashas Lech Lecha

וַיֹּאמֶר ה' אֶל־אַבְרָם לֶךְ־לְךָ מֵאַרְצְךָ וּמִמּוֹלַדְתְּךָ וּמִבֵּית אָבִיךָ אֶל־הָאָרֶץ אֲשֶׁר אַרְאֶךָּ — *Hashem said to Avram, "Go for yourself from your land, from your birthplace, and from your father's house to the land that I will show you"* (12:1).

The Mishnah states in *Avos* (5:4): Our forefather Avraham was tested with ten trials, and he withstood them all. According to the commentaries, Hashem's command that Avraham should leave the land of Charan constituted one of these trials. This is somewhat difficult to understand. Hashem promised Avraham that should he leave Charan and travel to Canaan, he would have children and become a great nation. In the presence of such a Divine promise, why was it seen as a trial for Avraham to heed Hashem's command?

The struggle that Avraham was faced with was not the physical hardships involved in uprooting himself from Charan and relocating to a strange country. Many people travel to strange lands in the hope of providing themselves and their families with a brighter future. The struggle that Avraham overcame, and the trial that was seen as a sign of Avraham's greatness, was a true test of Avraham's faith. Avraham knew beyond any possible doubt that Hashem, the Creator of the world, was capable of doing anything that He desired. Avraham was therefore faced with the following dilemma: Granted that it was the will of Hashem that Avraham have children that were destined to become a nation devoted to the service of Hashem, why was it necessary to first travel to the land of Canaan? Avraham knew that the power of Hashem is not dependent upon location. Whatever Hashem could bring about in

Canaan, He could just as easily bring to pass in Charan. Furthermore, not only were the inhabitants of Canaan no better off spiritually than the people of Charan, they were, as *Rashi* tells us (*Vayikra* 18:3), even worse. All things considered, why was it necessary for Hashem to command him to travel to Canaan, rather than staying right where he was?

Similarly, the main trial of the Akeidah was also a trial of faith. Hashem challenged Avraham with statements that seemed to be contradictory. Hashem had told Avraham, *"through Yitzchak will offspring be considered yours"* (21:12), and, *"I will maintain my covenant through Yitzchak"* (17:21). How was it possible to reconcile these statements with Hashem's request that he should sacrifice the very same Yitzchak upon Mt. Moriah?

To Avraham's credit, none of these questions bothered him. If it was the will of Hashem that he go to Canaan, then that is what he would do. Not only did he immediately heed the command of Hashem and go to Canaan, he retained the unblemished belief that Hashem could have granted him everything that he promised him in Charan as well. If Hashem desired the sacrifice of Yitzchak, then Avraham would sacrifice Yitzchak while preserving in himself the absolute belief that all of Hashem's promises would undoubtedly come true.

Indeed, it is because the Akeidah was not only a test of the strength of Avraham's devotion to Hashem versus the love of his only son, but rather a direct challenge to his faith, that Hashem asked of Avraham, "Stand firm for me in this trial, so that they should not say that the first trials were not substantial" (*Sanhedrin* 89b). Should Avraham have failed to withstand this trial, and showed even the slightest doubt, Heaven forbid, in the ability of Hashem to fulfill His word, it would have indicated that his faith had been incomplete all along.

❧ ❧ ❧

וַיִּבֶן שָׁם מִזְבֵּחַ לַה' הַנִּרְאָה אֵלָיו . . . וַיִּבֶן־שָׁם מִזְבֵּחַ לַה' וַיִּקְרָא בְּשֵׁם ה' — *So he built an altar there to Hashem Who appeared to him . . . and he built there an altar to Hashem and invoked Hashem by Name* (12:7-8).

Avraham built two altars in honor of Hashem's Name in a short span of time. The verse tells us that he invoked Hashem by Name when building the second, something he apparently did not do when building the first. What is the meaning of this "invoking" and why did he do it by the second altar but not the first?

The Talmud tells us (*Avodah Zarah* 9b) that the emergence of Avraham as a teacher of Torah brought about the end of the Era of Desolation, and the beginning of the Era of Torah. Now, this is difficult to understand: Were there not other righteous people who taught Torah prior to the emergence of Avraham? Noah, Shem, and Ever were all righteous people who studied and taught Torah and lived hundreds of years prior to the birth of Avraham. Indeed, we know that Yaakov studied in the study halls founded by Ever for 14 years before traveling to the house of Lavan. Why, then, is the Era of Torah considered to have begun only in the time of Avraham?

To answer this question, we may explain that there was a major difference between the methods of those earlier *tzaddikim* and the methods of Avraham. It is true that there were many teachers of Torah prior to Avraham, but they only taught the Torah to those people who came to them in search of the way of truth. While this may have been a noble undertaking, it was not sufficient. The ranks of people who were sufficiently self-motivated to come searching of their own accord would simply be too thin to guarantee the spread of Torah. This stands in contrast to the methods of Avraham. Avraham developed a new approach. He was the first person who *actively sought out* individuals to whom he could teach Torah and thereby bring them closer to Hashem.

It is this that the verse refers to by saying that Avraham "invoked Hashem by Name." Avraham erected an altar and publicly declared it to be in honor of the Name of Hashem. No longer would the recognizing of Hashem's greatness be limited to the self-motivated few; Avraham instead would strive to introduce recognition of Hashem's Name to the masses.

However, Avraham could not begin this monumental task immediately. The Talmud tells us (*Bava Metzia* 107b): Correct yourself and then correct others; that is, if you wish to teach a concept to others, you must first be sure to master it yourself. For this reason, Avraham first built his own personal altar; only then did he build one upon which he "invoked Hashem by Name" to teach others.

Soon after Avraham arrived in the land of Canaan and began his teaching, there was a hunger in the land that forced Avraham to temporarily move to Egypt. Upon his return to Canaan the verse tells us (13:4) that he went *to the site of the altar which he had made there at first, and there Avraham invoked Hashem by Name. Rashi* comments that the phrase, *and there Avraham invoked Hashem by Name,* can be interpreted in two ways. Either it refers to Avraham's invocation of God's Name when he first erected the altar, or it means that Avraham invoked God by Name now, upon his return. Now, why is the verse telling us this here? If it is referring to the past, why is it necessary to tell it to us again? And even if it refers to the present, is it necessary to tell us that Avraham continued to do that which we already know he was doing?

To answer these questions, we must attempt to analyze events from Avraham's perspective. Heeding God's command, Avraham traveled to Canaan. As soon as he arrived and began teaching Torah, Hashem brought a hunger to the land, forcing Avraham to relocate to Mitzrayim. *Rashi* tells us (21:34) that Avraham was only in Mitzrayim for three months. This was because soon after Avraham arrived in Mitzrayim, Hashem miraculously caused the hunger to end. This sequence of events could easily have been seen by Avraham as a sign that Hashem did not want him to be the one to convey Hashem's glory to the world. Avraham rejected this thought. Despite all the adversity that Avraham faced, when he came back to Canaan he immediately returned to the site of his altar and continued his holy work. This, then, is the message of the verse. As *Rashi* explains, the verse can be understood as referring both to the past as well as the present. Thus, the verse states, and there Avraham invoked Hashem by Name: That is, he did it now in the same way and for the same reasons that he had done it before. Nothing was changed by his forced relocation to Mitzrayim.

This is a lesson that we all must learn. We are all obligated to influence and teach others to follow the ways of Hashem. This concept is contained in our morning prayers, in the blessing before the recital of *Shema*. In this prayer, each and every one of us asks Hashem to grant us the ability to both teach and learn. Just as our forefather Avraham rejected any indication or thought that he might not be obligated to teach, we, his children, must also strenuously avoid all such thoughts.

❧ ❧ ❧

וַיִּקְרָא פַרְעֹה לְאַבְרָם וַיֹּאמֶר מַה־זֹּאת עָשִׂיתָ לִּי לָמָּה
לֹא־הִגַּדְתָּ לִּי כִּי אִשְׁתְּךָ הִוא. לָמָה אָמַרְתָּ אֲחֹתִי הִוא
וָאֶקַּח אֹתָהּ לִי לְאִשָּׁה — *Pharaoh summoned Avram and said, "What is this you have done to*

me? Why did you not tell me that she is your wife? Why did you say 'She is my sister,' so that I would take her as my wife?" (12:18-19).

Twice, Avraham and Sarah were forced by hunger to leave the land of Canaan for neighboring kingdoms. In both instances they employed the ruse that Sarah was Avraham's sister, and in both instances she was taken captive by the king. Both Pharaoh and Avimelech king of Gerar, after being punished and finding out that Sarah was actually Avraham's wife, reacted with surprise and righteous indignation. Indeed, both kings asked Avraham why he had hidden the fact that Sarah was really his wife, thus creating a situation where immoral behavior could result. This, though, is where the similarity between the two stories end. While Avraham did not respond to Pharaoh's query in the above-mentioned verses, he did respond to Avimelech's. The verse tells us that Avraham answered Avimelech, *"Because I said, 'There is but no fear of God in this place and they will slay me because of my wife'"* (20:11).

Why did Avraham answer Avimelech and ignore Pharaoh? The answer is that Pharaoh knew full well the ill state of the moral fabric of his country. Had they known that Sarah was a married woman, they simply would have done away with Avraham and then taken Sarah captive. Pharaoh's words to Avraham were nothing more than mere bluster, neither requiring nor worthy of any response.

Avimelech, on the other hand, seemingly conducted the affairs of his land with some semblance of decency. He truly felt that had Avraham told them the truth, he and his wife would have been safe in his land. Because he felt this way, he asked Avraham: *"What did you see that you did such a thing?"* (20:10). Avraham therefore answered him, explaining that *"there is no fear of God in this place."* As explained by *Rashi*, Avraham perceived this weakness from the actions of the local inhabitants. Arriving in Gerar as a guest, Avraham expected to be questioned regarding his need for food and drink — not the marital status of his traveling companions. Sensing the priorities of the locals, Avraham feared that whatever decency existed there was only surface deep. Should they desire his wife, he worried that they would kill him based on some false pretense, thus justifying his death to the populace.

There is an interesting lesson to be learned here. Not always must we succumb to the urge for self-justification. There are times when the questions being asked of us do not deserve answering. These questions are rhetorical, meaningless bluster, and they are not to be answered.

❦ ❦ ❦

וְגַם־לְלוֹט הַהֹלֵךְ אֶת־אַבְרָם הָיָה צֹאן־וּבָקָר וְאֹהָלִים — And also Lot who went with Avram had flocks, cattle, and tents (13:5).

While it would appear that Lot also believed in Hashem and fulfilled the *mitzvos*, he was only able to adhere to Hashem's will when there was no difficulty involved in doing so. Where can we see this in the verse? The verse tells us that Avraham and Lot were forced to part ways as a result of a disagreement between their shepherds. The verse prefaces this by telling us, *And the land could not support them dwelling together for their possessions were abundant and they were unable to dwell together.* What was their disagreement? *Rashi* explains that Lot's dishonest shepherds grazed their flocks in other people's pastures. When Avraham's shepherds rebuked them for this, they responded that Hashem had promised the land to Avraham, and since he was childless, Lot was his heir. Avraham himself, however, disagreed with this rationale, and his flocks only grazed in public fields. The question arises: How was Lot able to justify the logic of his argument when Avraham himself — the supposed owner of the land — would not allow his shepherds to use the land? And the answer is as the verse states — because *the land could not support them.* Land suitable for grazing was in short supply. To find public land for all his flocks presented too much of a difficulty for Lot. He therefore succumbed to temptation, and allowed his shepherds to follow their twisted reasoning.

In the beginning of *Parashas Vayeira* (18:4), *Rashi* draws a contrast between Avraham and Lot. Avraham, fearing that his guests might be wilderness dwellers that worship the dust of their feet, first asked them to wash their feet and then invited them to stay the night. Lot, however, first invited his guests in, and only then asked that they wash their feet. The clear implication of this *Rashi* is that while Avraham was concerned with the prospect of a false deity entering his house, Lot was not. Further in the Parashah (19:2), however, *Rashi* seems to contradict this, for he explains that Lot had good reason to want the guests to refrain from washing their feet until they were ready to leave his house. Lot feared that, should the guests be seen in his house with clean feet, the infamous residents of Sodom, who abhorred acts of kindness, would attack him, saying: "Two or three days have already passed since they came to your house, and you did not let us know!" Unlike the previous *Rashi*, this *Rashi* implies that Lot's actions were indeed justified. How can we reconcile these two seemingly contradictory *Rashis*?

Apparently, *Rashi* understood that Lot did not feel physically threatened by the prospect of the Sodomites catching him hosting guests. (It is not possible to say that this was a life-threatening situation, for if so, Lot would *not* have been obligated to risk his life and require them to wash prior to entering. The law of "be killed and do not transgress" would not apply here, since there was no question of worshiping a false deity — only of one entering the house. Furthermore, since the guest would be bringing in the dust and not Lot himself, this would not even be considered ancillary to worshiping a false god. For Lot it was simply a question of being discomfited by a confrontation with his neighbors. *Rashi* therefore draws his contrast as follows: Avraham would have demanded that his guests wash their feet prior to entering his home despite any discomfort that this might cause him. Lot, on the other hand, was not willing to pay the price of discomfort to assure that no false deity would enter his home. (While this contrast is not clearly depicted in the verse, i.e., Avraham did not have to risk any discomfort and Lot did, *Rashi* based his comment on our knowledge of the truth — that the risk of discomfort would in no way deter Avraham from preventing a false deity from entering his home.)

※　※　※

וַיֹּאמֶר אַבְרָם אֶל־מֶלֶךְ סְדֹם הֲרִימֹתִי יָדִי אֶל־ה' קֵל עֶלְיוֹן קֹנֵה שָׁמַיִם וָאָרֶץ. אִם־מִחוּט וְעַד שְׂרוֹךְ־נַעַל וְאִם־אֶקַּח מִכָּל־אֲשֶׁר־לָךְ וְלֹא תֹאמַר אֲנִי הֶעֱשַׁרְתִּי אֶת־אַבְרָם
Avram said to the king of Sodom: "I lift up my hand to Hashem, God, the Most High, Maker of heaven and earth, if so much as a thread to a shoestrap; or if I shall take from anything of yours! So you shall not say, 'It is I who made Avram rich' " (14:22-23).

Avraham made it clear to the king of Sodom that he would not retain anything that had belonged to Sodom, lest the king claim that he was the cause of Avraham's wealth. Avraham wanted all to know that his sole benefactor was Hashem, and that He alone was responsible for any wealth that he may have. Yet, in contrast to this, we find that when Avraham and Sarah traveled to Mitzrayim, Avraham told Sarah that she should claim to be his sister, "so that it may go well with me" (12:13). Indeed, the verse relates that Avraham left Mitzrayim a wealthy individual, having received riches from Pharaoh. Similarly, Avraham willingly accepted a thousand pieces of silver from Avimelech the king of Gerar. Why is it that Avraham willingly accepted these gifts while adamantly refusing to keep any of the spoils of Sodom?

The answer lies in the intentions of Pharaoh and Avimelech when they gave their gift, as opposed to those of the king of Sodom. Hashem had promised Avraham great wealth. There are many ways that Hashem can grant a person riches. One way is through the receipt of gifts. When an individual receives a gift, it is only as a result of the fact that Hashem made the giver decide to give the gift to the recipient. Avraham thus accepted the gifts of Pharaoh and Avimelech with the realization that they were Divinely inspired — a part of the fulfillment of Hashem's words.

This thinking held true with respect to the gifts of Pharaoh and Avimelech. They had given Avraham their gifts as a means to accomplish their own ends. Pharaoh desired to honor Avraham for the sake of Sarah. Avimelech wished to appease Avraham after taking Sarah as a wife. Neither one of them had as their ultimate goal the enriching of Avraham. This, however, was not the case by the king of Sodom. What was he thinking? Avraham had just returned after defeating the kings that had made off with the spoils of Sodom. By right, the wealth of Sodom was now Avraham's to do with as he pleased. Why then did the king tell Avraham, "Give me the people and take the possessions for yourself"? It is obvious that the king, in his twisted, Sodomite way of thinking, had somehow decided that the wealth of Sodom was still his. Why, then, did he see fit to grant riches to Avraham? If the wealth was his and the people were his, why give Avraham anything? Avraham therefore realized that it was the king's intention not to make a deal with him, but rather to enrich him in return for the favor of saving his people. Such a gift Avraham knew he could not accept — lest the king say that it was he and not Hashem that had made Avraham wealthy.

※ ※ ※

וַיַּעַל אֱלֹקִים מֵעַל אַבְרָהָם — *God ascended from upon Avraham* (17:22).

There are two places where this phraseology (*from upon*) appears. The first is after Hashem gave Avraham the commandment of circumcision. The second is in *Parashas Vayishlach*, after Hashem speaks with Yaakov (35:13). On the first verse, *Rashi* comments that the phrase "from upon Avraham" is a "clean," i.e. respectful, term used to describe the way the Divine Presence took leave of Avraham. *Rashi* would seem to be basing this on the fact that the verse could have said "from Avraham" without using the seemingly extraneous word "upon." By choosing to include this word, the verse gives emphasis to God's superiority. *Rashi* comments further that we learn from this verse that "the righteous are the chariot of the Divine Presence." This is to say that in a sense, God's presence was "riding upon" Avraham, since the righteous are the means of conveying God's presence into the world. Certainly, we can say that *Rashi's* explanation holds true for the verse about Yaakov as well.

There is an underlying message to be learned here. The two appearances of the above phrase in the Torah refer to two ways a person can become worthy of being called the "chariot of the Divine Presence." As we mentioned previously, the first verse is to be found after the commandment of circumcision. The Torah refers to the commandment of circumcision as a *bris* — a covenant. This is because when the father of the child performs the circumcision, he enters into a covenant with Hashem. He accepts upon himself the responsibility to raise the child as a servant of Hashem — someone who will observe the laws of the Torah and follow the ways of Hashem all his life. This is what is necessary to become the "chariot of Hashem" — the total dedication of a person's life to the service of Hashem. This is a task that can be accomplished by anybody, in any time, and in any place. The only prerequisite is a person's own commitment to the service of Hashem.

This is the message of the first verse. The second verse appears in *Parashas Vayishlach,* at the conclusion of Yaakov's successful return trip from the house of Lavan. Yaakov traveled with his family to Beth-el and erected an altar in honor of Hashem's Name. After he did so, Hashem appeared to him and blessed him. It is at the conclusion of this blessing that we find the verse we are discussing. The verse reads as follows: *Then God ascended from upon him in the place where He had spoken with him* (35:13). Now, this verse requires explanation. Why does the verse emphasize that this occurred *in the place where he had spoken with him*? What is the point of the end of the verse (*in the place. . .*)? *Rashi,* too, seems troubled by this and comments, "I do not know what it teaches us."

The building of an altar represents the second method of gaining closeness to Hashem. Hashem, in His infinite wisdom, saw fit to grant us the ability to bring ourselves closer to Him by bringing sacrifices. This, however, is a method with limits and guidelines set down by the Torah. Sacrifices cannot be brought just anywhere. They must be brought in the *Beis Hamikdash* exclusively. For this reason Yaakov was told to proceed to Beth-el, the site of the *Beis Hamikdash.* Indeed, one who brings a sacrifice outside of the *Beis Hamikdash* is liable for the strict punishment of *kares.* It is for this reason that the verse concludes by saying *"in the place where he had spoken with him,"* to signify that the preceding actions were dependent upon the place where they were performed.

❀   ❀   ❀

פרשת וירא
Parashas Vayeira

וַיֵּרָא אֵלָיו ה׳ — *Hashem appeared to him* (18:1).

The verse tells us that Hashem appeared to Avraham, without recording any dialogue that may have taken place between them. For this reason, *Rashi* explains that Hashem was coming to Avraham in order to fulfill the commandment of *bikur cholim,* visiting the sick. A novel law can be learned from this. There are two reasons given for the *mitzvah* of *bikur cholim* : attending to the patient's needs, and praying for his recovery. Obviously, neither one of these reasons applies to Hashem. Accordingly, *Rashi* is telling us that Hashem's actions constituted *bikur cholim,* even though the reasoning did not apply — and we may learn therefrom that the *mitzvah* of visiting the sick indeed applies in all cases.

Perhaps we can offer another reason for Hashem's visit. It is possible that Hashem visited Avraham because he wished to observe how a *tzaddik* of Avraham's caliber performed *mitzvos.* As the verse tells us, *Then those who fear Hashem spoke to one another, and Hashem listened and heard (Malachi 3:16).* Hashem is attentive to the *mitzvos* performed by the righteous. Indeed, this is not a phenomenon restricted to Avraham alone — Hashem watches the actions of every one of us on a constant basis, as it says, *The eyes of Hashem — they scan the whole world! (Zechariah 4:10).* Avraham, however, unlike us, was on so high a spiritual level that he merited perceiving the presence of Hashem observing him.

For this reason, we must realize that it is incumbent upon each and every one of us to carefully weigh our actions on a constant basis.

Indeed, this is true even of our very thoughts, for before Hashem all is equally clear, thought as well as deed.

❧ ❧ ❧

וַיֵּרָא אֵלָיו ה' בְּאֵלֹנֵי מַמְרֵא וְהוּא יֹשֵׁב פֶּתַח־הָאֹהֶל כְּחֹם הַיּוֹם — *Hashem appeared to him in the plains of Mamre, while he was sitting at the entrance of the tent, in the heat of the day* (18:1).

Rashi comments that Avraham wished to stand out of respect for the Divine Presence. Hashem instructed him to remain sitting, telling him: Sit, and I will stand; you are a foretoken for your children, for I am destined to stand in the assembly of the judges while they are sitting. What is the connection between Hashem's appearing to Avraham and the Divine Presence standing in the assembly of judges?

Why does the Divine Presence rest among the judges while they hold court? The Divine Presence comes to the court to observe how the judges involve themselves in the law, and to Divinely assist them in arriving at the proper halachic decision. Judging the laws of the Torah requires a calm, settled mind; something best achieved while sitting. In addition, the Divine Presence wishes to give honor to the judges. Therefore, the judges are required to sit, despite the fact that the Divine Presence is among them.

Avraham, seeing guests approaching his home, had to judge how best to fulfill the *mitzvah* of *chesed*. The judging of how to best fulfill a law of the Torah requires the same settled mind as does judging between two litigants. Since he was involving himself in fulfilling the *mitzvos* of Hashem, he too was deserving of great honor; and for this reason Hashem instructed him to sit. We can therefore see that these two seemingly divergent things are actually very similar to each other.

❧ ❧ ❧

וַיִּשָּׂא עֵינָיו וַיַּרְא . . . וַיַּרְא וַיָּרָץ לִקְרָאתָם — *He lifted his eyes and saw . . . He saw and he ran toward them* (18:2).

Why does the verse tell us twice that Avraham saw his guests approaching? We may explain that the Torah wishes to underscore the degree of preparation undertaken by

Avraham before performing an act of *chesed.* There are two types of "seeing" that must take place before one takes action. The first is simply to take notice of *what* it is that must be done. The second is to figure out *how* the deed would best be done. The verse testifies that Avraham prepared for his guests in a properly thorough fashion.

This lesson can be applied to all of our worthy endeavors. If we invest the proper amount of preparation in our actions, we can be assured that we will be successful in accomplishing our intended goals; moreover, we will also merit to be a source of inspiration to others, who will follow in our footsteps.

❀ ❀ ❀

יֻקַּח־נָא מְעַט־מַיִם — *Let some water be brought* (18:4).

Rashi tells us that by choosing the passive form (*Let some water be brought*) rather than the active form (*I will bring some water*), the verse tells us that Avraham chose to have the water brought by a messenger rather than bringing it himself. It is for this reason, says *Rashi,* that when Avraham's descendants required water in the desert, it was given to them by means of a messenger — Moshe Rabbeinu — who, upon Hashem's command, struck the rock and brought forth water. This stands in contrast to Avraham's actions when serving food to his guests. Avraham chose to serve the food himself, as attested to in the next verse, *I shall take a morsel of bread.* As a result, *Bnei Yisrael* received the manna directly from Hashem, as the verse says (*Exodus* 16:4), *Behold! — I shall rain down for you food from the heavens.*

Certainly, Avraham, the paragon of *chesed,* would not entrust even a part of the task of caring for his guests to a messenger unless he knew that it would be performed in a perfect manner. Nevertheless, it is apparent from this *Rashi* that it pleases Hashem more when a person performs a good deed on his own, rather than delegating the deed to another.

There is another valuable lesson to be learned here. The best way to educate children is to give them the opportunity to observe their mentors performing good deeds. This affords them the ability not only to learn *what* deeds are proper and worthy of doing, but to observe *how* they are to be done. Imagine the educational impact of watching Avraham perform an act of *chesed!* Watching a child fulfill Avraham's command to do *chesed* would teach you that it is proper to do *chesed,* but what kind of *chesed* would it be? It would be the act of a child, lacking energy and joy. Watching Avraham *himself* do *chesed* would grant one insights into *chesed* not available in any other way. How much enthusiasm would Avraham bring to the task? How much would his "rejoicing in doing a *mitzvah*" be apparent? The only way to teach these all important lessons is to teach by example. This is the true challenge, and indeed, responsibility, of *chinuch* — the teaching of total involvement through example, not the oftentimes dry teaching of mere concepts.

While the above-mentioned *Rashi* seems to indicate that Avraham was wrong to delegate the task of bringing the water, it is possible to understand this *Rashi* differently. Avraham's decision to involve Yishmael in this task was certainly made with noble intentions. Avraham wished to train and encourage his son to perform *mitzvos*. After all, we see that much of the work involved in feeding the guests was done by Avraham himself. Indeed, it would seem that Avraham chose the more difficult tasks to perform by himself. Had Avraham's actions been guided by an unwillingness to work, he would have delegated the entire preparation to others.

Why, then, were *Bnei Yisrael* destined to receive their water through a messenger? We can explain that while this certainly was a *result* of Avraham's actions, it need not be viewed as retribution for a misdeed. As we know, one of Hashem's attributes is that He rewards both good as well as evil deeds measure for measure. It therefore follows that although there was nothing lacking in Avraham's actions, his children were simply rewarded measure for measure — thus they received their water through a messenger.

❧ ❧ ❧

There was another factor that influenced Avraham's decision to delegate some of the acts of *chesed* to his son Yishmael. Consider: When a father chooses to do a *mitzvah* himself rather than delegating the task to his son, he shows his son that the *mitzvah* is beloved to him; that he wishes to work at fulfilling it himself rather than allowing someone else to do it for him. If the father instead chooses to delegate the task, the child may think that the fulfillment of a *mitzvah* is not beloved, it is rather a bother — a task to be "unloaded" into the hands of whoever may be available. Why, then, did Avraham choose to allow Yishmael to make some of the preparations for the guests?

The answer is that while this is a valuable lesson, it is one that not every child is capable of perceiving. There are those children that will conclude otherwise, reasoning that their father does not entrust them with the performance of mitzvos because mitzvos are only the responsibility of greater people — and that simpler people need not concern themselves with their fulfillment.

It was this determination that Avraham had to make with regards to Yishmael. Which lesson did he need more? If Avraham would do everything himself, what would Yishmael think? Would he learn the precious nature of Hashem's mitzvos? Or would he think that mitzvos were only for people of his great father's stature?

Avraham, deciding that Yishmael needed to learn his own personal responsibility to fulfill mitzvos, opted to ask Yishmael to assist him in serving his guests. While Avraham's actions were based on his understanding of what his son needed most, Hashem knew that he was mistaken. Hashem, in His wisdom, knew that Yishmael had to be taught the value of a mitzvah — a lesson that he would have learned by watching Avraham enthusiastically do everything on his own. For this reason, the actions that Avraham delegated to Yishmael were not as precious to Hashem as those that he performed himself. Thus, as noted above, when Avraham's children were rewarded for their forefather's deeds, their reward for these acts came at the hands of messengers.

❧ ❧ ❧

וַתִּצְחַק שָׂרָה בְּקִרְבָּהּ לֵאמֹר . . . וַיֹּאמֶר ה' אֶל־אַבְרָהָם לָמָּה זֶּה צָחֲקָה שָׂרָה לֵאמֹר הַאַף אָמְנָם אֵלֵד וַאֲנִי זָקַנְתִּי. הֲיִפָּלֵא מֵה' דָּבָר — *And Sarah laughed at herself, saying . . . Then Hashem said to Avraham, "Why is it that Sarah laughed, saying: 'Shall I in truth bear a child, though I have aged?' Is anything beyond Hashem?!"* (18:12-14).

I t is of course impossible to say that our matriarch Sarah, who was an extremely righteous woman as well as a great prophetess, harbored any doubts as to the capabilities of Hashem. Furthermore, if indeed Hashem had truly found anything lacking in Sarah's words, would He have addressed His admonition to Avraham? The Talmud tells us (San-hedrin 43b) that when Hashem informed Yehoshua that someone had sinned and stolen from the consecrated spoils of the city of Ai, Yehoshua asked Hashem to tell him who had sinned. Hashem responded by asking

Yehoshua, "Am I an informer?" Hashem does not reveal the identity of a sinner to another party. Hence, had Hashem felt that Sarah had done anything wrong he would have directed His words to her, not to Avraham.

Why, then, did Sarah laugh? And what was the meaning of the admonition Hashem presented to Avraham? Let us analyze the events that occurred and try to answer these questions.

In the end of *Parashas Lech Lecha* (17:19), Avraham was told by Hashem that Sarah would give birth to a son. Why, then, was it necessary for Hashem to send an angel to inform Avraham of Yitzchak's birth? The answer is that while Avraham knew about the coming birth of Yitzchak, Sarah did not. It is possible that Avraham was not commanded to relate the prophecy he had received to Sarah. It is further possible that he was preoccupied with the fulfillment of the commandment of circumcision; whatever the reason, Sarah was not aware of the prophecy. The angel was therefore sent by Hashem to inform *Sarah* — not Avraham — of the coming miracle. Sarah, however, did not realize that the guests Avraham was serving were angels. Thinking that the guests were at best ordinary travelers, and at worst Arabians who were known to worship foreign gods, Sarah thought that the guest's statement was merely a blessing, not words of prophecy. Because of this she laughed, not giving the blessing any credence. Thus, it is clear that in no way did Sarah display any lack of faith in Hashem's ability to perform miracles; she was simply not aware that she was hearing words of prophecy stated by an angel at Hashem's behest.

This explains why Sarah laughed. Our second question, however, is now even stronger. What was the meaning of Hashem's admonishment, and why was it directed at Avraham?

The Talmud relates (*Taanis* 25a) that one *erev Shabbos* Rav Chanina ben Dosa noticed that his daughter was upset. When he asked what was troubling her, she responded that she had mistaken a vessel full of vinegar for one of oil, and used it for her Shabbos lights. Rav Chanina asked her, "Why should you care? He who said that that oil should burn will say that vinegar should burn!"

It is clear from his words that Rav Chanina saw no difference between oil burning and vinegar burning. This is because he understood that oil possesses the ability to burn only because God decrees that it must. Thus, R' Chanina told his daughter: He who said that oil will burn — Hashem — is equally capable of granting that ability to vinegar.

Hashem felt that Sarah should have realized this as well. Sarah's laugh was a laugh of disbelief. She reacted in this manner because she felt that she had heard their guest predict the occurrence of something that could not happen. Although Sarah did not know this was a message from Hashem Himself, Hashem was angered by her reaction; for Hashem demands an extremely high level of faith from people of Sarah's stature. As Rav Chanina noted, there really is no difference between what we see as miraculous, and what we consider to be the normal course of events; both are equal before Hashem. Accordingly, Sarah should not have found the possibility of bearing a child at her age surprising at all. Instead of laughing, her reaction should have been to say, "Amen! May it be Hashem's will to make it so." The responsibility of teaching this lesson belonged to Avraham, since he was greater than Sarah in Torah knowledge. For this reason Hashem admonished Avraham for this lapse, not Sarah.

The fact that Hashem expects the righteous to live with the understanding that the commonplace is no less miraculous than the miracle does not license the righteous to expect to live through miracles. Indeed we see that when Canaan was struck by famine Avraham traveled to Mitzrayim. Likewise, when he felt threatened by the Egyptians on account of his wife, he lied and said that Sarah was his sister. In both of these instances Avraham could have hoped to be saved through the performance of a miracle. This, however, would be wrong. When what is needed can be accomplished through the normal way of the world, there is no need to depend upon, or request, the performance of a miracle. Hashem created the world to operate according to the rules and norms which He designed. For one to needlessly say that he does not wish to live by those norms would be haughty; it would be akin to saying that one is above the creations of Hashem, and considers them unnecessary.

❈ ❈ ❈

כִּי־מַשְׁחִתִים אֲנַחְנוּ אֶת־הַמָּקוֹם הַזֶּה — *For we are about to destroy this place* (19:13).

Why did the angels credit themselves with the destruction of the five cities? Surely they did not intend to deliberately mislead people into thinking that they were capable of taking action on their own without being sent by Hashem!

The Talmud tells us (Shabbos 119b) that angels are divided into two categories — good and bad. Although both types of angels simply carry out the will of Hashem, there is a difference between them. The angels that carry out Hashem's will for good can be referred to as angels of Hashem, while the angels sent by Hashem for punishment do not carry Hashem's Name. Possibly, it was for this reason the angels did not say that Hashem was going to overturn the cities. They felt that it would be improper to mention the Name of Hashem regarding such an act of punishment.

With this idea we can explain another verse as well. When Yaakov returned to *Eretz Yisrael* from the house of Lavan, he encountered a camp of angels. The verse tells us (32:3) that when Yaakov saw them he exclaimed, *"This is a Godly camp!"* What is the meaning of this exclamation? We can now explain that Yaakov was not merely pointing out that they were angels — that was obvious as soon as he met them, as the verse states: *angels of God encountered him.* Yaakov's intent was to say that they were good angels — a *Godly camp* — for the name of God was visible upon them.

❀ ❀ ❀

וַיָּשֶׂם אֹתוֹ עַל־הַמִּזְבֵּחַ — *And he placed him on the altar* (22:9).

Ideally, sacrifices are not slaughtered on the altar itself. Rather, they are slaughtered in the location specified by the Torah, and only then are they put on the altar for burning (*Zevachim* 58a). Why, then, did Avraham wish to sacrifice Yitzchak on top of the altar that he had constructed?

A person who merits giving up his life for Hashem is without blemish. There is nothing undesirable or impure about him that prevents him from being brought up on the altar. Indeed, it is preferable to bring such a person up on the altar itself. An animal is only worthy of being raised upon the altar once it has been sanctified through slaughtering. A person, however, through his readiness for self-sacrifice, is capable of instantly attaining this degree of sanctification while still alive. Yitzchak, who attained this level of sanctification and was never actually slaughtered, retained this holiness for the rest of his life (see *Rashi* to 26:2).

❀ ❀ ❀

הִנֵּה יָלְדָה מִלְכָּה גַם־הִוא בָּנִים — *Behold, Milcah, she, too, has borne children* (22:20).

T he commentators tell us that the extra words "she, too," tell us that when Sarah was remembered by Hashem and bore children at an advanced age, Milcah too bore children.[1] Rashi tells us that this was an actual miracle because like Sarah, Milcah was not only old, she was unable to bear children naturally. It is interesting to note that while Sarah only bore one child, Milcah, whose miracle was only an outgrowth of Sarah's, gave birth to eight children. If we count the four children borne by Nachor's concubine Reumah, we see that Nachor had a total of 12 children — something that did not occur in the family of Avraham until Yaakov was more than 90 years old. Let us explore several possible reasons for this.

Rambam, in the preface to his *Commentary on the Mishnah,* tells us that all of the creations that are to be found in the world have a distinct purpose. Wheat was created to feed the inhabitants of the world. Certain plants are necessary for medicinal purposes. What, asks the *Rambam,* is the purpose of man? He answers that man was granted wisdom, and the purpose of man is to utilize that wisdom as a means of becoming closer to Hashem. Having said that, *Rambam* ponders the reason that Hashem sees fit to maintain in this world the many people who either do not contain or do not utilize such wisdom. What purpose do such people have in this world?

To answer this, *Rambam* uses the example of a wealthy man who commands his servants to build him a huge palace. To accomplish this task, he spends huge sums of money and hires a myriad of workers. At the time, it is difficult to see what contribution this person is making to the world. However, suppose years later a God-fearing man is taking a walk in the hot sun, and he pauses to rest in the shade of the palace. Suddenly, the life of the fool, who spent his days creating his lavish estate, has taken on new meaning. For while it may be true that during his lifetime he never displayed any wisdom of his own, he nevertheless has filled a higher purpose — serving the needs of one who has dedicated his life to serving Hashem. The same is true of the many workers who took part in the construction of the building. The people who worked in the lumberyards that supplied the materials for the project, the loggers who chopped down the trees from which the beams

---

1. See *Ramban* and *Targum Yhonasan.*

were later formed — they all are necessary to provide the needs of those who serve their Creator.

In light of this *Rambam,* we can understand that it may take hundreds, if not thousands, of people to serve the needs of even one God-fearing Jew over the course of his lifetime. Perhaps this is why while Sarah was remembered and blessed with one child, it was necessary for Hashem to grant Milcah eight children. Hashem knew that the descendants of Yitzchak were destined to be a nation of people dedicated to His service. He made sure to provide for their needs by granting Milcah eight children destined to form the infrastructure of a world capable of supporting such a nation.

There is another possible reason that Milcah was blessed with so many children. *Rashi* tells us that the Torah mentioned the genealogy of Nachor's family only because of the verse that tells of Rivkah's birth. The simple interpretation of this is that in order to refer to Rivkah's birth the Torah begins from Nachor, whom we already are familiar with as Avraham's brother, and works its way down to Rivkah. There is, however, another possible interpretation of this *Rashi.*

We know that the presence of a tzaddik acts as a source of positive inspiration capable of counteracting much evil.[1] Rivkah was a righteous woman destined to be one of the mothers of *Klal Yisrael.* The presence of a source of such positive inspiration would likely upset the balance of good and evil influences necessary for the continuation of individual free choice.

Based on this, we can now understand that *Rashi* is not only telling us that Nachor's genealogy was listed because of Rivkah. Rather, Nachor's family line owed its entire existence to Rivkah. For once Rivkah was born, it was necessary for Hashem to allow Nachor to have 12 children — thereby counterbalancing the effects of Rivkah.

In a similar vein, we must take into account the effect that the miraculous birth of Yitzchak had upon the people living at the time of Avraham and Sarah. When people saw that the God-fearing Avraham and Sarah had a miracle performed for them, they too began to believe in Hashem and follow His *mitzvos.* It is the will of Hashem that people believe and have faith in Him as a result of learning and understanding — not

---

1. An example of this can be seen in Avrohom's *tefillah* on behalf of the people of Sodom. Avrohom prayed that the presence of 10 God-fearing people should suffice to save the entire city. He understood this to be a reasonable request because 10 righteous people are capable of inspiring the rest of the inhabitants of a city to mend their ways.

because they witnessed the occurrence of miracles. Therefore, just as it was necessary to counterbalance the positive influence of the presence of Rivkah, so too the miracle performed for Avraham and Sarah had to be counterbalanced through the occurrence of a similar miracle for the undeserving Nachor — thus preserving people's free choice.

❀ ❀ ❀

וַתָּבֹא וַתַּגֵּד לְאִישׁ הָאֱלֹקִים וַיֹּאמֶר לְכִי מִכְרִי אֶת־הַשֶּׁמֶן וְשַׁלְּמִי אֶת־נִשְׁיֵךְ וְאַתְּ וּבָנַיִךְ תִּחְיִי בַּנּוֹתָר — *She came and told the man of God, and he said, "Go sell the oil and pay your creditor, and you and your sons will live on the remainder"* (Malachim II 4:7 — Haftaras Vayeira).

After the Shunammite woman did as told by Elisha, the *passuk* says that she came and told the man of God, and he said, "Go sell the oil." Why did she need to ask for permission to sell the oil? The whole point of the miracle was so that she should have the oil for her needs! Chazal also say "and you and your sons will live on the remainder" means until the dead are revived, which is also difficult to understand. It appears that she meant to ask what to do first, whether to pay her debts, or to first take what her children needed. Elisha told her to first pay off her debt, and ensured her that she and her sons would live on the remainder. This means that the *Navi* instructs all generations till the revival of the dead that first we must pay our debts — not only debts we recognize as obligations, but also those obligations the Torah imposes, such as charity, and the support of *yeshivos* and the like. When we fulfill these obligations, we are ensured that we will live on the remainder in comfort.

❀ ❀ ❀

פרשת חיי שרה
Parashas Chayei Sarah

וַיִּהְיוּ חַיֵּי שָׂרָה מֵאָה שָׁנָה וְעֶשְׂרִים שָׁנָה וְשֶׁבַע שָׁנִים שְׁנֵי חַיֵּי שָׂרָה — *Sarah's lifetime was one hundred years, and twenty years, and seven years; the years of Sarah's life* (23:1).

Rashi tells us that the verse breaks down the years of Sarah's life into categories, to teach us that each category is to be expounded on its own. When she was one hundred years old, she was similar to a twenty-year-old with respect to sin.[1] When she was twenty years old, she was like a seven-year-old with regard to beauty.

It is clear from this *Rashi* that the verse considers Sarah's beauty worthy of praise, despite the fact that beauty is merely a physical attribute, one that we would not ordinarily expect the verse to make mention of. We can explain the reason for this as follows.

Sarah's beauty was worthy of praise because she glorified the name of Hashem through her beauty. This occurred when Sarah was taken captive by the kings Pharaoh and Avimelech. In both of these instances, Sarah, who was an extremely attractive woman, could have been tempted to use her beauty to her advantage by seducing her captors. Sarah, to her praise, did not have any such thought. By defeating this temptation, she elevated her beauty from a mere physical attribute to a spiritual one worthy of great praise.[2] [One might ask: How can we be sure

---

1. One is not liable to punishment until the age of twenty.

2. A person living in this world is constantly surrounded by things that, at first glance, appear to be purely physical, as opposed to spiritual, in nature. Eating, sleeping, all of a person's physical requirements — they all seem to be activities devoid of any spiritual

that Sarah did not entertain such thoughts? This can be inferred from the fact that in both of these cases Hashem performed miracles on Sarah's behalf; and Hashem would not have performed a miracle for someone who had the slightest thought of sin. This can be seen from that which we find in *Daniel* (ch. 3), that the evil King Nebuchadnezzar ordered the prophets Chananiah, Mishael, and Azariah to bow down to a pagan statue. When they refused to do so, the king told them that they would be thrown into a furnace. The prophets understood that Hashem would not perform a miracle for them if they went into the furnace expecting Hashem's protection. For this reason, they told Nebuchadnezzar that while they knew that Hashem has the power to protect them, they would refuse to worship foreign gods even with the understanding that they would be put to death for their rebelliousness. From this we see clearly that Hashem does not make miracles, even where the miracle would result in the honor of His own Name, if the thoughts of the recipient are less than purely selfless in nature. In light of this, it is surely obvious that Hashem would not have performed miracles for Sarah had she been harboring even the slightest thought of sin.]

✿ ✿ ✿

Rashi comments further that the apparently superfluous phrase, "the years of Sarah's life," teaches us that all of Sarah's years were "equal for goodness." It would seem that it is not *Rashi's* intent to comment on the pleasantness of Sarah's personal physical existence, for as we know, there were periods of her life that were not pleasant. Sarah endured the anguish of years of being childless. She also endured aggravation from her maidservant Hagar. These years were certainly not "equal for goodness" to the rest of Sarah's life. What, then, is the meaning of *Rashi's* comment?

---

value. This, however, is far from the truth. As a person grows in spirituality, it is his responsibility to take all of the seemingly mundane physical aspects of life, and sanctify them through their use as a means of serving Hashem.

A simple example can be given with regard to eating. It is a physical necessity for every human being to eat. Yet, eating can take place in different ways, with different goals in mind. A person who sits down to a lavish feast with the sole intent of indulging his palate and filling his stomach is indeed performing an action totally devoid of any spiritual benefit. That is the *physical* form of eating. There is, however, a way to elevate the act of eating from the physical to the spiritual level. A person who eats with the intent of strengthening his body so that he will have the ability to do Hashem's bidding has indeed turned eating into a spiritual exercise.

Perhaps we can explain that *Rashi* is referring to a different "goodness"; namely, the goodness that Sarah shared with the world. No matter what was happening in Sarah's personal life, whether she was joyous or troubled, her actions towards other people were the same. The acts of goodness that Sarah regularly performed, the kindness that she bestowed upon her guests — all remained totally unaffected by the trials and tribulations of her personal existence. In this way, says *Rashi*, all of the years of Sarah's life were indeed "equal for goodness."

❦ ❦ ❦

בְּמִבְחַר קְבָרֵינוּ קְבֹר אֶת־מֵתֶךָ — **In the choicest of our burial places bury your dead** (23:6).

The verse tells us that Avraham did not close a deal with Ephron until he agreed to pay an exorbitant purchase price for Sarah's burial plot. This is difficult to understand. Why would Ephron and the *Bnei Cheis,* after offering to give Avraham the burial plot for free, demand payment of an exorbitant sum?

The truth is that the *Bnei Cheis* were willing to give Avraham a free burial plot only on one condition. They wanted Sarah to be buried amongst *them* in *their* burial ground.[1] This was a condition that Avraham would not agree to. The *Bnei Cheis* would have gloried in the fact that they had such a righteous woman buried among them. Avraham, knowing that they were not deserving of such a high honor, insisted on purchasing a plot from them. To this, the *Bnei Cheis* were not so agreeable; thus, they demanded what they considered full payment — an exorbitant price. In fact, the reason that the purchase of the field is counted among the ten trials of Avraham is because such an exorbitant price was asked.

❦ ❦ ❦

וַיָּקָם שְׂדֵה עֶפְרוֹן — **And Ephron's field stood** (23:17).

Rashi, troubled by the verse's use of the word "stood" in reference to a field, comments that this means the field had an ascension, in that it left the possession of a commoner for the possession of

---

1. This can be seen in their choice of words: In the choicest of *our* burial places.

a king. This *Rashi* is difficult to understand. In what way can a material item have a spiritual "ascension" through the change of ownership from Ephron to Avraham?

Let us analyze this further. The innate holiness of *Eretz Yisrael* can be divided into two categories. First, there is the holiness that existed from the beginning of Creation. This holiness would be present irrespective of Avraham's purchasing of the field. Second, there is the holiness which was placed on the land when Yehoshua and *Bnei Yisrael* conquered it. This holiness, too, would not have been effected by Avraham's purchase of the land. This being the case, how was an "ascension" of the field effected by Avraham's purchase?

The answer to our question is that *Rashi* is not discussing the holiness of *Eretz Yisrael*. Rather, he refers to the potential for holiness that exists in every material object created by Hashem. Whether or not an item is considered "holy" depends on the end use of the item. If the item is used in a way that allows it to fulfill a higher purpose, it can be said to have had an ascension. A simple example of this would be the parchment used in the writing of a *Sefer Torah*. The parchment is sanctified through its use for such a lofty purpose. The same is true of any item that is used for the benefit of a righteous person. *Rashi* is telling us that Ephron's field had an ascension because it would now be used by Avraham as a burial plot for the righteous Sarah.

With this idea, we can explain another concept that we find in the Talmud. The Mishnah (*Sanhedrin* 90a) lists three Jewish kings that have no share in the World to Come. The Talmud asks (*Sanhedrin* 104a) why the evil king Amon was not listed among them. The Talmud answers that Amon was not listed, in honor of his righteous son Yoshiyahu. The Talmud then asks that Menashe too should not have been listed, in honor of his righteous father Chizkiyah. To answer this, the Talmud explains that a son can earn merit for a father, but a father cannot earn merit for a son.

We can now explain this as follows. A son can earn merit for a father, because the son would not exist without the father. Thus, while Amon himself was an evil individual, he was a necessary factor in the righteousness of his son Yoshiyahu. When a father raises a righteous son, the son sanctifies and elevates the spiritual level of the father much the same way that writing a *Sefer Torah* sanctifies the parchment it is written on. A father, however, cannot earn merit for a son, because in no way is the son a necessary factor in the creation of the father. For this reason, although the evil Menashe had a righteous father, this could not spare him from being mentioned in the Mishnah. [This should not be seen as being contradictory to the concept of *zchus avos*. *Zchus avos* is a promise that Hashem made that He would provide for the needs of children who are not personally meritorious, in their *father's* merit. Merely having a meritorious father, however, does not make a son meritorious himself.]

There is another way we may understand the ascension Ephron's field underwent through its transference to the ownership of Avraham. The Torah at times presents us with physical reminders of the Torah way of life. One example of this would be the *mitzvah* of *tzitzis*. The verse states that the *tzitzis* are supposed to have the effect of reminding a person of his obligation to the Torah and *mitzvos*. How do the strings of the *tzitzis* accomplish this task? The Talmud (*Sotah* 17a) provides us with the answer. According to the Torah's specifications, one of the strings on each corner of a garment with *tzitzis* is to be dyed with *techeiles*. The Talmud teaches that the color of the *techeiles* reminds a person of the ocean. The ocean's color in turn reminds a person of the sky. The sky then makes a person think of the Heavenly Throne — which of course serves as a reminder to adhere to the requirements of Hashem's Torah.

The *Me'aras Hamachpeilah* and the land upon which it stood would now serve a similar function. They would act as a landmark — not a physical but rather a mental landmark — causing people to think of Avraham and his faith in Hashem. This would result in people following the ways of Avraham, thus glorifying the Name of Hashem. It is for this reason too that the verse mentions the trees that stood in the field — they are visible from afar and often serve as the landmark which delineates a person's property.

The concept of a place serving as a reminder triggering the fear of Hashem can be found in the instance of Shmuel Hanavi. Dovid Hamelech ran to Shmuel's home, hoping to escape persecution at the hands of Shaul and his followers. He was followed there first by Shaul's messengers and eventually by Shaul himself. The verse relates that as each individual approached Shmuel's home — even before they saw Shmuel himself — they were overcome by the spirit of Hashem. The sight of Shmuel's dwelling place alone was sufficient to cause them to remember Shmuel. This triggered in them the desire to follow in his ways — to rid themselves of all evil and search for the truth.

❀ ❀ ❀

וַיָּרָץ הָעֶבֶד לִקְרָאתָהּ — *The servant ran towards her* (24:17).

Rashi comments that the servant (Eliezer) ran towards Rivkah because he saw something that suggested to him that this was the young lady he was searching for; namely, he observed the water in the well miraculously rise up when Rivkah approached to draw water. This poses a difficulty for us. If Eliezer saw that a miracle was performed for Rivkah, what need was there for him to proceed with the rest of his test? Surely, if Hashem was performing miracles for this girl, this should be sufficient indication that she was a righteous person, and a suitable match for Yitzchak!

The answer to our question is that the occurrence of the miracle did not serve to prove that Rivkah possessed the trait of kindness, and it was this specific trait that Eliezer was searching for. Indeed, we find that the occurrence of a miracle on behalf of an individual serves only to prove that he has performed a good deed at some point in his life. We find this to be the case by the evil king Nebuchadnezzar. Nebuchadnezzar, as we know, was the king of Babylon who destroyed the First Temple. We can be sure that such a person was thoroughly evil. The Talmud relates (*Sanhedrin* 96b) that while there were other evil people who merited having descendants who were God fearing, Nebuchadnezzar was so evil that it was decreed he would never be so fortunate. Yet, the fact remains that he fulfilled the will of Hashem by punishing the Jews for their evil ways. In another instance, we find that Nebuchadnezzar ran four paces for the honor of Hashem's Name (*Sanhedrin* 96a). As payment for these good deeds, we find that he was rewarded with the occurrence of several miracles, including being granted dominion over wild beasts.[1] Obviously, if an infamous person such as Nebuchadnezzar could merit the performance of miracles, the same could be true of a simple girl who may have done a good deed, albeit not one involving an act of kindness. Eliezer understood this, and as such felt it necessary to proceed with the rest of his test.

❀ ❀ ❀

---

1. The Talmud (*Shabbos* 150a) relates that Nebuchadnezzar rode upon a lion, using a snake for the reins.

פרשת תולדות
Parashas Toldos

וַיֵּרָא אֵלָיו ה' וַיֹּאמֶר אַל־תֵּרֵד מִצְרָיְמָה שְׁכֹן בָּאָרֶץ אֲשֶׁר
אֹמַר אֵלֶיךָ. גּוּר בָּאָרֶץ הַזֹּאת וְאֶהְיֶה עִמְּךָ וַאֲבָרְכֶךָ כִּי־לְךָ
וּלְזַרְעֲךָ אֶתֵּן אֶת־כָּל־הָאֲרָצֹת הָאֵל . . . וְהִרְבֵּיתִי אֶת־
זַרְעֲךָ כְּכוֹכְבֵי הַשָּׁמַיִם וְנָתַתִּי לְזַרְעֲךָ אֵת כָּל־הָאֲרָצֹת הָאֵל
. . . עֵקֶב אֲשֶׁר־שָׁמַע אַבְרָהָם בְּקֹלִי . . . — *Hashem*
appeared to him and said, "Do not descend to
Egypt; dwell in the land that I shall indicate to
you. Sojourn in this land and I will be with you and
bless you; for to you and your offspring will I give
all these lands . . . I will increase your offspring
like the stars of the heavens; and will give to your
offspring all these lands . . . Because Avraham
obeyed My voice . . . " (26:2-5).

I n both v. 3 and v. 4, instead of using the word הָאֵלֶּה, the usual
Hebrew word for "these," the verse uses the word הָאֵל. What is the
reason for this distinction?

Yitzchak, living in the land of Canaan, was faced with a famine that
forced him to leave his home. *Rashi* tells us that Yitzchak's first thought
was to go to Egypt for the duration of the hunger, following the lead of
his father Avraham. Hashem, however, commanded Yitzchak to remain
within the boundaries of the land of *Eretz Yisrael.* For this reason Yitzchak
traveled instead to Philistia, a kingdom existing within these boundaries.
Why was Yitzchak forbidden to leave *Eretz Yisrael? Rashi* explains that
Hashem told Yitzchak, "You are a blemish-free offering, and territory
outside *Eretz Yisrael* is not worthy of you." Since Yitzchak had been offered to Hashem as a sacrifice at the time of the *Akeidah,* he was sanctified,

and consequently was unable to leave *Eretz Yisrael*. He was required to live in *Eretz Yisrael* because the land of *Eretz Yisrael* is itself sanctified, and was therefore a suitable home for a person of Yitzchak's holiness.

For this reason the verse uses the word הָאֵל instead of the familiar הָאֵלֶּה. הָאֵל is a word which can also be Hashem's Name. The verse is hinting at the reason behind Hashem's command that Yitzchak remain in *Eretz Yisrael*. The lands of *Eretz Yisrael* are the lands of "הָאֵל" — they are Hashem's lands, the only suitable home for Yitzchak.

In v. 5, the final verse of the above prophecy, Hashem tells Yitzchak that he will receive all of this reward in the merit of his holy father Avraham. Why was it necessary for Hashem to invoke the merit of Avraham to reward Yitzchak? Surely Yitzchak was worthy of such reward based on his own merits![1]

The answer is that Yitzchak's level of spirituality precluded a reward of material nature being addressed to him. The level of sanctification that Yitzchak attained at the *Akeidah* was so high, that while physically he lived on this world, spiritually he was as if next to the Heavenly Throne itself. As such, material blessings such as the ones included in this prophecy could not be bestowed upon Yitzchak in his own merit. Hashem therefore granted these blessings to Yitzchak in the merit of Avraham.

❧ ❧ ❧

וְעַתָּה בְנִי שְׁמַע בְּקֹלִי לַאֲשֶׁר אֲנִי מְצַוָּה אֹתָךְ — *So now, my son, heed my voice to that which I command you* (27:8).

I t is apparent that Rivkah was concerned about the possibility of Eisav receiving Yitzchak's blessing.[2] Moreover we find that it was not only Rivkah that was concerned. The Targum tells us (*Bereishis* 27:13)

───────────

1. The *Sforno* asks this question, and answers that Yitzchak at that stage of his life did not yet merit such reward. This, however, cannot be correct. It is absolutely impossible to say that Yitzchak, having already experienced the *Akeidah* at which he attained an extremely high level of holiness, did not yet merit this reward. Indeed, in the prophecy Avraham received following the *Akeidah*, the verse says *Bless, I shall bless you* (22:17). *Rashi* says that the repetitious language indicates that there was a blessing for the father as well as a blessing for the son — they were both equal. Just as Avraham merited blessing himself, so too Yitzchak fully deserved reward in his own right.

2. *Ramban* comments that Rivkah told Yaakov that should the blessings be given to Eisav, since they are given through Divine inspiration, they will certainly be fulfilled by him and all his future generations, and you will not be able to stand before him.

that Rivkah told Yaakov she had received a prophecy approving of her actions. Would they indeed have been fulfilled? Had Yaakov blessed Eisav it would have been predicated on his assumption that Eisav was truly worthy of receiving them. Since this was not the case, the blessing would be one given based on a false premise, and as such should not be fulfilled!

The answer to this question is that the blessings of a righteous person are always accepted by Hashem — even if they are given mistakenly. We find this to be true concerning the curse of a righteous person as well. Even if the curse was given conditionally and the condition is not met, the curse can still be fulfilled. [An example of this would be Yaakov's curse to whoever stole Lavan's idols, which later resulted in Rachel's death. Yaakov's words were fulfilled although he uttered them while unaware of Rachel's actions.] The explanation for this phenomenon is as follows: When a righteous person prays to Hashem on behalf of an individual, Hashem is favorably disposed to heed his prayers. Therefore, if the person has any merits at all, a blessing can be fulfilled on account of those merits. The same is true of a curse; should the person have performed any misdeeds, a curse can be fulfilled on account of those misdeeds.

This, then, is why Rivkah was concerned. She recognized that Eisav was evil, and she knew that Yitzchak's blessing would be based on the assumption that he was righteous. Yet she also understood that Eisav must have some merit, and that on account of that merit the blessing of a person of Yitzchak's stature would surely be fulfilled.

We find that Yitzchak, too, understood this to be true. After Eisav came to Yitzchak and exposed his brother's trickery, Yitzchak exclaimed, *"Indeed, he shall remain blessed!"* (27:33). *Rashi* comments that Yitzchak said this in order that one should not say, "Had Yaakov not deceived his father, he would not have received the blessings. This is why Yitzchak consented to what Yaakov had done, and blessed him knowingly." It is clear from this *Rashi* that the only reason Yitzchak said, *"He shall remain blessed,"* was so that no one should be able to say that Yaakov received the blessings only through trickery. *Rashi* does *not* say that it was necessary for Yitzchak to bless Yaakov again because the first blessing was given with the understanding that the recipient was Eisav, and was therefore invalid. This is because, as we explained, the blessings of the righteous are fulfilled by Hashem even when they are given mistakenly.

There is, however, one more difficulty still to be dealt with. Thus far we have explained that the blessings could have been fulfilled for Eisav, despite the fact that they were given mistakenly. What we have not taken into account is the fact that Yitzchak incorporated into the blessings a safeguard to guard against them working for someone undeserving of them. For when Yitzchak gave the blessing, he said: "And may God give you . . ." (27:28). The Name of God used in the verse is *Elokim,* the Name used to refer to Hashem's attribute of judgment. *Rashi* explains that Yitzchak's intent was to say, "May you only receive the benefits of the blessings if you are worthy of them by law. If, however, you are found to be unworthy, may you receive nothing at all." Seemingly, this caveat would serve as adequate protection against the blessing being fulfilled for Eisav. Surely the evil Eisav would not meet the criteria set down by Yitzchak for fulfillment of his blessings! If so, we must once again ask our original question: Why the concern for the possibility of the blessings being fulfilled for Eisav?

The answer is that it is quite possible that Eisav would have been found worthy of the blessings despite his evil tendencies. God's attribute of judgment functions differently for different people. The Talmud tells us (*Yevamos* 121b) that Hashem is very strict with those close to Him. It therefore follows that Yaakov, who was close to Hashem, would be judged very strictly, while Eisav, who was removed from Hashem, would be judged more leniently. For this reason, while it is true that in order for Yaakov and his descendants to be deserving of the blessings, they would have to keep the entire Torah, Eisav, on the other hand, could conceivably be found deserving of the blessings on account of any one great commandment he may have fulfilled. His famous attention to the commandment of honoring his father may have sufficed to allow him to reap the benefits of the blessings.

It was for these reasons that Rivkah's actions were necessary. She understood — and indeed saw prophetically — that it was vitally important to prevent the blessings from falling into the hands of Eisav, for she knew that this occurrence and its ramifications would be to the detriment of Yaakov and his descendants for all time.

❧ ❧ ❧

פרשת ויצא
Parashas Vayeitzei

וַיֵּצֵא יַעֲקֹב מִבְּאֵר שָׁבַע וַיֵּלֶךְ חָרָנָה — *Yaakov departed from Beer-sheva and went to Charan* (28:10).

The Torah tells us that Yaakov left Beer-sheva, and that he traveled to Charan. Clearly, it would have been sufficient to tell us that he traveled to Charan — it would then be self-evident that he had left Beer-sheva. It would appear that the Torah wishes to compare the two; telling us that Yaakov's travel to Charan was with the same will and desire to serve Hashem as his departure from Beer-sheva. Yaakov left Beer-sheva knowing that he would have to prepare himself for his stay in Charan. Yaakov had to strengthen himself — lest he be influenced by the actions of the wicked people he would be surrounded by.

In a similar vein, we can explain a verse in *Parashas Shemos*. We find that both in *Parashas Vayigash* as well as in *Parashas Shemos,* the verse refers to *Bnei Yisrael* as those "who were coming" to Egypt. While this appellation is appropriate in *Parashas Vayigash*, which tells of *Bnei Yisrael's* arrival in Egypt, it hardly seems appropriate in *Parashas Shemos,* when they had already been living there for many years.

This can be explained as follows: Even after many years of life in Egypt, *Bnei Yisrael* had not changed. Just as Yaakov traveled to Charan with the same mindset with which he left Beer-sheva, so too *Bnei Yisrael,* even after many years of living in Egypt, maintained the same mindset as when they first arrived. They came to Egypt with the intent of remaining sojourners in the land, and so they remained — never adopting Egypt as their home.

This also explains Moshe Rabbeinu's method of naming his children. Moshe named his oldest child Gershom, a contraction of the Hebrew words *ger* and *shom,* literally: "a stranger there." As the verse explains, Moshe said of his stay in Midian: "I have been a stranger in a strange land." His second son he named Eliezer, a contraction of the words *Eili* and *ezer,* literally: "my God the helper." With this name, Moshe acknowledged the hand of Hashem that saved him when Pharaoh had sought to have him killed. The order of these names is difficult to understand. Moshe had been saved from the sword of Pharaoh *before* he was a stranger in the land of Midian. Why, then, did he use the name Gershom commemorating his status as a stranger for his eldest son, prior to using the name Eliezer in commemoration of his salvation?

The answer is that Moshe understood well the lesson we have explained above. Moshe knew that unless he managed to remain the same "stranger" to Midianite ways that he was when he first arrived in Midian, his salvation from Pharaoh would be worthless. Therefore, he named his first child Gershom. When, after years of living in Midian, he saw that he was able to maintain his righteousness in the face of the evil influences surrounding him, he named his second son Eliezer — thanking Hashem for his salvation.

❧ ❧ ❧

וַיַּחֲלֹם וְהִנֵּה סֻלָּם מֻצָּב אַרְצָה וְרֹאשׁוֹ מַגִּיעַ הַשָּׁמָיְמָה וְהִנֵּה מַלְאֲכֵי אֱלֹקִים עֹלִים וְיֹרְדִים בּוֹ — *And he dreamt, and behold! A ladder was set earthward and its top reached heavenward; and behold! angels of God were ascending and descending on it* (28:12).

What was the meaning of this dream? Although the verse records Yaakov's dream, the Torah does not give any indication of what we are to learn from it.

Rashi tells us that this dream actually took place after Yaakov had already arrived in Charan. Upon reaching Charan, Yaakov realized he had passed by the place where his ancestors had prayed — *Har Hamoriyah* — and regretted not stopping there himself to pray. For this reason, he resolved to immediately return to *Har Hamoriyah.* As soon as he set out, the land of *Har Hamoriyah* miraculously came to him. This type of miracle, where a person's trip is miraculously shortened, is generally referred to as *kfitzas haaretz*, contraction of the land. There is a difference, though, between the type of *kfitzas haaretz* experienced by Yaakov and the type usually performed by Hashem. We find in other places that a person travels to a place, but finds that his traveling time was miraculously shortened. This is not what happened to Yaakov. *Rashi* tells us that in this instance, Yaakov's destination, Har Hamoriyah, came to him.

There is a lesson to be learned from this difference. Hashem wanted to teach Yaakov that even the holiness of Har Hamoriyah was capable of surviving in the decadent environment of Charan. Yaakov had experienced the holiness of Yitzchak's house and the holiness of the *yeshivah* of Shem and Ever; now he was going to be exposed to the absence of holiness exemplified by the people of Charan. Yaakov was worried, and for good reason. How was he going to fulfill his task of raising 12 God-fearing Torah-observant tribes in such a place? Hashem showed him that no matter the type of place one happens to be in, there is no atmosphere in which Torah cannot survive.

This was the lesson of Yaakov's dream. Hashem showed Yaakov that no matter where you may be on the earth, it is always possible to reach the heavens. All that is necessary is the proper ladder. If you have a ladder that is firmly grounded in a foundation of Torah learning and adherence to Hashem's commandments, you will always be able to use it to ascend to higher levels of closeness to Hashem.

As we know, Yaakov was ultimately successful. He raised his children in Charan and yet was able to tell Eisav, "I lived with Lavan, and I kept all 613 commandments of Hashem" (see *Rashi* to 32:5) The holiness of Yaakov persevered even in Charan.

❧ ❧ ❧

וַיִּיקַץ יַעֲקֹב מִשְּׁנָתוֹ וַיֹּאמֶר אָכֵן יֵשׁ ה׳ בַּמָּקוֹם הַזֶּה וְאָנֹכִי לֹא יָדָעְתִּי — *Yaakov awoke from his sleep and said, "Surely Hashem is in this place and I did not know!"* (28:16).

For what purpose did Yaakov mention this seemingly insignificant fact? *Rashi* explains that Yaakov's intent was: Had I known, I would not have slept in a holy place such as this. This is very difficult to understand. The Gemara tells us (*Chullin* 91b) that Hashem caused the sun to set early in order to cause Yaakov to sleep in this particular spot (*Chullin* 91b). The Talmud further teaches that the stones Yaakov had placed surrounding his head miraculously joined, forming one large stone. As the verse narrates, it was during this sleep that Yaakov merited receiving a prophecy from Hashem, as well as a promise of protection during his numerous travels. From all of these miraculous occurrences it should have been clear to Yaakov that it was the will of Hashem that he should sleep in this spot. Why, then, would Yaakov say that had he known of Hashem's presence he would have done otherwise?

The proper way to understand Yaakov's words is as follows. Yaakov thought that one is only considered to be serving Hashem when involved in spiritual pursuits such as *tefillah* and Torah study. Involvement in physical matters such as eating and sleeping, however, could not be considered serving Hashem, since they are not themselves *mitzvos.*

By performing miracles and causing Yaakov to *sleep* (a purely physical activity) on the future site of the *Beis Hamikdash,* Hashem sought to teach Yaakov that this is not the case. Hashem gave His Torah to human beings knowing that they are creations whose physical needs must be satisfied to facilitate their continuing ability to fulfill His commandments. It is His Divine will that these physical activities should be sanctified through their use as tools assisting people in their service of Hashem. In this way, these activities can be raised to the level where they themselves become the fulfillment of Hashem's will.

It was this that Yaakov alluded to when he exclaimed "*and I did not know.*" Yaakov exclaimed that prior to being taught this lesson, he did not know that a physical act such as sleeping could be sanctified to such a degree. *Rashi* (quoted above) explains that commensurate with Yaakov's prior understanding, had he known of the holiness of the site he would not have thought it proper to sleep there.

Taking note of this lesson, Yaakov said that the stone upon which he rested his head while sleeping should be a *Beis Elokim.* It was Yaakov's wish that the stone should serve as a reminder to the fact that a *Beis Elokim* is not only a place where one is involved in Torah and *mitzvos.* Even the seemingly mundane act of sleeping must be done with the proper intentions — so that a sleeping place, too, can reach the level of *Beis Elokim.*

❧ ❧ ❧

וַיֹּאמֶר לָבָן לֹא־יֵעָשֶׂה כֵן בִּמְקוֹמֵנוּ לָתֵת הַצְּעִירָה לִפְנֵי הַבְּכִירָה — *Lavan said, "Such is not done in our place, to give the younger before the elder"* (29:26).

Rabbeinu Tam, in a *Tosafos* to Tractate *Kiddushin* (52b), implies that we learn from this verse that it is in fact customary to marry off the older daughter before the younger.[1] This is difficult to understand. Why would we deduce the truth from the words of Lavan the quintessential liar!?

The answer is that we must analyze Lavan's words in their context. Upon discovering that he had been given Leah as a wife instead of Rachel, Yaakov asked Lavan, "*Why have you deceived me?*" (29:25). *Rabbeinu Tam* understood that with his reply (our verse), Lavan was not merely explaining to Yaakov *why* he did what he did; rather, Lavan sought to respond to Yaakov's accusation that he had tricked him. After all, said Lavan, "*Such is not done in our place. It is well known* that we do not marry off the younger daughter before the older. Since this is such a well-known custom, you surely understood that I would do whatever necessary to assure that Leah would marry first." It is upon this statement of Lavan's — that it was a *well-known* custom that elder daughters were married first — that *Rabbeinu Tam* bases his ruling.

❧ ❧ ❧

וַיִּשְׁמַע אֱלֹקִים אֶל־לֵאָה וַתַּהַר וַתֵּלֶד לְיַעֲקֹב בֵּן חֲמִישִׁי — *God hearkened to Leah; and she conceived and bore Yaakov a fifth son* (30:17).

What was it that Hashem "hearkened to"? *Rashi* explains that Hashem saw that Leah was desirous and put forth effort to increase tribes. Hashem therefore granted her wish and she conceived another son.

Rashi specifies that Leah's desire was not merely to have more children; rather she desired to have more *tribes*. Men or women that

---

1. Based on this verse, *Rabbeinu Tam* says that should a person give a man money with the intent of marrying one of his daughters without in any way specifying which one, the *halachah* would dictate that the marriage would take effect on the older daughter.

already have children are usually not distressed if they do not have any additional children. By this time Leah already had borne four children. *Rashi* therefore says that the motivating factor behind Leah's desire for children was not the usual joy that every woman has from her children. It was the wish to produce more tribes — the progenitors of *Klal Yisrael* who were so beloved by Hashem — that drove Leah's desires.

❀   ❀   ❀

פרשת וישלח
Parashas Vayishlach

כֹּה תֹאמְרוּן לַאדֹנִי לְעֵשָׂו כֹּה אָמַר עַבְדְּךָ יַעֲקֹב עִם־לָבָן
גַּרְתִּי וָאֵחַר עַד־עָתָּה — *"Thus shall you say: To my
lord, to Eisav, so said your servant Yaakov: I
have sojourned with Lavan and have lingered
until now"* (32:5).

Rashi presents us with two possible interpretations of this verse.
The first is that Yaakov meant to say, "I did not become a
dignitary or a noble, but a mere sojourner. Thus, it does not befit
you to hate me on account of the blessings of your father who blessed
me by saying, "Be a lord over your brothers," for it has not been fulfilled
in me." In the second interpretation, *Rashi* points out that the numerical
value of the Hebrew word for "sojourned" is 613, which corresponds to
the number of commandments in the Torah. Accordingly, Yaakov's
intent was to tell Eisav, "I sojourned with Lavan, the evil one, yet I kept
all 613 commandments and did not learn from his evil ways."

Both of these interpretations present us with difficulties. According
to the first interpretation, Yaakov appears to be telling Eisav that the
results of Yaakov's blessing never came to pass. It is not possible to
suggest that Yaakov would say such a thing. Belief in the words of a
true prophet is one of the pillars of our faith. Indeed, it would be
reasonable to suggest that one must surrender his life prior to denying
the truth of the words of a prophet! Certainly, in a situation such as the
one Yaakov found himself, where his statement did not even assure his
salvation, it would be forbidden to say that the words of a prophet were
not fulfilled.

The second interpretation, too, is difficult to understand. Why would Yaakov send Eisav a message informing him that he was still observant of all 613 commandments of Hashem? In what way did Yaakov think this would serve to placate Eisav?

We can answer both of our questions by explaining that the two interpretations of *Rashi* come together to express Yaakov's true intent. We know that when Yitzchak blessed Yaakov he did so conditionally. For this reason he incorporated into the blessing the word "Elokim" — the Name of Hashem that connotes the attribute of judgment. Yitzchak's intent was clear: The blessings would only be fulfilled if and when Yaakov was judged to be worthy of them. The blessing given to Eisav, however, was unconditional. Yitzchak understood that the evil Eisav would never be found worthy, and therefore did not hold him to such a standard.

With this in mind, we can now explain that Yaakov's intent was to tell Eisav as follows: "Had I not taken your blessing, our father, thinking that you were righteous, would have blessed you with the conditional blessing that I received. Our father's standards of righteousness are so high, that even I, who observe all 613 commandments, have not been judged as worthy to reap the benefits of his blessing. This is obvious from the fact that I was forced to be a sojourner in the house of Lavan. There is no question that you — who not only does not keep Hashem's commandments, but even commits sins — would never have benefited from such a blessing. As a result of my actions, however, our father realized that you are not the righteous individual he thought you to be, and he therefore blessed you with an unconditional blessing."

Moreover, Yaakov was able to show Eisav that while it would seem that his own conditional blessing had not been fulfilled, Eisav's unconditional one was already yielding dividends. At the time that Yaakov sent his messengers to Eisav, Eisav had already conquered the inhabitants of Seir. Thus Yaakov was able to tell him, "While my blessing has not been fulfilled due to the constraints placed upon them by our father, your blessing of *by the sword you shall live* has helped you to conquer the inhabitants of Seir."

This was the true meaning of Yaakov's message. He sought to convince the evil Eisav that he had not lost anything through Yaakov's actions — to the contrary, he had only gained.

❀ ❀ ❀

וַיַּשְׁכֵּם לָבָן בַּבֹּקֶר . . . וַיָּשָׁב לָבָן לִמְקֹמוֹ — *And Lavan awoke early in the morning . . . then Lavan went and returned to his place* (32:1).

The verse tells us that after all that had transpired, "Lavan returned to his place." Lavan remained the same person he had been prior to his dealings with Yaakov — nothing impressed him, and he had not improved himself at all. Even the appearance of Hashem in his dream warning him not to harm Yaakov had no positive effect on Lavan. Quite the opposite; since Hashem warned him against harming Yaakov without actually preventing him from doing so, Lavan felt that he indeed possessed the power to harm Yaakov. For this reason Lavan told Yaakov, "It is in my power to do you all harm; but the God of your father addressed me last night, saying: 'Beware of speaking with Yaakov good or bad' " (31:30). Lavan felt that the choice was his — he could obey the command of Hashem, or he could choose to disobey and do to Yaakov as he pleased. While Lavan — who was not ordinarily inclined to follow Hashem's commands — ultimately decided to obey and not harm Yaakov, Hashem's words did not move him to repent.

❀ ❀ ❀

We see that Yaakov too recognized that while Hashem had sent angels to escort him on his travels, they would not Divinely intercede on his behalf. In the end of *Parashas Vayeitzei*, the verse relates that Yaakov encountered an angelic guard sent by Hashem to escort him into *Eretz Yisrael*. In the beginning of *Parashas Vayishlach*, Yaakov dispatched this group of angels on a mission to his seemingly hostile brother Eisav. While the angels faithfully fulfilled Yaakov's charge — delivering a large gift to Eisav — they did not appear to Eisav as angels, but as simple messengers. Had the angels told Eisav that they had been sent from Heaven by Hashem to help Yaakov, he certainly would have been frightened. In this way they could have assured that Eisav would not dare to confront Yaakov in a hostile manner. Why, then, did the angels hide their true identities from Eisav? The angels were following the instructions that they had received from Hashem — that they not assist Yaakov through their status as angels.

In light of this, we can understand why Yaakov, knowing that he had angels in his camp, still feared his confrontation with Eisav. This is unlike the prophet Elisha who, while surrounded by the armies of Aram, told his servant that he need not have any fear, because they had angels protecting them (*Melachim II* 6:8-18). To Yaakov, however, it seemed as if Hashem had no desire, Heaven forbid, to assist him. Indeed, in this we can see the greatness of Yaakov. Although it seemed that Hashem was not willing to help him, Yaakov at no time questioned the ways of Hashem.

❧ ❧ ❧

וַיִּירָא יַעֲקֹב מְאֹד וַיֵּצֶר לוֹ — *And Yaakov became very frightened, and it distressed him* (32:8).

When Yaakov was traveling to the house of Lavan, Hashem appeared to him saying: *"Behold, I am with you; I will guard you wherever you go, and I will return you to this soil; for I will not forsake you until I will have done what I have spoken about you"* (28:15). After receiving such a promise from Hashem, why was Yaakov afraid of confronting his brother Eisav? The sages therefore explain that Yaakov was frightened despite Hashem's promise, because he was afraid lest a sin cause him to lose this protection. This explanation of the Sages is somewhat difficult to understand. *Rambam* tells us (*Hilchos Yesodei HaTorah* 10:4) that any good decree that is made by Hashem is never rescinded. Even if the recipient of the goodness sins before the decree is fulfilled, the good promised by Hashem will still take place.[1] In light of this *Rambam*, we must once again ask: Why was Yaakov afraid that Hashem's decree might possibly be rescinded?

We must therefore explain that while Yaakov was indeed certain that the promises of Hashem would be fulfilled, there was no guarantee that the fulfillment would come painlessly. While Hashem had promised him that he would return to the land of Canaan, Yaakov feared that perhaps a sin would cause him to first suffer distress at the hands of Eisav. This was one fear that Yaakov had — but there was another, more serious one. Let us explain:

As part of the preparations that Yaakov made for his confrontation with Eisav, he divided his family into two camps. The verse relates that Yaakov said, "If Eisav comes to the one camp and strikes it down, then the remaining camp shall survive" (32:9). *Rashi* comments that Yaakov's

---

1. This concept can also be seen in a conversation between Yirmeyahu and a false prophet in *Yirmeyahu* ch. 28.

intent was that the remaining camp would survive "against Eisav's will, because I will do battle with him." This is very difficult to understand, for, if Yaakov was afraid that a sin might cause him to be unworthy of Hashem's blessing, how could he then be so confident as to say, "the remaining camp will survive" because he will do battle with Eisav? Perhaps a sin would cause Eisav to Heaven forbid defeat Yaakov totally! The answer is that Yaakov knew Hashem's promise granting him children compared to the sand of the sea and possession of the land of *Eretz Yisrael* was guaranteed to be fulfilled. For this reason he was certain that at least one camp of his family would survive. His fear was that perhaps, Heaven forbid, only part of his family would survive, with the rest falling to Eisav as the result of some sin.

❀ ❀ ❀

Rashi comments that Yaakov was frightened lest he be killed, and he was distressed over the thought that he might have to kill others. There was certainly no reason for Yaakov to be distressed should he be forced to kill Eisav. Not only was Eisav coming to kill him, he was also a wicked murderer who undoubtedly deserved just such a fate. Rather, the cause of Yaakov's distress was the thought that while Hashem would save him from the hands of Eisav, it might only be through his having to do battle and kill Eisav. Yaakov knew that Hashem could just as easily save him by granting knowledge to Eisav, so that he would not wish to fight at all. What Yaakov understood — and indeed what we all must realize — is that Hashem's goodness need not be tainted with any anguish or loss at all. If we receive goodness from Hashem in a way that necessitates any difficulty at all, we must realize that the difficulty is a result of a sin, for which we are being punished. It is this thought that distressed Yaakov: Why should Hashem put him in a position where he would have to do battle? Why should his salvation be dependent upon his having to kill? Since Hashem could certainly save him in a more pleasant fashion, this would only be the result of some misdeed for which he was being punished.

An example of this can be seen in the events that occurred when *Bnei Yisrael* first entered *Eretz Yisrael*. As Hashem had foretold to Moshe in a prophecy (*Vayikra* 14:34), when *Bnei Yisrael* entered the land, their houses were afflicted with *tzaraas*. The laws of *tzaraas* require that the afflicted area of the house, and at times the entire house, must be demolished. Upon demolishing the homes, *Bnei Yisrael* found treasures sealed inside the walls. The inhabitants of the land had hoped to hide their valuables from the advancing *Bnei Yisrael*. Had the homes not been Divinely smitten with an affliction, these treasures might have remained hidden for years to come. While at first this would seem to be a wonderful gift from Hashem, it came at the expense of the Jews having to knock down their homes. We can therefore see that while they certainly merited the gifts of the treasures, they also had sinned; therefore, they deserved the punishment of the affliction along with all the aggravation it entailed.

❈ ❈ ❈

לֹא יַעֲקֹב יֵאָמֵר עוֹד שִׁמְךָ כִּי אִם־יִשְׂרָאֵל כִּי־שָׂרִיתָ עִם־אֱלֹקִים וְעִם־אֲנָשִׁים וַתּוּכָל — *"No longer will it be said that your name is Jacob, but Israel, for you have striven with the Divine and with man and have overcome"* (32:29).

We find two places where Jacob learned of the changing of his name: once, in the above verse, from the angel who fought with him prior to his confrontation with his brother Eisav; and once by Hashem Himself. There is an interesting difference between the two. When the angel informed Jacob about the impending change, he supplied Jacob with a reason, as stated in the end of the verse (*for you have striven. . .*). Hashem, on the other hand, gave no reason for the change at all.

In order to understand the reason for this differentiation, we must first explain the meaning of the reason given to Jacob by the angel. The angel told Jacob that he was worthy of receiving the name Yisrael because he "strove with the Divine and with man and overcame." What was the nature of the "striving" to which the angel referred?

A person is faced with many challenges in this world. It is his role to meet those challenges and remain steadfast in his faith and fear of Hashem. These challenges mainly fall into two categories. First, there are the personal struggles that every person has within himself. Our Evil Inclination is always trying to tempt us to transgress the laws of our Torah in search of imagined material gain. Hashem granted us this Evil Inclination for our benefit, to ensure that we would always have free choice — and thus, be deserving of reward in the World to Come.

This is one type of challenge a person is often faced with. There is, however, another that is sometimes even more difficult to face than the first. This second type of challenge is the challenge of people. In every generation, there are those people who try to persuade and prevent us from adhering to the tenets of our Torah. This, too, is a type of adversity we must constantly face and, with much effort, defeat.

The angel told Jacob that in the *past* he had been successful on both of these fronts. "For you have striven with the Divine" refers to the Divinely given Evil Inclination. "With man" refers to the various people who tried to stop Jacob from pursuing his spiritual goals. For this reason, the angel told Jacob, he was worthy of having his name changed to Yisrael. Hashem, on the other hand, was not discussing the past. Hashem was assuring Jacob that all the *future* generations of *Klal Yisrael* would be worthy of the name Yisrael; that they all would contain learned, God-fearing individuals who would neither give in to the persuasions of the Evil Inclination nor bend to the will of corrupt people. By giving the name Yisrael to Jacob, Hashem promised him that in every generation anyone who could be said to have "striven" would be guaranteed to "overcome."

❧ ❧ ❧

וַיֹּאמֶר עֵשָׂו יֶשׁ־לִי רָב אָחִי יְהִי לְךָ אֲשֶׁר־לָךְ. וַיֹּאמֶר יַעֲקֹב . . . וְלָקַחְתָּ מִנְחָתִי מִיָּדִי כִּי עַל־כֵּן רָאִיתִי פָנֶיךָ כִּרְאֹת פְּנֵי אֱלֹהִים וַתִּרְצֵנִי — *Eisav said, "I have plenty. My brother, let what you have remain yours." But Yaakov said, ". . . Please accept my gift which was brought to you, inasmuch as God has been gracious to me and inasmuch as I have everything"* (33:9-11).

Eisav said, "I have plenty." Yaakov responded, "I have everything." Each one, in his individual choice of words, spoke volumes about his perception and understanding of the world in which he lived. What is the difference between Eisav, who felt that he had plenty, and Yaakov who stated that he had everything? Let us analyze the two different world-views that are represented by this difference in phraseology.

A person that truly believes in Hashem and His Torah, who knows that all that he has is Divinely ordained, should realize that whatever he has, that is exactly what it is that he needs. The wealthy person has not one cent above, nor does the pauper fall one cent short of what is necessary to fill his needs. While it may seem to the rich person that he has much more than he needs to provide for his family's needs, he must realize that this is not the case. If Hashem blessed him with riches, those riches are accompanied by additional obligations. The support of the indigent, the spreading of Hashem's Torah through the financial support of *yeshivos* — these things are not to be seen as optional; rather they are part and parcel of financial success. For this reason the *tzaddik* who understands this knows that he never has plenty, he simply has everything — everything that he needs to fill *all* of his obligations.

This stands in stark contrast to the perspective of the wicked. The wicked live under the mistaken premise that their wealth came to them not as a gift from Hashem, but rather as a product of their own efforts and abilities. Accordingly, they do not feel that the possession of material wealth comes with any obligations at all. For, in their minds, if they earned their wealth, who has the right to tell them how to use it? Such a person, when he sees that he has more than is required to fill his needs, will think that he has plenty — because he does not accept the fact that he has any other obligations besides those dictated by his own personal priorities.

This was the difference between Yaakov and Eisav. Yaakov understood that he possessed everything. He had in his possession everything that he needed to do the things that Hashem wanted him to do. He had wealth, to be sure, but in his mind every cent was accounted for — they all had a purpose in the service of Hashem. Eisav on the other hand thought that he had plenty. He thought that he was free to do as he pleased with all that he had, and that he had more than he needed to do so.

Each person must take this lesson to heart, and realize that Hashem does not give any person more than he needs. Accordingly, when a person is blessed with prosperity, he must recognize his responsibility, and strive to build Torah and do good works. For in truth, this is the very purpose of his prosperity.

❦ ❦ ❦

וַתָּמָת דְּבֹרָה מֵינֶקֶת רִבְקָה וַתִּקָּבֵר מִתַּחַת לְבֵית־אֵל תַּחַת
הָאַלּוֹן וַיִּקְרָא שְׁמוֹ אַלּוֹן בָּכוּת — *Devorah, the wet
nurse of Rivkah, died, and she was buried below
Beth-el, below the allon; and he named it Allon-
bachuth* (35:8).

The Hebrew word *"bachuth"* means weeping. Yaakov named the
entire plain Allon-bachuth, to commemorate the crying and
mourning that took place there.

It is interesting to note that Yaakov chose to commemorate the
weeping that took place; not the fact that Devorah was actually buried
there. This is difficult to understand. Why didn't Yaakov use a name
alluding to the fact that Devorah was interred there? Surely that would
be a more permanent way to preserve her memory! After all, while the
weeping was a one-time occurrence that would likely be forgotten with
the passage of time, her physical remains would always be there.

There is a simple answer to our question. Yaakov understood that the
permanence of a physical memorial is only superficial. While it may be
true that by creating a physical monument to Devorah's burial place her
grave would be forever memorialized, it would soon become simply
another grave of some long-forgotten person.

This was not the type of memorial that Yaakov was looking for. He
knew that the eternal memorial to Devorah would be the results of the
weeping over her memory. Eulogizing her, speaking about her good
deeds and positive character traits would serve to inspire countless
generations of people. This is the sort of memorial Yaakov wished for
Devorah, that the people who knew her should mourn her loss and take
to heart the ideals she had stood for during the course of her life. If they
would do so, and seek to instill those ideals into the hearts and minds of
their children, they would perpetuate the memory of Devorah for all
eternity.

☙ ☙ ☙

As we have noted above, Yaakov named the plain after the weeping
that took place there over the passing of Devorah. When Yaakov buried
Rachel, however, he chose to name the place after her burial — not after
the mourning over her loss. This is despite the fact that the mourning
over her loss must have been even greater than the mourning over the
loss of Devorah.

The reason for this difference is simple to understand. Rachel, being one of the Matriarchs of *Bnei Yisrael,* was one of the greatest women of all time. Furthermore, she passed away in her younger years. This was obviously a tragedy of great proportions. Yaakov and all who were with him certainly mourned her loss greatly, observing the 30-day mourning period that is obligatory after the loss of a righteous person. It was therefore unnecessary for Yaakov to call our attention to the fact that the people wept over her loss. What was important was to call attention to the location of Rachel's burial place — so that the future generations of *Klal Yisrael* would know where they may pray for Hashem's mercy in her merit.

The same could not be said of the passing of Devorah. Yaakov wished to publicize the fact that she was a virtuous woman, one who merited being the nursemaid of one of our Matriarchs — a person whose loss was worthy of being mourned. To do so, Yaakov named the entire plain Allon-bachuth, the plain of weeping.

❦ ❦ ❦

פרשת וישב
Parashas Vayeishev

וַיֹּאמֶר יִשְׂרָאֵל אֶל־יוֹסֵף הֲלוֹא אַחֶיךָ רֹעִים בִּשְׁכֶם לְכָה וְאֶשְׁלָחֲךָ אֲלֵיהֶם וַיֹּאמֶר לוֹ הִנֵּנִי — *And Yisrael said to Yosef, "Your brothers are pasturing in Shechem, are they not? Come, I will send you to them." He said to him: "Here I am!"* (37:13).

e find in the Midrash (*Bereishis Rabbah* 84:12): Reb Chama ben Reb Chaninah said: "Our forefather Yaakov would remember these words (after the sale of Yosef) and his insides would be chopped up (with anguish). You (Yosef) knew that your brothers hated you, yet you answered me, 'Here I am!' " Yosef knew that his brothers were not favorably disposed towards him. He therefore realized that by fulfilling his father's mission he was quite possibly heading into danger. Even so, he did not hesitate to honor his father's request. While this may seem a very commendable fulfillment of the *mitzvah* of *kibbud av*, honoring your father, it is actually very puzzling. How was Yosef permitted to enter into danger? Understandable as it may be that Yosef did not wish to reveal to his father the hatred that he knew his brothers felt towards him, he should have found some other pretext excusing himself from entering into such a dangerous position. If he could not contrive any other excuse, then he should have told his father the true state of affairs that existed between him and his brothers, and his father — while undoubtedly being upset — would have told him not to go.

We can answer this as follows. We explained earlier that Yaakov was frightened of his confrontation with Eisav because he worried that perhaps a sin would cause him to lose some aspect of the Divine protection that he had been granted. While Yaakov was able to entertain such fears, his son Yosef was not. It would have been forbidden for Yosef to suspect his father — who was also his teacher as well as a prophet — of any wrongdoing. Therefore, Yosef reasoned, he had nothing to fear. For since Yaakov was not deserving of any punishment, he, being his father's beloved son, could not possibly be killed. Even if he himself was guilty of sin, and therefore liable for punishment in his own right, that would not be cause for Hashem to rescind His promise to Yaakov that all his children would survive. It was still possible that Yosef would have to suffer other forms of distress at the hands of his brothers, but since he knew that he would not be killed, he was prepared to suffer, rather than reveal to his father the enmity that existed between him and his brothers.

❀ ❀ ❀

פרשת מקץ
Parashas Mikeitz

הֲשָׁלוֹם אֲבִיכֶם הַזָּקֵן אֲשֶׁר אֲמַרְתֶּם הַעוֹדֶנּוּ חָי. וַיֹּאמְרוּ שָׁלוֹם לְעַבְדְּךָ לְאָבִינוּ עוֹדֶנּוּ חָי — *"Is your aged father of whom you spoke at peace? Is he still alive?" They replied: "Your servant our father is at peace; he still lives"* (43:27-28).

Yosef's question and the brothers' answer are very puzzling. If Yaakov could be said to be at peace, certainly it follows that he was alive! Yet for some reason Yosef and his brothers felt they had to mention both.

In order to answer this, we must understand that both Yosef and his brothers knew that there is more to life than superficial existence. Yosef was asking his brothers: Your father may be at peace — but is he alive? Has he been able to maintain his righteousness and complete faith in Hashem in the face of all the troubles he has had to bear?

His brothers answered him with a resounding yes. "Our father is at peace; he still lives"; that is, our father's righteousness remains unaffected by all that has happened to him. This is because at all times, no matter what transpires, our father accepts the justice of Hashem's actions.

❧ ❧ ❧

וַיִּשְׁתּוּ וַיִּשְׁכְּרוּ עִמּוֹ — *They drank and became intoxicated along with him* (43:34).

Yosef, who had the ability to reveal his identity to his brothers at any time, no longer felt the sorrow of his long separation from his brothers. The rest of the Tribes, however, were as yet unaware that the Egyptian viceroy with whom they were dealing was actually their long-lost brother. Why, then, did they break their practice of not drinking intoxicating beverages — a practice they had adopted on the day they sold Yosef into slavery?

Prior to the Tribes' departure from the land of Canaan, Yaakov prayed that they should be successful in their endeavors, that they should find favor in the eyes of the Egyptians, and that they should return with Binyamin, as well as their "other brother." *Rashi* explains that this was a reference to Yosef, their "other brother" who was also missing. Arriving in Egypt, the brothers watched as the first part of Yaakov's *tefillah* was fulfilled. When they had previously arrived in Egypt, they had been threatened and falsely accused of attempting to spy on the land. Not only were they now greeted in a favorable fashion, they were going to dine together with the very person that had seemed to be their nemesis — the powerful viceroy of the country. Seeing that part of Yaakov's blessing was fulfilled, the brothers felt assured that the rest of Yaakov's blessing — that they should find and return with Yosef — would also be fulfilled. With this in mind, the Tribes felt confident enough to indulge as they had not done since they were separated from their brother.

There is an important lesson to be learned here. Just as the Tribes celebrated when they perceived the onset of their salvation, so too one must not wait for the completion of his salvation to give thanks to Hashem; rather, one must already thank Hashem at the onset of salvation.

❀ ❀ ❀

פרשת ויגש
Parashas Vayigash

הֵן כֶּסֶף אֲשֶׁר מָצָאנוּ בְּפִי אַמְתְּחֹתֵינוּ הֱשִׁיבֹנוּ אֵלֶיךָ
מֵאֶרֶץ כְּנָעַן וְאֵיךְ נִגְנֹב מִבֵּית אֲדֹנֶיךָ כֶּסֶף אוֹ זָהָב
*"Here, look: The money that we found in the
mouth of our sacks we brought back to you from
the land of Canaan. How then could we have
stolen from your master's house any silver or
gold?"* (44:8).

This is one of the instances in the Torah where the verse
documents the use of a *kal vachomer* (an *a fortiori* argument).
The brothers argued that if they had come all the way back from
Canaan to return money that they had not even taken, how could they
now be accused of having stolen? In another instance where we find use
of this type of reasoning, Moshe asks Hashem (with regard to Hashem's
command that he instruct Pharaoh to release the Jews from captivity):
*"Behold, the Bnei Yisrael have not listened to me, so how will Pharaoh
listen to me?"* (*Shemos* 6:12).

In both of the above-noted instances, the logic of the arguments would
seem to be flawed. In the case of the brothers, Joseph's men could have
retorted that they had a compelling reason to return the money they
found in their sacks. Perhaps they feared that it was placed there to test
their honesty. Or perhaps, as they themselves suggested upon reaching
Canaan, the money was placed there to frame them — in which case
they certainly would wish to return the money! Likewise, there is a
logical flaw in the *kal vachomer* argument advanced by Moshe. The
verse records a specific reason why *Bnei Yisrael* did not listen to Moshe:
but they did not heed Moshe, because of shortness of breath and hard

work (*Shemos* 6:9). Surely Moshe understood that this reasoning did not apply to Pharaoh!

To answer our question, we must explain that the Torah is introducing to us an important concept necessary to those involved in the intricacies of Torah study. Often, when involved in the study of Torah, one desires to make logical comparisons between two cases or laws. The *kal vachomer* argument mentioned above is one example of the type of arguments frequently employed in the course of Torah study. By showing us the use of arguments that are apparently logically flawed, the verse wishes to teach us that the use of such arguments is not an exact science. There are times when the inherent truth of something must suffice to identify it as correct, even after closer analysis reveals the presence of what appears to be a serious flaw. At the same time, this should not be taken as an indication that the Torah does not require deep thought — quite the contrary, one must delve into the depths of the Torah's meaning as deeply as possible. What is necessary, though, is a heart capable of discerning the truth, and distinguishing between that which *seems* true only on the surface, and that which *is* true despite what further analysis seems to reveal.

❈ ❈ ❈

וַיֹּאמֶר יוֹסֵף אֶל־אֶחָיו אֲנִי יוֹסֵף — *And Yosef said to his brothers, "I am Yosef"* (45:3).

וַיֹּאמֶר אֲנִי יוֹסֵף אֲחִיכֶם אֲשֶׁר־מְכַרְתֶּם אֹתִי מִצְרָיְמָה — *And he said, "I am Yosef your brother — it is me, whom you sold into Egypt"* (45:4).

Why did Yosef twice tell his brothers "I am Yosef"? We can answer this by explaining that there are two facets in the makeup of an individual. When Yosef first told his brothers that it was him, they only knew that it was the "physical" Yosef. They were unsure, though, whether or not the "spiritual" Yosef was still intact. For this reason, while the brothers no longer feared retribution from him, they nonetheless felt that he might harbor ill feelings towards them. Yosef, however, told them that he was still the same Yosef that they always knew, the one who inherited his traits and beliefs from his forefathers — Avraham, Yitzchak, and Yaakov. Having heard that, the brothers realized that they no longer had anything to fear.

❈ ❈ ❈

וַיֹּאמֶר פַּרְעֹה אֶל־יַעֲקֹב כַּמָּה יְמֵי שְׁנֵי חַיֶּיךָ. וַיֹּאמֶר יַעֲקֹב אֶל־פַּרְעֹה יְמֵי שְׁנֵי מְגוּרַי שְׁלֹשִׁים וּמְאַת שָׁנָה מְעַט וְרָעִים הָיוּ יְמֵי שְׁנֵי חַיַּי וְלֹא הִשִּׂיגוּ אֶת־יְמֵי שְׁנֵי חַיֵּי אֲבֹתַי בִּימֵי מְגוּרֵיהֶם — *Pharaoh said to Yaakov, "How many are the days of the years of your life?" Yaakov answered Pharaoh, "The days of the years of my sojourns have been a hundred and thirty years. Few and bad have been the days of the years of my life, and they have not reached the life spans of my forefathers in the days of their sojourns"* (47:8-9).

R*amban* asks: Why would Yaakov complain to Pharaoh? We shall see that Yaakov's statement was much more meaningful than a mere complaint.

When a group of people immigrate to a new country, it is natural and expected that they desire to better their chances of success in their new surroundings, through assimilation into their new nation. Certainly Pharaoh would have expected that Yaakov and his children, who were family to the royalty of the country, would wish to explore all of the opportunities open to them in their new home. This, however, was not Yaakov's desire at all. He understood that in order for his family to fulfill the will of Hashem and become "*A kingdom of ministers and a holy nation*" (*Shemos* 19:6), they would have to remain a people apart from the Egyptians. Indeed the Haggadah, expounding the verse that says "*And there he became a nation*" (*Devarim* 26:5), tells us that the children of Yaakov were successful at this and therefore became "distinctive" there. It was this that Yaakov wished to convey to Pharaoh — that he was not coming to Egypt with the same intent as most immigrants, and that his actions were not guided by what would allow him to live a comfortable life. *Few and bad have been the days of the years of my life* — my goal has never been to lead a comfortable existence. Rather, my way has been to live apart from others, even though it would seem to be to the detriment of my family's prosperity.

In this, Yaakov differed from the ways of his forefathers Avraham and Yitzchak. We know that Avraham and Yitzchak worked continuously to spread recognition of Hashem and adherence to His commandments among all of the nations. Yaakov, however, harbored no desire to do the same for the Egyptians. The reason for this lies in the fact that the world had undergone a major change from the time of Avraham and Yitzchak to the time of Yaakov.

Prior to the birth of Yaakov's twelve tribes, it was incumbent upon the righteous to teach and encourage others to follow the will of Hashem. Thus, Avraham and Yitzchak strove to teach others to recognize their Creator and obey the seven Noachide laws God had placed upon them. Once the twelve tribes had been born, however, there was now a specific nation, independent of the other nations of the world, that was to be dedicated to the service of Hashem. Their job was not to teach others, but rather to perfect themselves. Yaakov knew that in order to reach and maintain this perfection, it is necessary to distance oneself from evil as much as possible. For this reason, Yaakov never attempted to exert any positive influence upon Lavan and his children when he was living in Charan. It was for this reason too that Yaakov's children would have to live apart from the rest of the Egyptians in the land of Goshen.

Indeed, this is the task of *Bnei Yisrael* as a nation; to insulate itself from that which is evil, and thereby excel at that which it knows is Divine. We find this idea clearly reflected in the verse: *Thus Israel shall dwell secure, solitary, in the likeness of Yaakov (Devarim* 33:28).

[While there is a commandment to admonish a sinner, and one might think that for this reason Yaakov should have sought to correct the evils of Egyptian society, the verse specifies that this commandment refers only to a fellow Jew; not to a gentile. An example of this can be seen in the case of Naomi and her two Moabite daughters-in-law, Ruth and Orpah. When Naomi's two sons died, Orpah returned to her gentile family and their practice of idol worship. Naomi encouraged Ruth to do likewise, despite the fact that idol worship is forbidden to all people as one of the seven Noachide commandments. Thus, it is clear that we are not obligated to care for the spiritual well-being of the gentile population.]

❀ ❀ ❀

פרשת ויחי
Parashas Vayechi

הֵאָסְפוּ וְאַגִּידָה לָכֶם אֵת אֲשֶׁר־יִקְרָא אֶתְכֶם בְּאַחֲרִית
הַיָּמִים — *"Assemble yourselves and I will tell you
what will befall you in the End of Days"* (49:1).

he Talmud teaches: Yaakov wished to tell his children when
Mashiach would come, but the Divine Presence deserted him.
Yaakov, wondering why the Divine Presence would leave him,
thought that perhaps one of his children were unworthy — another
Yishmael or Eisav. In response to their father's fears, the Tribes
exclaimed, *"Shema Yisrael, Hashem Elokeinu, Hashem echad!* Just as
in your heart you recognize only one true God, so too, we in our hearts
only recognize one true God!" Yaakov, seeing that his fears were
unfounded, responded in gratitude, "בָּרוּךְ שֵׁם כְּבוֹד מַלְכוּתוֹ לְעוֹלָם וָעֶד,
Blessed is the Name of His glorious kingdom for all eternity" (*Pesachim*
56b).

It is interesting that while it is clear from the Talmud that Yaakov
uttered these famous words, Moshe was not commanded by Hashem to
record them in the Torah. It would seem that the reason for this lies in
the very nature of this phrase. The exclamation *Baruch Shem* etc. is one
which is used by a person when he feels that he must strengthen his faith.
When someone watches the successes of the gentiles living around him,
he often needs to verbalize and acknowledge the Kingship of Hashem as
a way of reaffirming and strengthening his belief in Hashem. The
generation of the Exodus, a generation that witnessed the miracles that
took place in Egypt and went on to accept the Torah, had no need for
such a tool to buoy their faith.

We find in *halachah* an indication that this is indeed the theme of Yaakov's words. The *halachah* teaches that one who needlessly utters a blessing containing Hashem's Name is required to immediately recite *Baruch Shem*. The ability to needlessly utter the Name of Hashem is indicative of a person lacking proper fear of Hashem. Such a person requires the recital of *Baruch Shem* etc. to reawaken in himself proper reverence for his Creator.

Based on the above, we can understand why, when we say *Baruch Shem* following the recital of the *Shema,* we do so in an undertone. Since the recital of this prayer indicates a need for our faith in Hashem to be strengthened, it would be both embarrassing to ourselves as well as disrespectful to Hashem to say it aloud. Indeed, the Talmud (*Pesachim* 56a) compares our recital of *Baruch Shem* etc. to a princess who is tempted by the aroma of a pot stew. The servants of the princess are faced with a dilemma: Should they serve the princess the dish — and by so doing embarrass her with food below her royal status? Or should they deny her that which tempted her, and possibly cause her distress? The solution that the servants find is to bring the dish to the princess discreetly — giving her what she desires without causing her unnecessary embarrassment. It is the same with *Bnei Yisrael.* While we require the positive effects of saying *Baruch Shem,* it is still something that we remain embarrassed about — and we therefore say it quietly. There is, though, an exception to this rule. On Yom Kippur, the day that we are commanded to candidly admit our sins and acknowledge our shortcomings before Hashem, we say *Baruch Shem* out loud for all to hear. On this day it is our desire to show Hashem that we are aware of our need to grow in our perception of Him — and that we are indeed searching for ways to strengthen our faith and our commitment to His Torah.

❧ ❧ ❧

ספר שמות ‏
Sefer Shemos

פרשת שמות
Parashas Shemos

וַיִּפְגְּשֵׁהוּ ה' וַיְבַקֵּשׁ הֲמִיתוֹ. וַתִּקַּח צִפֹּרָה צֹר וַתִּכְרֹת
אֶת־עָרְלַת בְּנָהּ . . . וַיִּרֶף מִמֶּנּוּ — *Hashem encoun-*
tered him and sought to kill him. So Zipporah
took a sharp stone and cut off the foreskin of her
son . . . So He released him (4:24-26).

T he Tanna R' Yehoshua Ben Korcha said: Great is the precept of
milah (circumcision), for Moshe the righteous did not have his
punishment suspended even for a single hour [when he failed to
circumcise his son in a timely manner]. It is interesting to note that
nowhere else do we find the appellation of "the righteous" used in
reference to Moshe. By using this terminology, the Tanna wishes to tell
us that even in this story, where as a result of his actions Moshe almost lost
his life, from a standpoint of *halachah* he was righteous. Let us explain:

What had Moshe done wrong? Moshe set out for Egypt with his family,
including his newborn son who had not yet been circumcised. He was
faced with a dilemma. Should he perform the circumcision before he
went, and then take the child with him? — but the infant would be in
danger for the first three days after the circumcision! Should he perform
the circumcision and then delay his trip for three days? — but Hashem
had commanded him to go! He decided to travel immediately and
perform the circumcision at the first available opportunity at the
conclusion of his trip. Although Hashem found no fault with Moshe's
decision to delay the circumcision, he was still held culpable, for when
they arrived at an inn, Moshe began making arrangements for his lodging
instead of performing the circumcision without delay.

From the standpoint of strict *halachah*, Moshe was correct. Since he had not yet finalized arrangements for lodging, his trip had not yet ended and his son was still halachically a traveler — unable to undergo the rigors of circumcision. At this point in his journey, however, Moshe had an option that was unavailable to him at the outset — prayer. When Moshe first set out on his journey to Egypt, he could have prayed to Hashem asking that his son not be harmed by the ordeal of circumcision; so that he would be able to perform the commandment in its proper time. Praying that Hashem should protect someone from a situation well known to be dangerous, however, would have been improper. This was not the case, though, when Moshe arrived at the inn. Now there were only minutes left to the journey — a situation that did not necessarily preclude the possibility of performing the circumcision. At that time the great Moshe — whose *tefillah* certainly would have been accepted by Hashem — should have prayed to Hashem for his son's protection and performed the circumcision.

פרשת וארא
Parashas Va'eira

וַיְדַבֵּר אֱלֹקִים אֶל־מֹשֶׁה וַיֹּאמֶר אֵלָיו אֲנִי ה' — *And God spoke to Moshe and said to him, "I am Hashem"* (6:2).

ashi comments: Hashem spoke to Moshe with words of rebuke for speaking harshly and saying, "Why have you harmed this people?" *Rashi's* deduction is apparently based upon the juxtaposition of the term, "וַיְדַבֵּר" a word usually used to indicate harsh speech, and the use of "Elokim," the name of Hashem that denotes justice. It is interesting to note that in the very same verse, in connection with the same conversation, we find the use of the word וַיֹּאמֶר, the term used to denote softer, more compassionate speech.

From this apparent discrepancy in the verse's terminology, we can learn an important lesson in the proper method to use when it is necessary to rebuke your fellow man. While it may be necessary to use harsh words, it is also necessary to immediately follow them with words of compassion and consolation. As the Talmud says (*Kesubos* 103b), it is at times necessary to "strike dread into the disciples"; yet, it is equally necessary to speak and act with compassion.

❧ ❧ ❧

וַיְחַזֵּק ה' אֶת לֵב פַּרְעֹה וְלֹא שָׁמַע אֲלֵיהֶם כַּאֲשֶׁר דִּבֶּר ה' אֶל מֹשֶׁה — *Hashem strengthened the heart of Pharaoh and he did not heed them, as Hashem had spoken to Moshe* (*Shemos* 9:12).

uring the first five plagues, Hashem did not interfere with Pharaoh's power of free choice. During the final five, however, when Pharaoh had already displayed his reluctance to repent,

Hashem punished him with the loss of his personal free will. For this reason we find that while following the third plague the verse tells us *Pharaoh's heart was strong* (8:15), after the sixth plague, the verse says, *Hashem strengthened the heart of Pharaoh* (9:12). No longer did Pharaoh possess the power to control his own heart — it was now being hardened by Hashem.

Although Pharaoh was no longer in control of his own destiny, Hashem punished him as though he continued to sin of his own volition. From Hashem's treatment of the wicked Pharaoh, we may determine how Hashem would treat the righteous in a similar situation.

Just as Pharaoh was punished for his evil deeds by losing the ability to fight his Evil Inclination, there are those who are rewarded by Hashem for their good deeds with the removal of their Evil Inclination. The Talmud tells us (*Bava Basra* 17a) that this is the meaning of David Hamelech's statement in *Tehillim* (109:22), *my heart has died within me.* David Hamelech said that through his good deeds he earned the removal of his Evil Inclination. Therefore his "heart," a reference to the Evil Inclination which until that point had resided in his heart, could be said to have died.

When Hashem rewards a person for his good deeds, He takes into account the amount of effort a person invests in his actions. The lame person who limps to *shul* every morning may earn more reward with his five-minute walk than the athlete who jogs two miles to *shul*. When Hashem removes the Evil Inclination from the righteous, it allows them to serve Hashem without any struggle at all. Will this lessen the amount of reward they will receive? Surely not. If Pharaoh, who no longer had the ability to fight his Evil Inclination, was punished as if he chose not to fight it, certainly the righteous, who no longer must fight their Evil Inclinations, will be rewarded as if they battled mightily — and won.

❦ ❦ ❦

וַיֵּצֵא מֹשֶׁה מֵעִם פַּרְעֹה אֶת־הָעִיר וַיִּפְרֹשׂ כַּפָּיו אֶל־ה' וַיַּחְדְּלוּ הַקֹּלוֹת וְהַבָּרָד וּמָטָר לֹא־נִתַּךְ אָרְצָה — *Moshe went out from Pharaoh, from the city, and he stretched out his hands to Hashem; the thunder and hail ceased and rain did not reach the earth* (9:33).

Rashi comments that the words *and rain did not reach the earth* teach us that the hailstones that were in midair at the time of Moshe's prayer immediately disappeared and never reached the earth. While at first glance this appears to be an unnecessary miracle, upon further reflection we will find that there are several important lessons we can learn from its occurrence.

Why do we view the discontinuation of the hail's earthward flight as miraculous? Only because we accept as fact the laws of physics, which demand that heavy objects such as hail that are suspended in midair must eventually fall. We must ask ourselves, however: Why is it that the laws of physics operate the way that they do? Who ordained that hail should fall and not float upon the wind? We must realize that these facts that we accept as natural and immutable are only the result of the word of Hashem, uttered during the six days of Creation. While it is true that Hashem ordained that heavy objects fall and lighter ones float, the fact remains that He could have just as easily done the exact opposite.

For this reason, Hashem did not allow the descending hail to fall. We cannot understand this as a miracle — for as we have noted, Hashem does not perform unnecessary miracles. How then are we to understand it? The answer is that Hashem wishes us to realize that this happening need not be considered more miraculous than nature itself; and this was the very reason that Hashem caused the hail to vanish.

We find this concept portrayed in the Talmud as well. The Talmud relates (*Taanis* 25a) that one *Erev Shabbos* Rav Chanina ben Dosa noticed that his daughter was upset. When he asked what was troubling her, she responded that she had mistaken a vessel full of vinegar for one of oil, and used it for her Shabbos lights. Rav Chanina asked her, "Why should you be concerned? He Who said that oil should burn will say that vinegar should burn."

Rav Chanina understood clearly that oil burns only because Hashem imbued it with the ability to do so; not because physics demands that it should. Were it to be the will of Hashem, He could easily invest vinegar with those same properties. Recognizing this, Rav Chanina found the phenomenon of vinegar burning no more surprising than the fact that oil burns. It is only as a result of this understanding that he was able to rely on Hashem's arranging that the vinegar would burn. Such a request would normally be considered a prayer for a miracle, something that the Talmud tells us (*Berachos* 60a) is not proper. In the case of Rav Chanina, however, it was not considered to be a prayer for a miracle, because to Rav Chanina it would seem no more miraculous than the usual occurrences of everyday life.

This is one lesson to be learned from this occurrence. Let us now explore another.

The verse in *Parashas Ki Savo* tells us, *Hashem will confirm you for himself as a holy people, as He swore to you — if you observe the commandments of Hashem your God, and you go in His ways* (*Devarim* 28:9). The Sages tell us that the phrase *and you go in His ways* is a Biblical commandment that we should emulate the ways of Hashem as much as possible. It is from this verse that we learn the importance of perfecting our character traits, as well as the importance of performing acts of kindness. In both of these areas, Hashem has set an example through His actions for us to follow. There is, however, one thing that is difficult to learn from Hashem — the proper way to fulfill His commandments. Where has Hashem set an example of how we are to respond to His commands?

Perhaps that is what Hashem wishes to teach us with the performance of this miracle. From the way Hashem responds to the *tefillos* of the righteous, we may learn how to respond to the commands of Hashem. Hashem accepted the *tefillah* of Moshe and immediately fulfilled it exactly as it had been expressed — without regard for the reasoning behind it. Moshe's intent when praying was simply that the plague should end (i.e. no new hail should come forth from the clouds). Hashem, however, having accepted Moshe's *tefillah* that the plague should cease, caused the plague to end immediately — immobilizing the hail in midair.

We find that Hashem acted similarly after Moshe prayed for an end to the plague of locusts. The *Ramban* says that as a result of Moshe's *tefillah*, locusts never again destroyed any crops in the land of Egypt. Clearly, Moshe was only praying for the removal of the locusts at that time, not for all future generations. Yet, since Hashem accepted the prayer that he offered without any specifications, He prevented locusts from causing damage in Egypt forever and ever.

When we do *mitzvos*, too, we should be motivated by our desire to fulfill the decree of Hashem our King — not by what we perceive to be the reason for His commands.

It is also possible that Hashem caused the miraculous disappearance of the hail to clearly illustrate to Pharaoh that Moshe was capable of controlling the hail with his prayer. Had the hail simply ceased, Pharaoh might have assumed that Moshe had timed his prayer to coincide with the time that he knew the plague would end; or that Moshe had only limited mastery over the plague. To dispel this notion, Hashem caused the hail to miraculously vanish in midair, leaving no doubt as to Moshe's ability.

פרשת בא
Parashas Bo

הַחֹדֶשׁ הַזֶּה לָכֶם רֹאשׁ חֳדָשִׁים רִאשׁוֹן הוּא לָכֶם לְחָדְשֵׁי הַשָּׁנָה — *This month shall be for you the beginning of the months, it shall be for you the first of the months of the year* (12:2).

ashi comments that this verse teaches us that the month of *Nissan* — the period in which the Exodus from Egypt took place — is to be counted as the first month of the year, *Iyar* the second and so on. This is somewhat puzzling. Of all the months, the most obvious choice to be the first month would have been *Tishrei*, since it was then that the world was created. One would have thought that the second choice would be the month of *Sivan* — the month in which the *Bnei Yisrael* accepted the Torah. Why is *Nissan* the second choice? After all, *Rashi* tells us in *Bereishis* (1:31) that the entire continuity of the Creation was dependent upon the acceptance by the *Bnei Yisrael* of the Torah. Surely this takes precedence even over the miraculous Exodus from Egypt!

The answer is that the acceptance of the Torah that took place in the month of *Sivan* cannot be viewed independently. For the *Bnei Yisrael* to reach a level of dedication where they were capable of accepting the Torah with a lasting commitment, great preparation was necessary. Their faith, their character traits — these things required great change prior to the Revelation at Sinai. In addition, they would have to learn and accept the need to separate themselves from the ways of the gentile nations. All of this was accomplished during the 49 day interval between the Exodus and the Revelation. How was this possible? Only because the Revelation was preceded by the tremendous lessons of the miraculous Exodus. For this reason the Exodus from Egypt was also the start of the acceptance of the Torah — and thus we count *Nissan* as the first month of the year.

We can learn from this an important lesson regarding the proper method of raising children. The teaching of proper character traits and *emunah* cannot wait until a child is ready to begin learning and understanding Torah. We must strive to imbue our children with these all-important ideals from birth — so that when the time comes they will be prepared to dedicate themselves fully to leading a life of Torah and *mitzvos*.

❧ ❧ ❧

וַיֵּלְכוּ וַיַּעֲשׂוּ בְּנֵי יִשְׂרָאֵל כַּאֲשֶׁר צִוָּה ה' אֶת־מֹשֶׁה וְאַהֲרֹן
כֵּן עָשׂוּ — The children of Israel went and did as
Hashem commanded Moshe and Aharon, so
they did (12:28).

Rashi comments that the seemingly repetitive phrase *so they did* teaches us that "even Moshe and Aharon did so." This *Rashi* is difficult to understand. Do we really need extraneous phrases to teach us that Moshe and Aharon fulfilled the commandment of Hashem? It is of course obvious that the teachers of *Bnei Yisrael,* Moshe and Aharon, fulfilled the commandments of Hashem without fail! *Rashi* is calling to our attention a deeper message that is hidden in the words of our verse.

The righteous and great people among the *Bnei Yisrael* carry a great responsibility. For them, it is not sufficient to fulfill the halachic requirements of a commandment. When they perform a good deed, it must be obvious to all that the commandment was fulfilled in a perfect manner. The reason for this is simple. The righteous among us are held up as an example for the rest of us to try and emulate. When such a person performs a commandment, he must serve as a source of teaching and inspiration to all who observe him. This is only possible if it is clear to all that the deed was performed properly. If, however, there is any room for one to think — even in error — that the deed was not performed properly, the result will be that nothing will be learned from any of his actions. Once people dismiss some of the righteous person's actions, they will dismiss the rest, saying, "Just as this portion of his actions is improper and unworthy of emulation, so too it is unimportant to learn from the rest of his actions."

The great Amora, Rav, understood this well. The Talmud tells us (*Yoma* 86a) that Rav was asked to depict a case of *chillul Hashem*, desecration of Hashem's Name. Rav answered that should he ever purchase meat on credit, that would constitute a desecration of Hashem's Name. But surely there is nothing wrong with purchasing goods on credit so long as both parties are agreeable to the terms! Why, then, would such an act be a desecration of Hashem's Name? The explanation is that Rav knew that a person of his stature dare not leave himself open to the accusation that he had no intention of paying for his purchase. Although there were obviously no grounds whatsoever for such an ugly accusation, should one unscrupulous individual forward such a thought, the path would be open to a devaluation of Rav and the Torah that he taught. That would indeed cause a tremendous desecration of Hashem's Name.

This, then, is the lesson of our verse. It is patently obvious that Moshe and Aharon fulfilled the commandments of Hashem, and no extra verse is needed to teach us this. Our verse wishes to testify that it was obvious to *all of the Bnei Yisrael* observing Moshe and Aharon, that they had fulfilled the will of Hashem in a proper and fitting manner.

❀ ❀ ❀

וַיֹּאפוּ אֶת־הַבָּצֵק אֲשֶׁר הוֹצִיאוּ מִמִּצְרַיִם עֻגֹת מַצּוֹת כִּי
לֹא חָמֵץ כִּי־גֹרְשׁוּ מִמִּצְרַיִם וְלֹא יָכְלוּ לְהִתְמַהְמֵהַּ
They baked the dough that they took out of Mitzrayim into unleavened cakes, for they could not be leavened; for they were driven from Mitzrayim, and they could not delay (12:39).

The Bnei Yisrael were surprised when they were told to leave Mitzrayim immediately following *makas bechoros*. Unaware that they would be leaving Mitzrayim so soon, they had kneaded dough and left it to rise; when they were miraculously and suddenly redeemed, they had only the unleavened dough with them.[1] They now took this unleavened dough with them. Although Hashem told Moshe that they would be leaving Mitzrayim after this final plague (11:1), he only related this prophecy to Pharaoh, not to the Jews.

There was, however, another command from which the Bnei Yisrael

---

1. See *Targum Yehonasan* to *Shemos* 12:34.

should have understood that they would be leaving Mitzrayim shortly. When relaying Hashem's instructions regarding the pesach-offering, Moshe tells the Bnei Yisrael, "and as for you, you shall not leave the entrance of your house until morning" (12:22). Why did Hashem wish the Bnei Yisrael to remain indoors for the entire night? Hashem foresaw that Pharaoh and his servants, after witnessing the calamitous events of makas bechoros, would demand that the Bnei Yisrael leave immediately. Hashem wished to make it clear to all that the Bnei Yisrael would leave Mitzrayim solely because of His command — not at the behest of Pharaoh. Hashem therefore commanded that they not even leave the entrances of their homes before morning, lest the Egyptians think they were bowing to their will and leaving the country.

The Bnei Yisrael, however, misunderstood. They thought that Hashem desired them to stay indoors so that they would not be swept up in the plague together with the Egyptians. Had the Bnei Yisrael properly understood Hashem's intentions, the implication of the verse would have been clear: Do not leave the entrance of your house until morning — in the morning, however, we will leave Mitzrayim entirely. As a result of this misunderstanding, the Bnei Yisrael had no way of knowing that they were about to leave Mitzrayim. Therefore, assuming they would be remaining in Mitzrayim until Pharaoh would agree to let them leave, they kneaded their dough and left it to rise.

Rashi, quoting the Mechilta, comments on the above verse (12:22): "This verse tells us once permission has been granted to the agent of destruction to damage, he does not differentiate between the righteous and the wicked." This same deduction can be found in the Talmud (Bava Kamma 60a). While this deduction is undoubtedly valid, it is not based on the real reason for Hashem's command. Rather, the Tannaim deduced this principle from what the Bnei Yisrael mistakenly thought Hashem's reasoning was.

While this is clearly the way the Bnei Yisrael understood the command of Hashem, this understanding is quite astonishing for a variety of reasons. Firstly, what agent of destruction was there to be afraid of? The plague that killed the Egyptian firstborn was not carried out by the Angel of Death nor by any other heavenly destroyers. This plague was performed by Hashem Himself, as attested to in the verse: "I shall go through the land of Egypt on this night . . ." (12:12). Secondly, when the plague struck the Egyptian populace, the firstborn inside the houses were no safer then those who were outside. In addition, we see that in fact the plague did strike selectively, differentiating between the firstborn

Egyptians and the rest of the population. Moreover, not a single Jew died on that night. Even those Jews who had reached their heavenly decreed time to die did not die on that night![1] For all of these reasons, the *Bnei Yisrael* should have realized that they had nothing to fear. Indeed this was the very night that Hashem describes as a *night of protection* (12:42). Certainly, no one from the *Bnei Yisrael* would be harmed in any way.

We are therefore forced to explain as we have above: This interpretation of Hashem's words was an error on the part of the *Bnei Yisrael*. And one may ask: Why didn't Hashem command Moshe to correct the people and teach them the proper understanding of His will? The answer is that Hashem wanted the *Bnei Yisrael* to be caught unawares so that we would be left with matzoh — the physical manifestation of the suddenness of the redemption.

❅   ❅   ❅

וְהָיָה לְאוֹת עַל־יָדְכָה וּלְטוֹטָפֹת בֵּין עֵינֶיךָ כִּי בְּחֹזֶק יָד
הוֹצִיאָנוּ ה' מִמִּצְרָיִם — *And it shall be a sign upon your arm, and for tefillin (totafos) between your eyes, for with a strong hand Hashem removed us from Egypt* (13:16).

Rashi, quoting Menachem ibn Saruk, comments that the Hebrew word *totafos*, used in this verse to mean *tefillin*, is an expression meaning speech. What speech is it that this verse speaks of? *Rashi* goes on to explain that in an earlier verse, tefillin are referred to as something which should serve as a *remembrance between your eyes* (13:9). It is the intent of the Torah that the *tefillin* should serve as a reminder of Hashem's miraculous redemption of the *Bnei Yisrael* from the hands of the Egyptians. Acting as such a reminder, the *tefillin* will also serve as a catalyst, causing people to speak of the great miracles that Hashem performed for us during the exodus. It is for this reason, says *Rashi,* that the verse calls tefillin "*totafos*" — for they are objects which are intended to cause speech.

It is interesting to note that the earlier verse quoted by *Rashi* begins, *And it shall be for you for a sign."* It is implicit in the verse that the tefillin are to serve as a sign not for others, but rather as a sign for the

---

1. See *Divrei Eliyahu.*

wearer himself. Thus, the verse teaches that each individual should *himself* learn the message of the *tefillin* that he wears — improving his ways through the remembrance of Hashem's miracles, and Hashem's gifting to us of His Torah. Through this introspection brought about by the *tefillin,* he will become a great person imbued with the lessons of the Torah. When people see such a person adorned with *tefillin,* they will surely speak of Hashem and His miracles, and desire to follow in his ways. If, however, the sign of the *tefillin* will not be heeded by the one who wears them, neither he nor his tefillin will have any effect on others at all.

פרשת בשלח
Parashas Beshalach

וַיִּבֶן מֹשֶׁה מִזְבֵּחַ וַיִּקְרָא שְׁמוֹ ה' נִסִּי — And Moshe built
an altar and called its name "HASHEM is My Miracle"
(17:15).

ashi explains that when one would recall the name of the altar,
he would be reminded of the great miracle God had performed.[1]
Through seeing Moshe's actions and his building of the altar,
people immediately recognized that Hashem does miracles with the
Jewish people, and it was through these miracles that they vanquished
the Amalekites.

This can teach us how important it is for each person to act in a manner
which is so exemplary that all who see him recognize that his behavior is
proper and is a model which should be emulated.[2]

As we have mentioned elsewhere, when people saw the prophet
Shmuel — and even more so, when they came into his company — they
forsook their bad character traits, and all envy and hatred abandoned
them. It was for this reason that David sought refuge with Shmuel when
he fled from Shaul Hamelech (I Shmuel 19:18). When Shaul's messengers and even Shaul himself, arrived in pursuit of David, they no longer
experienced hatred, envy, enmity or discord. Upon seeing Shmuel, they
immediately perceived the true and proper way to act, and peace and
harmony reigned.

The need to set such a powerful example is taught specifically when the
Torah recounts the incident with Amalek, because Amalek was worse
than the others who threatened the Jews. Despite the great awe inspired
by the wondrous miracles which they saw — the signs and wonders which
the Jews experienced during their Exodus from Egypt and the Splitting of

---

1. This is similar to the altar which Yaakov built, which would cause people to recall
that "God is the God of Yisrael" (Bereishis 33:20).
2. See also Shabbos 153a.

the Sea, as recounted in the Song of the Sea — Amalek attacked in an effort to cause a loss of faith in Hashem. Indeed, *Rashi (Devarim* 25:18) notes that Amalek's attack can be compared to a lawless person who springs into a bath of scalding water. While he gets burned, the water is cooled to the point that others will now be able to enter. Although Amalek recognized that it would be inflicting damage upon itself, it chose to attack the Jews, in order to make it easier for others to do so.

In a time such as this — where those who sought to uproot belief in Hashem demonstrated self-sacrifice — it was of the utmost importance to strengthen good efforts and to exhibit self-sacrifice for Torah and *mitzvos*, as I have explained at length regarding Hashem's response to Bilaam's saddling his own donkey on his way to attempt to curse the Jews.[1]

❧ ❧ ❧

כִּי־יָד עַל־כֵּס יָ"הּ . . . — *For the hand is on the throne of God . . .* (17:16).

The verse uses an abbreviated form of the Hebrew word for throne (כִּסֵּא), and the Two-letter Name of Hashem (יָ"הּ) rather than the full Name (the Tetragrammaton). *Rashi* explains that the abbreviated forms indicate that Hashem's Name and throne are diminished as long as Amalek exists.

With this in mind, the statement of the Gemara in *Sotah* (17a), that Hashem placed the letter *yud* in the Hebrew word for "man" (אִישׁ) and the letter *hei* in the Hebrew word for "woman" (אִשָּׁה), so that the Name of Hashem would be formed upon their union in marriage, seems, at first, somewhat perplexing. If Hashem desired the union of husband and wife to be graced with His Name, why would he choose the incomplete Two-letter Name as the signature of His Presence?

Upon reflection, however, the matter can be explained simply. While it is true that Hashem graces each Jewish couple with His Name, He provides only a foundation, upon which the couple must build, constructing a true Jewish home. Hashem's contribution, while basic and essential, is only a beginning — it is only the good works of the couple that can complete the Name that is present in their home. If they succeed in doing so, then true blessing will surely follow — as the verse states elsewhere (20:21):*wherever I permit My Name to be mentioned, I shall come to you and bless you.*

---

1. See *Darash Moshe* Volume I, page 257.

פרשת יתרו
Parashas Yisro

וַיִּשְׁמַע יִתְרוֹ כֹהֵן מִדְיָן חֹתֵן מֹשֶׁה — *Yisro, the minister of Midian, the father-in-law of Moshe, heard* (18:1).

Rashi asks: What was it that Yisro "heard" that had the effect of inspiring him to join the *Bnei Yisrael* in the desert? *Rashi* answers that he heard reports of the splitting of the Yam Suf and the war with Amalek. The Talmud tells us (*Zevachim* 116a) that there are three opinions among the Tannaim as to what it was that Yisro heard. *Rashi* mentions only two of them; the third opinion is that Yisro heard tidings of the giving of the Torah to *Bnei Yisrael*. We must ask ourselves: Why is it important for us to know exactly what it was that motivated Yisro?

It is axiomatic that different people are inspired by different things. The three events mentioned by the Tannaim in the Talmud represent three distinct categories of Divine behavior. There are those people that would gain inspiration from observing the destruction of evil, as in the war against the evil nation of Amalek. Then there are those who would find greatness in the salvation of the oppressed, such as could be seen in the salvation of the Jews from the hands of the Egyptians at the Yam Suf. There are also those people that would discern the true greatness of Hashem in the Torah that He gave us at the Revelation at Sinai.

For this reason, it is more than merely incidental to discuss what it was that inspired Yisro. Indeed, knowing what it was that triggered in him the desire to come and join the *Bnei Yisrael* would grant us insight into the very heart of Yisro.

Similarly, among righteous people there are distinct personalities and abilities. [There are those whose main strength and greatness lie in their prowess in Torah learning. Others excel in their capability to combat those who wish to perpetuate evil ideals. A third group may be known for their deeds of great kindness. All of these are high ideals, worthy of great praise. [There is, of course, one righteous person who is greater then the rest — he who possesses all of these traits at once.]

We mentioned above *Rashi's* comment that Yisro was inspired by tidings of Hashem's splitting of the Yam Suf, as well as news of the *Bnei Yisrael's* victorious war with Amalek. While we can easily understand the inspirational effect of the miracles performed by Hashem during the Exodus and the Splitting of the Sea, the inspirational value of the war with Amalek is somewhat difficult to perceive. The Exodus was replete with open miracles, and the Splitting of the Sea was an obvious act of Hashem — but this was not the case in regard to the war with Amalek. The fact that the *Bnei Yisrael* emerged victorious from their conflict did not portray the hand of Hashem in as open and readily recognizable a fashion. To the contrary, fear of the *Bnei Yisrael* was so great among the nations of the world that it seems most astonishing that Amalek would dare provoke them — it therefore should not have seemed shocking or particularly inspiring that they were met with defeat. In what way, then, did this news serve to inspire Yisro?

To answer our question, we can explain that Yisro was influenced in a different way by each piece of news that he received. It was the open miracles of the Exodus and the Splitting of the Sea that opened Yisro's eyes to belief in Hashem. This can be seen in Yisro's own words — for it is this that Yisro mentions when giving thanks to Hashem for His salvation of the Jewish nation. Yet, while Yisro now firmly believed in Hashem and His omnipotence, these events alone may not have persuaded him to accept upon himself the obligations of a full fledged Jew. Indeed, even now, Yisro had no responsibility to do any more than adhere to the seven Noachide laws that even gentiles are commanded to follow. It was, however, the war with Amalek that ultimately persuaded Yisro to join ranks with the *Bnei Yisrael* completely. What was it about this event that had such a tremendous effect on Yisro? Let us explain:

Rashi, speaking of Amalek's attack on the *Bnei Yisrael,* comments that the actions of Amalek can be compared to that of a person who leaps into a tub of boiling water. Prior to his foolish act, everyone else is fearful of jumping in and getting burned. Once this fool jumps in, although he may get burned, he has the effect of cooling off the waters in the eyes of others. So too, the same thing was the aim and accomplishment of Amalek's ambush of the *Bnei Yisrael.* In the aftermath of all the miracles that Hashem had performed for the *Bnei Yisrael,* the nations had tremendous fear of Hashem and His nation. Amalek, by sacrificing themselves to defeat in order to attack them, took the edge off this fear and showed that war with the *Bnei Yisrael* — while certainly difficult — was not unthinkable. What kind of people would so totally ignore the lessons of the Exodus that they would be willing to sacrifice themselves simply to dull the effects of those lessons on others?

This is what Yisro saw in the war with Amalek, that people who live without Hashem's Torah are capable of sinking to depths beyond our imagination. From hearing of the decadence of Amalek, Yisro realized that it would be impossible for him to raise a new generation properly without accepting the Torah first. He might have been able to fulfill his responsibility to Hashem by simply adhering to the seven Noachide laws, but he knew that this would not give him the ability to properly train his children and grandchildren.

This concept is not a new one. Centuries earlier, when Avraham traveled with his wife to the land of Gerar he told Avimelech the king that he felt it necessary to hide the fact that Sarah was his wife because, "There is but no fear of God in this place, and they will slay me because of my wife" (*Bereishis* 20:1). Avimelech was not Pharaoh, and his country was not as immoral as Egypt. Avimelech administered his land in a basically moral and just way. Yet, Avraham knew that because there was no fear of Hashem among the people, they were capable of perpetrating as base an act as killing him to take his wife.

❧ ❧ ❧

וַיֵּצֵא מֹשֶׁה לִקְרַאת חֹתְנוֹ וַיִּשְׁתַּחוּ וַיִּשַּׁק־לוֹ וַיִּשְׁאֲלוּ אִישׁ־לְרֵעֵהוּ לְשָׁלוֹם וַיָּבֹאוּ הָאֹהֱלָה — *Moshe went out to greet his father-in-law, and he bowed and kissed him, and they inquired, one man to the other, about the other's well-being; then they came to the tent* (18:7).

Rashi comments that since the verse uses ambiguous wording (*he bowed and kissed him*), we have no way of knowing who bowed to whom. When the verse follows with the words, *one man to the other*, we can infer that it was Moshe who bowed to Yisro. How can we see this? *Rashi* explains that Moshe is referred to in another verse as the "man," as it says, "*And the man Moshe*" (*Bamidbar* 12:3). According to *Rashi's* interpretation of the verse, Moshe first kissed and bowed to Yisro, and the two men then spoke to each other. However, a difficulty arises here. While we can understand that out of proper respect for Moshe, Yisro did not approach and kiss Moshe, he certainly should have responded to Moshe's bowing by bowing to Moshe in return! Indeed, it seems most astonishing that he did not do so.

We can answer that Yisro's actions were guided by his prior life experiences. Yisro had been a worshiper of foreign gods, and as such he had a very clear understanding of the causes and ways of thinking that are able to lead to such worship. In the early days of the world, the concept of worshiping false deities began when people began to worship the sun and the moon. They knew that Hashem had created the world as well as all of the heavenly bodies. Their mistake lay in the thought that it would be proper to worship these creations of Hashem as intermediaries — as opposed to worshiping Hashem directly. This led eventually to the worship of all sorts of false deities — and the total denial of Hashem's creation of the world.

Yisro was well aware of this — and it was this knowledge that led to his decision not to bow to Moshe. Yisro recognized the greatness of Moshe, the servant of Hashem. Moshe had been the messenger of Hashem in performing the miracles of the Exodus, and it was through him that Hashem gave the *Bnei Yisrael* the manna. Yisro feared that should he bow to Moshe, it would be looked upon as if he was bowing not out of respect for Moshe, but as an act of worship. Because of this, Yisro actually felt that it would be forbidden for him to bow to Moshe, for it would be a case of something forbidden because of "appearance of wrongdoing."

❧ ❧ ❧

עַתָּה שְׁמַע בְּקֹלִי אִיעָצְךָ — *Now heed my voice, I shall advise you* (18:19).

Seemingly, Moshe, the preeminent teacher of the *Bnei Yisrael,* did not require the advice of Yisro in order to be able to devise a plan to best judge and teach *Bnei Yisrael.* Why, then, did he wait for this advice before putting such a system in place?

We know that Moshe never took action without being commanded to do so by Hashem. The verse itself testifies to this fact in *Parashas Mattos,* when Moshe arranged for the conditional receipt of land across the Yardein by the tribes of Reuven and Gad. From a simple reading of the text, it appears that Moshe issued that famous decision on his own —

without consultation with Hashem. Yet, the representatives of Reuven and Gad speaking to Moshe said, *"As Hashem has spoken to your servants, so shall we do"* (Bamidbar 32:31). They knew that Moshe's every decision was rooted firmly in the word of Hashem. They therefore understood that Moshe must have received instructions from Hashem at the very time they were speaking with him. As we are taught, "the Divine Presence spoke from the throat of Moshe."

Moshe knew that if it was the will of Hashem that he establish a system of judgment for the *Bnei Yisrael,* He would have commanded him to do so. Since he had not yet received any such command, he refrained from doing so on his own. Indeed, when Moshe eventually did institute his system, it was not as a result of Yisro's advice — rather it was because Hashem then commanded him to do so.

Yisro, though, did not comprehend this. The verse quotes Yisro as saying, *"If you do this thing — and God shall command you — then you will be able to endure (18:23). Rashi* comments on the phrase *and God shall command you,* that Yisro told Moshe to bring the matter before Hashem for His consideration. Clearly, while Yisro knew that Moshe would not act without direction from Hashem, he thought it necessary for Moshe to approach Hashem in order to request that direction.

Although in the final analysis the establishment of the judicial system was in no way due to the advice of Yisro, he still received credit for his efforts. Since he gave Moshe sound advice — albeit unnecessarily — the verse names him Yeser, crediting him with the addition of this chapter of the Torah to him.

❧ ❧ ❧

וְכָל־הָעָם רֹאִים אֶת־הַקּוֹלֹת — *The entire people saw the thunder* (20:15).

Rashi comments on this verse that at the time of the Revelation the people "saw that which is audible, which is impossible to see elsewhere." For what purpose did Hashem perform this seemingly unnecessary miracle?

Hashem wished to teach the *Bnei Yisrael* an important lesson in how to properly approach Torah study. It is not sufficient for a person to have a superficial understanding of the Torah. Rather a person must strive, using all of his energies and intellectual abilities, to understand the lessons of the Torah clearly — as if they were spelled out to him in front of his very eyes. The common ability to hear thunder represents a simple level of understanding, the miraculous ability to actually *see* thunder — that represents the level of understanding for which we must reach.

While this should be the goal for anyone involved in Torah study, it is especially necessary for those whose responsibility it is to teach others. Parents who must teach their children, *Rabbanim* who must judge and lead their congregations — if they will themselves reach this high level of clarity, they will then be able to give their knowledge over to others in an equally clear manner.

❦ ❦ ❦

וְאִם־מִזְבַּח אֲבָנִים תַּעֲשֶׂה־לִּי לֹא־תִבְנֶה אֶתְהֶן גָּזִית כִּי חַרְבְּךָ הֵנַפְתָּ עָלֶיהָ וַתְּחַלְלֶהָ — *And when you will make an altar of stones for Me, do not build them hewn, for you will have raised your sword over it and desecrated it* (20:22).

Rashi quotes the Tanna Rabbi Yishmael: Every example of the word אִם in the Torah is referring to something which is optional, except for three times. One of the times mentioned by Rabbi Yishmael is here in our verse. When the verse says *and if you will make an altar of stones*, the word אִם cannot be understood literally as meaning "if," for indeed it is incumbent upon *Bnei Yisrael* to build an altar of stones, as the verse states: *Of whole stones shall you build the altar of Hashem* (*Devarim* 27:6). Rather, as used in this verse, the word אִם must mean "when."

The question must be asked: If the Torah meant to say *when*, why did the Torah choose to use a word that usually means *if*? To answer this, we must first explain a key fact about the type of altar to which the Torah is referring.

When one erects a stone altar, it must be constructed out of many individual stones put together. An altar built of one single stone is a monolith, the erection of which is prohibited as is stated in the verse *and you shall not erect for yourselves a monolith which Hashem your God hates* (*Devarim* 16:22). The reason for the distinction between a monolith and an altar of many stones may be explained as follows: A monolith is something that is finite; it is complete and nothing can be added to it. As such, it is representative of a static existence, a life of no spiritual growth whatsoever. This is not the type of existence Hashem desires us to lead. As long as a person is alive in this world, he is obligated to constantly grow, to always add to his store of Torah and good deeds. This is represented by an altar of many stones. Such an altar can always be built upon further by the addition of more and more stones. This is the only type of altar that Hashem desires us to build. Indeed, the message of the monolith is so despised that the Torah teaches us that Hashem "hates" the monolith.

It is in reference to this lesson that the verse uses the word אִם. Growth is not something that can be regulated through the use of positive or negative precepts. Rather, a person must understand this lesson and seek to grow on a daily basis, both in his knowledge and understanding of Torah, as well as in the quantity and quality of his good deeds. Our verse hints at this, saying *"If" you will make an altar of stones,* for while the physical erection of the altar is something that will surely take place, the heeding of the lesson behind the altar is in the hands of each and every individual.

The verse goes on to say that the altar must not be constructed of hewn stones. The Tanna Rabbi Shimon ben Elazar explains that the reason for this is that while the altar was created to lengthen the life of a person, the steel blade was created to shorten the life of a person. Therefore it is not proper to wave that which shortens over that which lengthens.

This law never applied to a monolith. [Prior to the acceptance of the Torah at Sinai, it was permissible to make use of this type of altar; it was likewise permissible to use a steel blade to cut the stone.] This is because the altar of many stones with its lesson of continual growth is capable of prolonging life. The monolith's lesson of status quo is deadly — there is no reason for Hashem to prolong the life of someone who is not utilizing his time and ability to grow.

פרשת משפטים
Parashas Mishpatim

וְאֵלֶּה הַמִּשְׁפָּטִים אֲשֶׁר תָּשִׂים לִפְנֵיהֶם — *And these are the ordinances that you shall place before them* (21:1).

R*ashi* comments that the word וְאֵלֶּה, *and these*, connotes an addition to what was said previously. Therefore, *Rashi* says we learn from here that "just as those which have been stated previously are from Sinai, so too, these are from Sinai." Taken at face value, *Rashi* seems to be saying: Just as it was obvious to all that the Ten Commandments, that are written earlier (in *Parashas Yisro*), were Divine, so too, the verse wishes to stress that the laws taught in *Parashas Mishpatim* are strictly of Divine origin.

This understanding of *Rashi,* however, is very troubling. In the beginning of *Parashas Behar* (*Vayikra* 25:1), *Rashi* tells us that we learn from the commandment of *shemittah* that *all* of the commandments were received by Moshe at Sinai. If so, in what way are the ordinances of *Parashas Mishpatim* unique?

We must therefore explain that *Rashi* is pointing us towards a deeper lesson that must be learned from the laws of *Mishpatim*. It is not the Divine origin of these laws that *Rashi* wishes to point out. Rather, *Rashi* is telling us that by virtue of their proximity to the Ten Commandments, these laws have been grouped together with them. Just as those — the Ten Commandments — are from Sinai, i.e. they were chosen to be given at the Revelation, so too, these — the laws of *Mishpatim* — were chosen to be a part of that same group. According to the commentary of the *Ramban,* these laws were told to Moshe to be taught to *Bnei Yisrael* immediately after the Revelation at Sinai. Why was it *Parashas Mishpatim* that was selected from all the laws of the Torah for this distinction?

The answer is that the lessons that lie in *Parashas Mishpatim* are indispensable to our understanding of the rest of the Torah. *Parashas*

Mishpatim contains the laws that govern everyday societal and financial interaction. By choosing to begin the teaching of the Torah with laws pertaining to the everyday interrelationships between people, Hashem taught us that our faith is not one restricted to the spiritual realm, having no place among the realities of everyday life. Quite the opposite is the truth; the majority of the Torah's laws deal with the material and financial concerns that people face every day of their lives. The laws of damages, loans, *shomrim* (custodians) — these are the laws that are placed adjacent to the Ten Commandments, because we must understand that the Torah governs every aspect of life — not just "religious" issues.

We may also learn from *Mishpatim* several important lessons regarding the teaching of Torah. Hashem chose to begin the teaching of the Torah with the practical applications of laws that affect everyday life. From this we learn that the laws of the Torah are not to be dealt with as theoretical concepts. They should be taught in an in-depth fashion, allowing the reaching of final conclusions that can be followed in real situations.

In the second *parashah* of *Mishpatim* we find a second lesson directed at the teachers of Torah. The verse, discussing the laws governing a Jewish maidservant, says: *If he does not perform these three things for her, she shall leave free of charge without payment* (21:11). The Sages derive from the end of this verse that she has a means of going free that does not apply to male bondsmen: She goes out when she begins to exhibit signs of puberty, even if she has not worked for the full six years of her contract.

The Talmud (*Kiddushin* 3b), troubled by the repetitious phrases *free of charge* and *without payment,* explains that the former refers to the law that frees a maidservant when she reaches full maturity, while the latter refers to the law that releases her when she first exhibits signs of puberty. At first, the Talmud seems not to have solved its problem at all. Why have a law specifying that a maidservant goes free upon reaching full maturity, when she already will have left six months earlier, when she first showed signs of puberty? The Talmud explains that indeed there is a need for both. Had the verse only used one phrase, there would have been room to argue that the Torah intended it to teach the release of full maturity. By using two phrases, the Torah presented its intent in as clear a way as possible. We may learn from this that when one is teaching, he must take care that the laws of the Torah are presented in as clear a manner as possible.

Further along in the *parashah,* the verse discusses the laws of a murderer. *Rashi* comments that in order to achieve a proper understanding of these laws, the verses written here must be balanced with the verses that appear elsewhere on the same subject. Here too, there lies a lesson for both the teachers and students of the Torah. Hashem could easily have arranged the Torah so that all of the details of each topic would appear together in one easily identifiable place. He chose not to, in order to teach us that to understand the individual laws of the Torah, it is necessary to learn the entire Torah.

Hashem, in His infinite wisdom, knew that we must learn these lessons immediately upon receiving His Torah. For this reason, they became inseparable from the Ten Commandments.

❀   ❀   ❀

כֹּל אֲשֶׁר־דִּבֶּר ה' נַעֲשֶׂה וְנִשְׁמָע — *Everything that Hashem has said, we will do and we will obey!* (24:7).

The acceptance of the Torah at Sinai was not a one-time occurrence that happened in the past. Rather it is an ongoing, continual process. For this reason, nowhere does the Torah refer to the holiday of *Shevuous* as the day the Torah was given — for to do so would seem to limit the event to one historical day. Indeed, the Sages teach us that we are to view each day as if it was the day that we first received the Torah. The Torah is not an ancient, obscure document that needs updates or revisions, God forbid. It is timeless, always relevant and ever requiring our obeisance.

Part of this ongoing process is the need for *every* generation to follow and accept the decisions and wisdom of their Torah leaders. When the Jews uttered the famous words *we will do and we will obey*, they obligated themselves to continuously obey the decisions of those wise men capable of rendering Torah decisions. In this way there is a constant, ongoing acceptance of the Torah, for a person must constantly accept that he will do as the sages tell him — despite the fact that he may not understand their reasoning. Even if a person feels that perhaps the decision rendered was in error, he must know that it is the Torah's will that we rely on the judgment of the *Gedolei HaTorah* of our generation.

Furthermore, the Torah requires that we constantly view all of our deeds through the lens of the Torah. The laws of the Torah must be everpresent in our minds. Every action that we undertake must be carefully considered to see that the requirements of the pertinent Torah are fulfilled as best as possible.

פרשת תרומה
Parashas Terumah

וְדִבַּרְתִּי אִתְּךָ מֵעַל הַכַּפֹּרֶת מִבֵּין שְׁנֵי הַכְּרוּבִים אֲשֶׁר
עַל־אֲרוֹן הָעֵדֻת אֵת כָּל־אֲשֶׁר אֲצַוֶּה אוֹתְךָ אֶל־בְּנֵי יִשְׂרָאֵל
— *And I shall speak with you from atop the
kapores, from between the two keruvim that are
on the Aron of the Testimony, and it is all that I
shall command you pertaining to the Bnei Yisrael*
(25:22).

Rashi explains that this verse is to be understood as follows: "And
that which I will speak to you there is all that I shall command
you pertaining to the *Bnei Yisrael.*" Accordingly, this verse would
seem to be exclusive, so that in effect Hashem was telling Moshe: That
which pertains to the *Bnei Yisrael* I will tell you in the *Mishkan.* That
which does not concern the nation as a whole, but is rather directed to
you personally, we will discuss elsewhere. Among the many things
Hashem told Moshe there were those that were beyond the scope of the
people's ability to comprehend. [Two such examples would be the
reasoning behind the commandment of *parah adumah,* and the fulfillment of Moshe's request to see Hashem's glory.] Since such prophecies
were intended for Moshe alone and were not for teaching to the rest of
Bnei Yisrael, they would be told to him outside of the *Mishkan.*

On the surface, it is difficult to understand the reason for this distinction. There is some disagreement among the commentaries concerning
precisely where in the *Mishkan* Hashem would converse with Moshe.
According to *Rashi,* Moshe stood outside the *Paroches* in the *Ohel Moed*
and heard the voice of Hashem emanating from within the Holy of Holies
between the *keruvim.* If this was so, Moshe, who was considered to be a
Kohen (even though his future generations were considered *Leviim*),
should have been able to enter the *Mishkan* for *all* of his conversations

with Hashem. Even according to those opinions that Moshe entered the Holy of Holies itself to speak with Hashem, that too should have been permitted. For as the Sages teach, the prohibition against entering the Holy of Holies did not apply to Moshe (see *Shemos Rabbah* 37:1 and *Zevachim* 101b).

Why, then, did Hashem see fit to make this distinction? Let us offer two possible reasons. Although the prohibition against entering the *Mishkan* did not apply to Moshe, even he was only permitted to enter if and when there was a need to do so. Needless entry into the *Mishkan* was prohibited to all. However, one might have thought that the acceptance of *any* prophecy would be reason enough to enter the *Mishkan*. This verse teaches us that this is not the case. Hashem told Moshe that only the prophecies that were intended for teaching to the rest of the nation would be received in the *Mishkan*. All other matters — no matter how great and holy they might be — would have to be spoken of elsewhere.

There is an important lesson to be learned here. Those messages of Hashem that were meant solely for the ears of Moshe were so holy that only Moshe, the greatest of all the prophets, merited hearing them. Yet, since they were for the personal growth of a single individual, they were not as significant as those which were intended for teaching to the masses. It is apparent from this that while personal study is undoubtedly great, teaching to others is even greater. Practically, this is a lesson that we must take to heart when setting our priorities. If we only have the opportunity to fulfill one of these lofty goals, we must take care to choose the right one.

There is another possible explanation of the reasoning behind this verse. The *Mishkan* was built with public funds donated by the entire nation. Thus, Hashem told Moshe that it would be improper to use it for the needs of a single individual. The *Mishkan* belonged to the entire nation, and thus was to be used only for things that benefited all.

❀ ❀ ❀

. . . וְעָשִׂיתָ לֹּו זֵר זָהָב סָבִיב . . . וְעָשִׂיתָ זֵר־זָהָב לְמִסְגַּרְתּוֹ סָבִיב — . . . *you shall make for it gold crown all around . . . and you shall make a gold crown on the molding all around* (25:24-25).

The Torah tells us twice to fashion a "crown" for the *Shulchan*. There was, however, only one crown. The same repetition occurs where the Torah describes the crown after it was made. It is not reasonable to interpret this repetition as being intended to explain and clarify what Hashem meant, because that *parashah* only describes what had already been done to fulfill His earlier commands. Moreover, *Rashi* (to 28:24) notes regarding the two golden ropes of the breastplate that since the ropes are mentioned twice only to make them, but not where they are described after they were made, this proves that there was only one set of ropes, and that the early repetition is for the purpose of clarity. If so, here, where the crown is also mentioned twice after the *Shulchan* was already made, it would be difficult to say that the double repetition is meant solely for purposes of clarity.

It appears that the reason the Torah mentions the crown twice is this: *Rashi* (to 25:25) explains that the *Shulchan* represents wealth and grandeur, as we find in the common expression, "the table of kings." *Rashi*, however, does not say that the crown refers only to royalty, but rather that it equally symbolizes any wealthy person. When a person uses his wealth, he certainly does acquire a "crown," because many people will praise and glorify him. But the use of wealth may bring one of two possible crowns. If he scatters his money for evil things, there will be some, and perhaps many, people who will be swayed by his influence, whose Evil Inclination will convince them that evil is actually good. But this is a crown of eternal curse, like the crowns of those wicked kings who earned eternal disgrace. However, if he scatters his money for the good things that Hashem has commanded, then even if he does not earn public adulation and praise, he earns a crown of eternal joy and blessing. By its repetition, the Torah tells us that all wealthy people earn one of these two crowns. And the Torah emphasizes that the crown should be fashioned "on the molding," to teach that we must see to it that the crown is on the molding, which was added for its beauty, so that the crown will forever be beautiful, praiseworthy, and glorified. [This concept of positive and negative crowns does not apply to Torah or the priesthood. Only one crown — that of beauty and praise — exists for Torah scholars and *Kohanim*.]

❀ ❀ ❀

It is also possible to interpret the Torah's double mention of the crown in another way. As *Rashi* explains, the crown represents the wealth of royalty, and indeed people do grant respect to wealth. But in truth, its possessor cannot glorify himself with it unless he has used his wealth as he should, as I have explained concerning the verse, *Let not the wise man glorify himself with his wisdom, and let not the strong man. . .with his strength, let not the rich man. . .with his wealth"* (*Jeremiah 9:22*). The next verse continues: *"For only with this may one glorify himself — contemplating and knowing Me."* This does not mean that contemplating and knowing Hashem is a reason to glorify one's self; for Rav Yochanan ben Zakkai has said, "If you have studied much Torah, do not take credit for yourself" (*Avos 2:9*). A Torah scholar must be humble. What is meant is this: With this may one glorify himself; in other words, only such a person deserves glory. Wealth, strength, and other skills and knowledge may give a person the ability to *claim* glory, but in reality all these attributes are futile — even if the person does no harm, and certainly if he uses these things for wickedness against the teachings of the Torah. But if a person uses his wealth, strength, or other skills to do the will of Hashem, then certainly their accomplishments deserve to be glorified. This is why the crown of the *Shulchan* is mentioned twice — to teach that along with the crown of the Torah, other crowns may be glorified.

We find similarly in the case of Shimshon that he never used his strength for his own needs. When the men of Yehudah came to bind him, he told them they would not be injured, for he would not use his power against them. His strength was granted by Hashem only so that he could save the Jewish People, and not for his own benefit. HaRav Nosson Lomner, has pointed out, this is why when Delilah caused him pain and suffering she was able to escape from him. Had he told her that if she would repeat her actions he would punish her, she certainly would not have performed such rebellious acts again. We see that Shimshon did not want to use his strength for any personal needs.

פרשת תצוה
Parashas Tetzaveh

וְאַתָּה תְּצַוֶּה אֶת־בְּנֵי יִשְׂרָאֵל וְיִקְחוּ אֵלֶיךָ שֶׁמֶן זַיִת זָךְ
כָּתִית לַמָּאוֹר לְהַעֲלֹת נֵר תָּמִיד — *Now you shall*
command the Bnei Yisrael that they shall take
for you pure, pressed olive oil for illumination, to
kindle the lamp continually (27:20).

There are three unusual expressions in the beginning of this
parashah. As the *Ramban* says, *Now you shall command*
implies that Moshe himself was required to communicate these
laws to the people. The phrase, *from the Bnei Yisrael* (in v. 21), also
appears unnecessary. Furthermore, why does the Torah say that the
Menorah was to be lit *outside the Partition?* It is obvious that it could not
be lit in the Holy of Holies, because we are told that it is forbidden to
enter there except on Yom Kippur!

The explanation is this: The oil used in the Menorah had to be
produced by pressing, not crushing. Even a higher-quality oil produced
by crushing was unfit for this use. Although it is true that crushing
produces an oil with sediment, this could be removed completely. After
all, oil produced by crushing can be used for the meal-offerings, even
though the slightest amount of sediment renders the oil unfit. Despite the
ability to completely remove sediment, oil produced by crushing remains
unfit. I have explained elsewhere that the reason for this is that a teacher
of Torah and faith must communicate his lessons so clearly that no
questions can arise because of a lack of clarity or ambiguity. Even in
regard to the greatest men, such as Antigonus, the leader of Socho,
Shemayah and Avtalyon said, "Scholars, be cautious with your words!"
To hint at this lesson, we were commanded to use for the Menorah only
pressed oil, which never contained any impurities. Oil that once
contained impurities is unfit, even if they were later removed. Using

crushed oil would require examination to verify that all sediment had been removed, and people would have a basis, though perhaps only due to stubbornness or argumentativeness, to claim that some impurity remains. Therefore, the Torah says that the Rav or teacher must try to ensure that their teaching is so clear and pure that it is as if it never contained any impurity. The students should also seek to learn in the same fashion, and not cloud their learning with stubbornness and argumentativeness. This is why the verse specifies here that Moshe should command, because he symbolizes the teachers of the *Bnei Yisrael*. The phrase, *from the Bnei Yisrael,* is included to teach us that their receptiveness should mirror Moshe's clarity of teaching. And the Torah states that the Menorah be lit *outside the Partition,* to teach that the earliest stages of learning and teaching should be preceded with a clear decision to proceed in the manner symbolized by the oil of the Menorah.

❧ ❧ ❧

וְהֵם יִקְחוּ אֶת־הַזָּהָב . . . — *They shall take the gold* . . . (28:5).

The command that the artisans should take the gold necessary for the making of the vestments of the *Kohanim* is difficult to understand. Is it not obvious that they needed access to the materials necessary for their work? The answer is that this is a commandment that the donors should not bring the gold to them, but rather that the artisans themselves, or their messengers, should go and take what they need. We find a similar idea in the case of the *metzora,* where the Torah states concerning every step of his purification: *The Kohen shall command.*

The explanation for this unusual requirement is this: Everyone knew that only those that Hashem had filled with the wisdom necessary to do this holy work and who were chosen by Moshe Rabbeinu were capable of doing it. Other people, having been neither chosen nor graced with the necessary wisdom, did not entertain the thought that they could do anything. The choosing and bringing of the materials, on the other hand, was not something that only the craftsmen were capable of doing. Still, the Torah says that this, too, was considered to be exclusively the responsibility of the craftsmen.

This can teach us an important lesson that applies to the Rabbi of a congregation and the community that has chosen him. Certainly, the members of the community or congregation know and understand that in matters of the Torah and *mitzvos* they must defer to the Rabbi's judgment, for he studied and knows, while they do not. But quarrels, and sometimes even divisive fighting, often arise concerning matters that appear to be exclusively of a worldly nature, such as how to decorate a synagogue, or how to raise money. In such matters, people often say that these are decisions that should be made by the laymen, because these matters are unrelated to Torah scholarship, and laymen have a greater expertise in such things. But the truth is that everything relates to the Torah, and the Rabbi must examine everything, even what may appear to be exclusively worldly matters, to ensure that they are done as the Torah directs. The community must heed the Rabbi's words, and then all will be peaceful and pleasant.

פרשת כי תשא
Parashas Ki Sisa

וְעָשִׂיתָ מִזְבֵּחַ מִקְטַר קְטֹרֶת . . . — *You shall make an Altar on which to bring incense up in smoke* (30:1).

ere, where the Torah commands us to make the vessels of the Temple, the golden Altar is mentioned last of all. Everywhere else, the golden Altar is mentioned first. Furthermore, the Torah tells us that the golden Altar had a "crown" along its top, which *Rashi* explains represents the crown of the priesthood. The outside Altar, used for other sacrifices, did not have any crown at all. This is because the golden Altar relates only to Aharon, since he is mentioned where the incense is discussed — *Upon it Aharon shall bring the spice-incense* (30:7). [The *Ramban* also notes this association.] This means that only *Kohanim* could offer the incense, and that even before the sin of the Golden Calf, during the time that firstborns could perform Temple service, they were not able to offer incense.

There is only one other similar case — that of the lighting of the Menorah. Even before the Temple service was taken away from the firstborns, the Torah says that the lighting of the Menorah was intended to be done specifically by Aharon. We see that these two services, the offering of the incense and the lighting of the Menorah, were intended to be done only by Aharon and his children, and could not have been done by firstborns even when they were fit for other Temple service.

The reason for both of these laws is the same. Aharon and his children were intended to be the teachers of the nation. Teaching involves two elements: One is the actual and direct teaching of the laws of the Torah and Ethics, and the other is the scrupulous personal behavior of the teacher, which the student must try to emulate. The responsibility and the talent to do both of these were given over particularly to Aharon and his children. This special character is symbolized by the golden Altar and the Menorah.

Incense differs from all else in that even people that are far away have pleasure from its strong fragrance — a bride needed no perfume in all of Yerushalayim, and even as far as Yericho, people enjoyed the fragrance. Also, it is a pleasure people enjoy unintentionally and even unwillingly, as we see in Tractate *Pesachim* 25b. Similarly, Aharon and his descendants, about whom it is written (*Devarim* 33:10), *They shall teach Your laws to Yaakov,* influenced even those who were far away, and even those who were not seeking or were unwilling to be influenced or to learn Torah. The story of the prophet Shmuel proves this: for in *Shmuel I*, Chapter 19 verses 18-24, we find that after Shaul attempted to kill David, David fled to Shmuel. Shaul sent messengers to arrest David, and when they came to Shmuel, they began prophesying. Even when Shaul himself approached Shmuel's abode, even from a distance, all his desires and envy and hatred left him, and all of them learned together with Shmuel, and merited prophesy while they were there. Firstborns did not have this power. So long as the firstborns had not been put aside in favor of Aharon, who on account of his righteousness and greatness had this power and transmitted it to his children, the golden Altar could not have been used for incense. There was no one who could influence the behavior of others from afar and without their acquiescence, as symbolized by the incense. After Aharon was anointed, they were commanded to bring the incense and the golden Altar became necessary. For this reason, the Altar was mentioned last. Henceforth, however, this Altar had precedence, for it was an inner Temple vessel with a high level of sanctity; moreover, the incense was most beloved of all sacrifices, as *Rashi* says in *Parashas Korach* (*Bamidbar* 16:6). This is also why of the two Altars, only the golden Altar of incense had the crown, for this service represented the most eminent aspect of the priesthood.

The other element of teaching is the direct inculcation of the laws of the Torah and Ethics. This involves a direct relationship, and is symbolized by the Menorah. When Aharon lit the Menorah, he was to hold the fire to the wick until the lamp's fire rose of itself. This means that the teacher must keep his hand on the student until he understands clearly what is taught, and can apply his learning to all situations. Further, the student must be able to assimilate his knowledge with every other thing he has learned, so as to make all his learning one integrated body of knowledge. Since this, too, represents this most important aspect of the purpose of Aharon and his children, it was intended specifically for them and was addressed to them. Both this and the incense service could not be performed by the firstborns, even when they were responsible for other Temple services.

❧ ❧ ❧

וְאַתָּה קַח־לְךָ בְּשָׂמִים רֹאשׁ — *Now you, take for yourself choice spices* (30:23).

The *Ohr HaChaim* comments that with the words, *take for yourself,* Hashem instructed Moshe that he should take these spices from his own personal possessions. Furthermore, Hashem indicated that He desired the *shemen hamishchah* to be prepared by Moshe himself — not by others. What was it about the *shemen hamishchah* that required the personal attention of Moshe, the great leader of the nation, more than any other part of the *Mishkan?*

The answer to our question lies in the purpose of the *shemen hamishchah.* The *shemen hamishchah* was used to anoint and sanctify all of the utensils of the *Mishkan.* The creation of something capable of imbuing physical articles with holiness required the efforts of a person of Moshe's stature — a human being who had reached a level of holiness even higher than that of angels. Indeed, the *shemen hamishchah* made by Moshe was never replaced; the original batch mixed by Moshe's hands will last forever.

This same lesson can be applied to the transmission of Hashem's Torah. Since growth in Torah is something that requires personal holiness, it follows that the Torah must be transmitted by a person of exceptional holiness — a person exemplary not only in learning ability, but in his deeds and attributes as well.

❧ ❧ ❧

וְנָתַתָּה מִמֶּנָּה לִפְנֵי הָעֵדֻת בְּאֹהֶל מוֹעֵד . . . — *and place some of it before the Testimonial-tablets in the Tent of Meeting . . .* (30:36).

In the *parashah* where we were commanded to make the *ketores* (incense), the Torah commands us to place some of it before the *Luchos* (Testimonial-tablets) in the Tent of Meeting, but it does not say that it must be offered on the golden Altar. Where the Torah tells us

of the golden Altar, in the end of *Parashas Tetzaveh* (30:6-7), it says that
Aharon should bring the *ketores* up on that Altar, and that the Altar
should be placed *before the Partition that is by the Aron of the Luchos,
in front of the Cover that is on the Luchos*. This is the same place
mentioned where the offering of the incense is discussed. Why, then,
does the Torah not mention the Altar when discussing the *ketores*?

It appears that the Torah, in the *parashah* of the *ketores,* omits
mention of the Altar to tell us that the reason the golden Altar was to be
placed in the Tent of Meeting in front of the Ark was because the *ketores*
had to be offered specifically there, and not vice versa. Since the *ketores*
had to be offered in front of the Ark, and the *ketores* could only be offered
on the golden Altar, the Altar was placed there. The reason for this is that,
as I have previously explained, the *ketores* symbolizes our obligation to
provide an example for others with the very conscientious and
scrupulous way we conduct ourselves. And the only way to acquire a
way of life that influences others by example is to constantly be involved
in the study of Torah before the great men of the generation — before the
Aron of the *Luchos,* as it were. To teach this lesson, the Torah requires
that the *ketores* be offered in front of the *Luchos* — and, as a result, the
golden Altar was situated there.

❧ ❧ ❧

לֻחֹת אֶבֶן כְּתֻבִים בְּאֶצְבַּע אֱלֹקִים — *stone tablets inscribed by the finger of God* (31:18).

The word used for the stone Tablets of Testimony, *Luchos* (which
is in the plural because it describes two Tablets), is written in the
deficient form without the vowel "vav." If not for the oral tradition
that it is read *luchos*, it could be read *luchas*, which means "the tablet"
in the singular form. *Rashi* explains that this unusual spelling is to teach
us that the two Tablets were identical. The literal understanding of this,
that the physical dimensions of the two Tablets were the same, while true,
is not of great importance. No one ever did or ever would move them
from where Moshe placed them, in the *Aron*. Rather, the lesson taught
here is that the commandments written on the two Tablets are to be
observed in the same fashion. While those on the first Tablet focus on
mitzvos between man and God, and those on the second focus on
mitzvos between man and his fellow-man, they should all be observed
only because they were commanded by Hashem through Moshe in the

Written and Oral Torah.

There is an important reason for this. The fact that a person does good deeds because of his good nature provides no basis for others to follow his example. Others who do not wish to emulate him will say: Just as he does good because that is his nature, we shall do the wicked things that *our* nature demands! If, on the other hand, one does good deeds because this is the will of Hashem, all will learn from his example to do good, for they have no basis for excusing themselves. Thus, performing the *mitzvos* between man and his fellow because Hashem commanded us to is of paramount importance.

This is what Hillel meant in his response to the proselyte (*Shabbos* 30a) who wanted to learn the entire Torah while standing on one foot: "That which is hateful to you, do not do to your friend." We might wonder: Why did Hillel not mention anything about *mitzvos* between man and God? This is because Hillel meant that whatever good deeds one does, he must know that he is doing them because the Torah commanded us to do them, and not because he has a good nature. As the *Rav* in the beginning of *Avos* explains, there are many among the nations that have authored books about good character traits, but the Torah wants us to strive to achieve those traits because "Moshe received the Torah from Sinai." The *Rambam* (*Hil. Melachim* 8:11) says the same thing concerning the seven Noachide *mitzvos*. Since we are to do these *mizvos* because we were so commanded by Hashem, there is then no difference between such *mitzvos* that are between man and God and those that are between man and his fellow-man.

❧ ❧ ❧

וַיֹּאמֶר ה' אֶל־מֹשֶׁה רָאִיתִי אֶת־הָעָם הַזֶּה וְהִנֵּה עַם־ קְשֵׁה־עֹרֶף הוּא — *Hashem said to Moshe, "I have seen this people, and behold! It is a stiff-necked people"* (32:9).

It is apparent from the text that Hashem considers being *stiff necked* a negative attribute. This is difficult to understand, for historically, this characteristic has served us well. Because we are a stiff-necked people, we are slow to be seduced by the ways of the gentile nations. It is therefore just this attribute that has prevented us from assimilating with the gentiles over the many years of *galus*. What is it about being stiff necked that Hashem finds undesirable?

The answer is that Hashem does not wish our *mitzvos* to be done out of stubbornness. When we do a *mitzvah*, Hashem wants it to be done out of joy, with all our heart and soul. Only in this way will we be successful in training our children to follow in our footsteps. If children see that a *mitzvah* is a burdensome chore only to be fulfilled after much perseverance and effort, they will wish to have no part of it. If, however, on the other hand, they are taught that a *mitzvah* is a thing of great beauty and worth, to be done with joy and happiness, they too will look forward to involving themselves in the Torah and its commandments.

It is for this reason that Hashem despises this attribute. For although it may occasionally result in some short-term good, the long-term threat to the perpetuation of Torah is too great to be ignored.

❀ ❀ ❀

וַיַּרְא אַהֲרֹן וְכָל־בְּנֵי יִשְׂרָאֵל אֶת־מֹשֶׁה וְהִנֵּה קָרַן עוֹר פָּנָיו וַיִּירְאוּ מִגֶּשֶׁת אֵלָיו. וַיִּקְרָא אֲלֵהֶם מֹשֶׁה וַיָּשֻׁבוּ אֵלָיו אַהֲרֹן וְכָל־הַנְּשִׂאִים בָּעֵדָה וַיְדַבֵּר מֹשֶׁה אֲלֵהֶם. וְאַחֲרֵי־כֵן נִגְּשׁוּ כָּל־בְּנֵי יִשְׂרָאֵל וַיְצַוֵּם אֵת כָּל־אֲשֶׁר דִּבֶּר ה' אִתּוֹ בְּהַר סִינָי. וַיְכַל מֹשֶׁה מִדַּבֵּר אִתָּם וַיִּתֵּן עַל־פָּנָיו מַסְוֶה —

Aharon and all Bnei Yisrael saw Moshe, and behold! — the skin of his face had become radiant; and they feared to approach him. Moshe called to them, and Aharon and all the leaders of the assembly returned to him, and Moshe would speak to them Moshe finished speaking with them and placed a mask on his face (34:30-33).

While involved in teaching Hashem's Torah to the *Bnei Yisrael*, Moshe did not wear the mask that hid the radiance of his face. Once he had completed his teaching, he immediately replaced the mask. There is a lesson here that applies not only to the generation of Moshe, but to all the future generations of the *Bnei Yisrael* as well.

The radiance that was evident upon the face of Moshe was actually the manifestation of the Divine Presence, resting upon Moshe in his capacity as a person involved in Torah study. While only Moshe had this Presence upon him to the extent that it was visible to all, every individual Jew has this aspect of the Divine Presence inside him — for it is an integral part of the holiness of the *Bnei Yisrael* given to us by the Torah. Indeed, this

Divine Presence is absolutely vital to the proper understanding of the Torah. One must approach Torah study with pure faith, knowing that every word of the Torah — including the words of our Sages — is true beyond any doubt, and that there is no possibility of them having made a mistake. It is this knowledge of the absolute truth of the Torah that should fuel the desire of a person to understand it. If a person approaches Torah in this way, then when he is confronted with a difficulty Hashem will assist him in his understanding, as part of the continuing process of the Revelation. It is for this reason that the Sages tell us, "If someone says there is Torah among the nations, do not believe them" (*Eichah Rabbah* 2:13). It is impossible for a non-Jew to truly understand Torah, for it is something that cannot be accomplished without having the Divine Presence at your side to assist you.

In light of this, we can understand why Moshe removed his mask while teaching Torah to the *Bnei Yisrael*. When not engaged in Torah study, the *Bnei Yisrael* were not deserving of experiencing the Divine Presence. When learning from Moshe, however, they too were experiencing the Divine Presence in themselves — thus, they were worthy of seeing the Divine Presence that rested upon Moshe.

פרשת ויקהל
Parashas Vayakhel

וַיַּעֲשׂוּ כָל־חֲכַם־לֵב . . . — *And the wise-hearted made . . .* (36:8).

“T*he wise-hearted*” are referred to in the plural (חַכְמֵי לֵב) only the first time they are mentioned (28:3), but in all other references they are referred to in the singular (חֲכַם לֵב). The *Ohr HaChaim* also remarks about this. It would appear that the explanation is this: Since there were many people responsible for the work that needed to be done, there might have been a concern that no individual would take responsibility; as *Chazal* say (*Bava Basra* 24b), food being cooked by partners is neither hot nor cold, because each depends on the other to take care of whatever needs to be done. This is why it uses the singular, to say that each considered himself responsible for all the work, and did not relax until he knew the work was being properly done.

As I have explained, the rule, that when a *mitzvah* that can be performed by another party arises one does not have to stop learning in order to do the *mitzvah,* only is true when he knows that the other will do it. Then, it can be considered doable by others. If it is not clear to him that it will be done, this is the same as a *mitzvah* that cannot be performed by others, for each will rely on the other, and it will remain “neither hot nor cold.”

פרשת פקודי
Parashas Pekudei

וַיָּבִיאוּ אֶת־הַמִּשְׁכָּן אֶל־מֹשֶׁה ... — *And they brought the Mishkan to Moshe* ... (39:33).

Rashi explains that the workmen were not able to erect the Mishkan due to its great weight. They therefore came to Moshe, who, with the help of Divine assistance, was able to erect the Mishkan. *Rashi* states further that Hashem deliberately brought this about so that Moshe, who had not contributed anything towards the construction of the *Mishkan,* would have a share in its construction.

This raises a question. Why, indeed, did Moshe not contribute anything towards the construction of the *Mishkan*? Furthermore, we find elsewhere that the tribal leaders were found lacking for their failure to come forward with their contributions until after the collection was complete, although they did so with good motives (see above, 35:27 with *Rashi* there); yet we do not find Moshe taken to task for what, upon the surface, would seem to be an even greater lapse!

The answer may be found in the wording of the commandment given to Moshe concerning the collection for the *Mishkan*. Hashem told Moshe, *"Speak to the Bnei Yisrael and let them take for Me a portion"* (25:2). From this Moshe understood that the requirement placed upon him was specifically to notify the Jews of their obligation — not to contribute himself. This can also be seen in the wording of a second passage (35:4-5), where Moshe proclaimed to the Jews: *"This is the word that Hashem has commanded, saying: 'Take from yourselves a portion for Hashem . . . ' "* *Rashi* there (ד״ה זה) explains: This is what Hashem commanded me to say to you; i.e. this obligation does not devolve upon me.

However, from this answer itself a larger question emerges. Why, when collecting for the construction of the *Mishkan*, was Hashem desirous of contributions from *every* Jew except Moshe himself? Surely the contribution of Moshe would have been tendered with greater sanctity of purpose than that of any other Jew!

To resolve this problem, we must understand Hashem's purpose in requesting contributions for the building of the *Mishkan*. A clue to His intent can be found in *Parashas Terumah*, where the verse records Hashem's initial instructions to Moshe. First, Moshe was instructed to tell the Jews simply that *any man whose heart would motivate him* was to contribute to Hashem, without telling them the use to which their monies would be put (25:2). Only later would they be told that their contributions were to be used to build the *Mishkan* (25:8). We can see from the unusual structure of the request that Hashem wished the Jews to give with the understanding that they were not entitled to ask the purpose of the contributions for they were to understand that all of their possessions were entrusted to them only to enable them to fulfill Hashem's will. By responding generously and with alacrity to Hashem's request, the Jews showed that they had attained this level of understanding.

With this in mind, we can understand why Moshe was not commanded to contribute to the *Mishkan's* construction. It was known to all that Moshe, the true servant of Hashem, had reached, and even surpassed, this level of understanding — for Moshe understood that not only his possessions, but even his very being existed only to further the will of Hashem. It was therefore not necessary to require Moshe to contribute to the *Mishkan*. However, so that Moshe should not be completely left out, Hashem accorded him with the honor of erecting the *Mishkan* for the very first time. [It is noteworthy that subsequently, the *Leviim* were able to erect and disassemble the *Mishkan,* when the Jews traveled in the Wilderness; it was only during its initial erection that Hashem caused Moshe's assistance to be required.]

It is also possible that Hashem wished to give the Jews a chance to atone for their grievous sin of donating their valuables towards the construction of the Golden Calf; their zeal in donating to the *Mishkan* served to help atone for their previous misdeed. This would also explain why Moshe was not required to contribute, as he was not even present when the collection for the Golden Calf took place.

ספר ויקרא ⟩⟨

Sefer Vayikra

פרשת ויקרא
Parashas Vayikra

וַיְדַבֵּר ה' אֵלָיו מֵאֹהֶל מוֹעֵד לֵאמֹר . . . — . . . *and
HASHEM spoke to him from the Tent of Meeting,
saying* (1:1).

In the beginning of *Parashas Vayikra*, where the Torah describes the
various types of sacrifices, we find that *every broad category begins
with the words, And Hashem spoke to Moshe*. When the Torah
begins the category of voluntary offerings those words occur, and then
later, when the Torah begins the category of sacrifices that can only be
brought under an obligation, those words occur once more. But when
the Torah comes to the three types of *asham* sacrifices, these words
appear not once, but twice; once when describing the *asham* for
inadvertent unauthorized use of sanctified material (*asham me'ilos*) and
the *suspended asham* (*asham talui*), for a person that thinks he may be
liable for a full guilt-offering but is not sure, and a second time when
describing the *asham* for one who uttered a false oath in an attempt to
deny monetary liability (*asham gezeilos*).

The reason two verses are required is because the two categories
of *ashamos* are completely different from each other, and require
the separation of a new introduction. One category includes the
asham me'ilos and *asham talui*, which are very similar. Had the person
intentionally used sanctified material, he would not be liable either
for the 25-percent fine nor eligible to bring a sacrifice, while
inadvertent use invokes both the penalty and the sacrifice. This is
because the main purpose of these obligations is to bring forgiveness for
the inadvertently caused desecration of Hashem's Name, not to atone

for the act itself. Similarly, the *asham talui* does not bring actual forgiveness; rather, it protects the person until such time that he finds out whether he sinned, at which point (if he indeed had sinned) he would bring a full guilt-offering, the *chatas*. *Asham gezeilos,* on the other hand, comes to bring forgiveness for a sin between man and his fellow man which was compounded by the sin of a false oath; indeed, this sacrifice is one of the few that can effect forgiveness even for an intentional sin. We see that the first type is brought not for the direct act itself, but for side effects or for temporary protection. The second type is brought directly for a sin, even if the sin was intentional.

❀   ❀   ❀

וְעָשָׂה מֵאַחַת מֵהֵנָּה — *and he commits one of them* (4:2).

In describing the circumstances which result in the obligation to bring a *chatas* (sin-offering), the Torah uses the words "*mei'achas mei'heinah*." The plain meaning of these words is that the person did "one of them," "them" being certain proscribed acts. However, the literal meaning would be "of one of them." *Chazal* derive several rules from this unusual wording. One is that the laws of Shabbos are comprised of both "Avos" and "Tolados." These are the primary and principal categories of forbidden work and their derivative subcategories. Another is that sometimes a person is liable to bring many sacrifices for his many sins — where he knew it was Shabbos but didn't remember that his acts were forbidden, and that sometimes a person brings one sacrifice for many acts — where he knew that such acts would be forbidden on Shabbos, but he forgot that the day was Shabbos (*Shabbos* 70a).

These lessons can be applied in everyday life. A person must establish "Avos"; he must clearly set out for himself what is important in life, and then make sure that all the many branches of his life stem from those fundamental principles. This is true in his own study and actions and also in his teaching and interactions with his students. Similarly, he must see to it that all of his actions are done in accordance with the "one" principle, and that the "one" should be the basis of the many — that all his traits should be developed and used to attain the goal of walking the path of the just and doing good deeds.

❀   ❀   ❀

פרשת צו
Parashas Tzav

. . . צַו אֶת־אַהֲרֹן וְאֶת־בָּנָיו — *Command Aharon and his sons . . .* (6:2).

The Torah divides the laws of the *korbanos* into two *parashios* — beginning the laws in *Parashas Vayikra,* and then reiterating them with some additions in *Parashas Tzav.* This is because many of the *korbanos* may be eaten, in part, by the *Kohanim* and owners, and the Torah wanted to teach that despite the fact that people eat the *korban,* it is wholly sanctified and dedicated to the Temple, and the people are only sharing the food at the table of Hashem. For this reason, in the case of the *korban olah,* which is completely burned, the Torah repeats nothing; and only adds the law that a defective *korban,* once on the Altar, may remain there, and the rule of the removal of a portion of the ash from the Altar (*terumas hadeshen*).

❧ ❧ ❧

זֹאת תּוֹרַת הָעֹלָה — *This is the law of the elevation-offering* (6:2).

These words teach us, as the Gemara in *Zevachim* states (84a), that certain defective sacrifices, which may not be placed on the Altar, are nonetheless not removed from the Altar if they were placed there. If they *were* removed, they are not put back on the Altar, unless they are charred on all sides, in which case they are once again placed on the fire of the Altar.

The reason for this law is intimated in *Parashas Tetzaveh,* where the Torah says, "whatever touches the Altar shall become sanctified" (*Shemos* 29:37). This is the crux of the mechanism by which the Altar requalifies unqualified sacrifices. The Altar is deemed "holy of holies," and this quality allows it to elevate sacrifices in its domain.

Every person must know this concept; if he wants to influence others, his actions must be "holy of holies." Then at least his students will act with holiness when they are in his presence, and eventually they will repent of any misdeeds and go on the path of Torah and *mitzvos.* If the *rebbi's* holiness is like a fierce flame, this will influence the student to the degree that even when the student is no longer together with the *rebbi,* he will remain on the path of truth.

※ ※ ※

מַחֲצִיתָהּ בַּבֹּקֶר וּמַחֲצִיתָהּ בָּעֶרֶב — *half of it in the morning and half of it in the afternoon* (6:13).

Every day of the year, the *Kohen Gadol* must bring a sacrifice called *Chavitei Kohen Gadol.* This is a *minchah-* sacrifice with the unique attribute that half is burned in the morning and half in the evening. This teaches us that people must see to it that when they go home in the evening, they have not descended from the high level of holiness they had when they left from home in the morning. The job of the *Kohen Gadol* is to ensure this occurs, through his Temple service, Torah, and holiness. And when there is no *Kohen Gadol,* the obligation to bring this sacrifice devolves upon all the *Kohanim.*

Even if a person finds it impossible to maintain his holiness at a constant peak level, he must not despair, for we find that if the entire sacrifice was brought in the morning, it is valid. This teaches that even if a man knows that he cannot be perfect, he should do whatever he can, and this will lead to perfection, because *mitzvos* bring other *mitzvos* in their wake.

※ ※ ※

פרשת שמיני
Parashas Shemini

קַח־לְךָ עֵגֶל בֶּן־בָּקָר לְחַטָּאת — *Take yourself a young bull for a sin-offering. . .* (9:2).

It would seem that inasmuch as this sacrifice was to atone for Aharon's participation in the sin of the Golden Calf, the use of a bull calf would be inappropriate, for as *Chazal* say (*Rosh Hashanah* 26a), a prosecutor cannot become a defender. Why, then, did Hashem choose this sacrifice for his atonement?

It appears that Aharon's participation in the sin of the Golden Calf had an aspect of transcendent importance and benefit. Aharon was willing to sacrifice all that he held dear to prevent the punishment of the nation with utter destruction, Heaven forbid. He saw this as a possibility when Chor was murdered by the worshipers of the calf, and he too was in jeopardy of being killed, which would result in the deaths of both a *Kohen* and a prophet (*Midrash Rabbah, Vayikra* §10). Thus, it was to his great merit that he was willing to literally offer his soul to protect the nation. Although his act was, in the final tally, impermissible, his motivation did provide a strong argument on his behalf. Accordingly, it is not problematic that the sacrifice for his atonement involves a calf. On the other hand, the episode of the Golden Calf was purely negative from the perspective of the nation as a whole. Therefore, the *Kohen Gadol* cannot wear gold, which recalls the Golden Calf, while he is in the Holy of Holies during the Yom Kippur service.

This explanation can help us understand another perplexing verse that is written concerning the Golden Calf. Moshe's complaint to Aharon, *"What did this people do to you?. . ."* (*Exodus* v. 32:21) is very difficult to understand; for seemingly, the act of Aharon was a grievous sin, one which we are enjoined to avoid even at the price of death! What Aharon did is certainly no less than appurtenant sins of idolatry, which also are never justified despite an imminent threat to life. But with the above in mind, we can understand the dialogue between Moshe and Aharon. Moshe complained that perhaps the nation would not have done anything to Aharon even had he refused to cooperate, and that Aharon was wrong in suspecting them of murder. Aharon answered, *"the people is disposed toward evil,"* stating that he believed that his evaluation of the situation was more accurate.

In Talmudic times, the custom was to translate the verses of the Torah when they were read in public. However, the Gemara in *Megillah* (25b) states that when we read the story of Aharon's involvement with the calf, we do not translate the verses in public, in order that no one should err, thinking that Aharon was blameworthy. By his evaluation, what he did had great justification. A similar concept is found in Tractate *Sanhedrin, Perek Chelek* (107a), where the Gemara relates that when King David fled for his life from his son Avshalom, he was very afraid that people who saw his suffering might decide, "If a righteous man such as David suffers so much, there must not be justice in the world!" He therefore considered acting as if he had become an idolater, so that this disgrace to the honor of Hashem would not result. We see that David, too, considered this a sin that would possibly be justified for the greater glory of G-d. Similarly, Aharon felt his actions were justified to enable the nation to survive.

In fact, the survival of the Jewish people is itself the greatest glorification of Hashem. This can be seen from the prayer offered by Moses while petitioning God on behalf of the nation. Moshe said, *"Why should Egypt say, . . .He brought them out in order to kill them in the mountains?"* (*Exodus* 32:12). This shows that the glorification of Hashem is tied to the survival of *Bnei Yisrael, and* their destruction, Heaven forbid, would result in a desecration of His honor. Indeed, even Moshe himself, when faced with the threat that *Bnei Yisrael* would be wiped out because of their terrible sin, said to Hashem: *"and if not, erase me from Your book. . ."* (ibid. v. 32) which means "from the books of the living and the dead" (*Rosh Hashanah* 16b). Moshe, too, offered the total destruction of his soul to prevent what he saw as a disgrace to the Glory of Hashem. This interpretation is correct and true.

❦ ❦ ❦

וַיֹּאמֶר מֹשֶׁה אֶל־אַהֲרֹן קְרַב אֶל־הַמִּזְבֵּחַ וַעֲשֵׂה אֶת־
חַטָּאתְךָ וְאֶת־עֹלָתֶךָ וְכַפֵּר בַּעַדְךָ וּבְעַד הָעָם — *Moshe said to Aharon: Come near to the Altar and*

perform the service of your sin-offering and your elevation-offering and provide atonement for yourself and for the people (9:7).

Moshe told Aharon to perform the service of the sin-offering at the end of the inauguration period for the Tabernacle, and said to him concerning that offering, "*provide atonement for yourself and for the people.*" But this is difficult to understand: The sin-offering calf that Aharon brought only provided forgiveness for Aharon, and not the people! The people's forgiveness was provided by the goat offering, as the end of this verse states.

Ibn Ezra and *Ohr HaChaim* have asked this question, and suggested answers. It appears to me that the answer is this: Atonement is not possible if one continues to sin. Therefore, if the leader and teacher of the nation, whose behavior is naturally emulated, is a sinner, then no one will even try to improve themselves. In Tractate *Bava Kamma* (52a) a Galilean said homiletically concerning Rav Chisda that when the shepherd is angry at the sheep, he blinds their leader, as *Rashi* explains there. If the case is that the leader is a sinner, the nation will not be forgiven for their sins because of the likely prospect that they will continue sinning. Therefore, Moshe said that first Aharon must purify himself and ensure that he is clean of sin, and then others will emulate him and follow the path of Hashem Yisbarach and His holy Torah. This would prepare the nation to receive atonement. Then, the only sins to be concerned about would be those from the past, which can be forgiven through the goat offering.

We see here how anyone who is influential on other's behavior, such as community leaders or teachers, must be extremely careful to achieve and maintain the highest purity possible, for what they do determines whether or not the repentance of others will be acceptable.

❧ ❧ ❧

הוּא אֲשֶׁר־דִּבֶּר ה' לֵאמֹר בִּקְרֹבַי אֶקָּדֵשׁ — *Of this did Hashem speak, saying: "I will be sanctified through those who are nearest Me"* (10:3).

In the *tefillah* of Rosh Hashanah and Yom Kippur we find the phrase "The holy God is sanctified with charity." This means that the fact that Hashem forgives sin, and does not punish sinners as they truly deserve to be punished, sanctifies Him. This seems to contradict the verses which tell us about the death of the children of Aharon. There, the verse states, *Of this did Hashem speak, saying: "I will be sanctified through those who are nearest me."* This verse teaches that Hashem's meting out strict justice to the righteous for even a minor infraction sanctifies Him.

We must answer the question thus: There are two forms of Hashem's trait of "strict judgment." One is that which Hashem desired to utilize in the creation of this world. Concerning this "trait of judgment," it is said that even our forefathers could not endure such strict justice. After the world was created with an admixture of the trait of "mercy," there still is a form of the trait of "judgment." Concerning this trait, the forefathers were called "the powerful one," who were far beyond any need for Hashem's charitable mercy. They could request recognition of their merit as a matter of right. Sometimes, however, it is Hashem's will to be sanctified through the application of the trait of "strict judgment" which existed before any admixture of mercy. But Hashem only does this when there are righteous people who can endure the more lenient level of "judgment." Most generations do not have men like this. In such times, sanctification of Hashem's Name comes through forgiveness and the withholding of punishment. If Hashem were to apply any trait of "judgment," people would despair from repenting, and so forgiveness increases holiness in this world by encouraging penitents. Therefore, the *tefillah* instituted for our generations is to ask for mercy so that Hashem's Name will be sanctified through forgiveness.

This also provides a strong reminder that if one has been granted the merit of influencing large numbers of people, he must be as strong and unrelenting as possible to habituate himself to act with the greatest possible holiness, far beyond the letter of the law.

❁　❁　❁

כִּי אֲנִי ה' הַמַּעֲלֶה אֶתְכֶם מֵאֶרֶץ מִצְרַיִם — *For I am* HASHEM *Who elevates you from the land of Egypt* (11:45).

In the section that deals with the prohibition from eating teeming creatures, the Torah uses the expression *For I am Hashem Who elevates you from the land of Egypt. . . . Rashi* quotes *Chazal*, who say that the merit of avoiding abhorrent creatures suffices to make the Exodus worthwhile. I have explained that even in matters where the nations of the world do as we do, the way we perform the *mitzvos* makes it evident that we do them to fulfill Hashem's wish, and not as natural behavior. For example, we worry even about the possibility that the vegetables we eat might contain some vermin.

This should be true in regard to the way we do charity and improve our character traits. Some of the nations give charity and act correctly because of a natural fineness in their personality. But we should realize that there is a difference between doing these things to quiet our consciences, and doing them to fulfill Hashem's wishes. We must always be concerned that we have not done enough, and seek to ensure that Hashem will testify that we did each *mitzvah* properly.

❧ ❧ ❧

לְהַבְדִּיל בֵּין הַטָּמֵא וּבֵין הַטָּהֹר — *to distinguish between the contaminated and the pure* (11:47).

At the end of the *parashah's* descriptions of the various kosher and non-kosher creatures, the verse says, *This is the law. . . to distinguish between the contaminated and the pure. . . . Rashi* explains that this means that it is not enough to merely list these differences; rather, we must become expert and experienced in discerning these differences. Along the same lines, he explains that *the contaminated and the pure. . .* refers to the difference in *shechitah* between an improperly half-cut trachea and a case where the majority was cut. *Between the animal that may be eaten and the animal that may not be eaten* refers to ostensible indicators of unfitness which may or may not actually render the animal unfit. Clearly, *Rashi* is teaching us the obligation to learn the Torah, which is that it is not enough just to know the law. Instead, one must be fluent, so that he is able to decide the law for others when asked. This requires actual knowledge of, and the ability to recognize, all of the various species, and to be able to measure the infinitesimal difference between half and majority, and to recognize by sight the indicators of unfitness. This knowledge must be immediately accessible to us, and not only after thought and investigation. This is a very novel way to understand the obligations set forth in this verse. It does help us to understand why Rav spent such a long time as a shepherd (*Sanhedrin* 5b) so that he could recognize those blemishes which release the first-born animal for personal use.

❧ ❧ ❧

פרשת תזריע
Parashas Tazria

תָּבִיא כֶּבֶשׂ בֶּן־שְׁנָתוֹ לְעֹלָה וּבֶן־יוֹנָה אוֹ־תֹר לְחַטָּאת —
she shall bring a sheep within its first year for an elevation-offering, and a young dove or a turtle-dove for a sin-offering (12:6).

The Torah says that a childbearing woman must bring two sacrifices, one an *olah* (an elevation-offering), and one a *chatas* (a sin-offering.) *Rashi* quotes the Gemara in *Zevachim* (90a) that says that the order of sacrifices in the verse is not the order of offering, for in practice the *chatas* always comes first. We must then understand why the Torah reversed the order of the sacrifices in the verse.

The answer is this: An *olah* works forgiveness only for minor sins, such as the omission of a positive commandment, or thoughts of doing a sin that were never carried out. A *chatas*, on the other hand, brings forgiveness for inadvertent actions, and involves such sins that would invoke the *kares* (premature death) penalty if done intentionally. We also know that our Sages say that these sacrifices are brought because when a woman begins the travail of childbirth, she swears to end her marital relationship with her husband. Now, this cannot have been a real oath, because if the woman had made a valid oath, either she would have to go to a court to annul the oath, or her husband would have had to invalidate it. *Chazal* must be referring to the thought that enters her mind during childbirth that it would be good if she would swear to avoid her husband. Therefore, the appropriate sacrifice is the *olah*, which comes for improper thoughts, and this is why the *olah* precedes the *chatas* in the verse.

Although according to this explanation the *chatas* sacrifice would seem to be inappropriate, still the Torah obligates her to bring a *chatas*, to let it be known that although bad thoughts usually only obligate an *olah*, there are times that bad thoughts are so inappropriate that they invoke the *chatas*. Childbirth is one of those times; for during childbirth, a woman needs the immediate mercy of Hashem. As the Gemara says in Tractate *Shabbos* (31b), "For three sins a woman might die during childbirth..," and *Rashi* there (32a) explains that at that dangerous time she should be praying for Hashem's assistance. At such a time, even thoughts take on a greater import, and can even invoke, to a degree, liability to a *chatas* sacrifice. Another possible approach is that such thoughts are especially inappropriate at the time the person should be recognizing Hashem's incomparable kindness in granting the ability to bear a child.

❧ ❧ ❧

וְכִסְּתָה הַצָּרַעַת אֵת כָּל־עוֹר הַנֶּגַע — *and the tzaraas will cover the entire skin of the affliction* (13:12).

The Torah says that a small spot of *tzaraas* renders the afflicted person a *metzora,* a designation which carries with it the highest degree of impurity possible in a living person. The Torah then tells us that if the small symptom spreads and the affliction covers the entire body, then the person loses his *metzora* designation, and may become pure. The words of the verse are: *If. . .the tzaraas will cover the entire skin of the affliction. . .then he shall declare the affliction to be pure.* This phrasing is perplexing, because certainly the meaning here is "if the *tzaraas* will cover the entire healthy skin" which had not yet been afflicted. Why, then, does the Torah say that it covered the *afflicted* skin?

The reason is this: The basis for the law which teaches that when the entire body is covered, the *metzora* becomes pure is not because it shows that he has repented. On the contrary: He is a great sinner who will not be helped by the regret most people feel upon becoming a *metzora.* Thus, Hashem causes his affliction to spread, and this unusual occurrence provides an infamous example that warns against slander and inspires repentance. As the *Rambam* says in the end of the sixteenth chapter of *Hilchos Tzaraas,* we learn from the *metzora* that if one does not repent, there will be no cure for his maladies. But the Torah does not create this state of impurity and isolation if it yields no benefit, for all of Hashem's punishments in this world must have some ultimate benefit. So, at first this man is afflicted because perhaps his anguish would inspire him to repent. If he does not repent, then healing him would be unreasonable, and punishing him more is useless. And so he remains a *metzora* without the impurity of *tzaraas*. This way, his condition remains a warning to others.

A similar idea is found in *Sanhedrin* 17. In one version of the Gemara, the Gemara brings the rule that if every member of the Sanhedrin holds that a man deserves capital punishment, he is not executed. Then the Gemara says that the way to remember this is by remembering that when a *metzora* turns all white (with *tzaraas*), he is pure. The reason for the law that when all hold guilty he is not executed is that the Torah decrees that a court which cannot possibly pay any attention to an argument for innocence may not sit in judgment. This is similar to the idea of *tzaraas*, in that his being completely covered with the affliction does not mean that he is any better, but instead that he is so wicked that *tzaraas* will not help him to repent. With this in mind, we can understand what *Rashi* means in verse 6. Where a possible *metzora* has been quarantined for two weeks, and the *Kohen* reexamines him, *Rashi* says that if the symptom remained the same size as it was at the last examination, he is impure and a *metzora*. Actually, the *halachah* is not so, for if the size remained constant he is pure and not a *metzora*. *Rashi* did not mean to state a *halachah* here, but to tell us what the Torah means to teach us: He is a *metzora* in the sense that he is the same wicked person as before, but there is no point in keeping him impure, and so he was neither healed nor declared a *metzora*.

Now we can understand why the Torah says that the affliction spread to cover "the entire skin of the affliction." This means that really he should be thought of as a *metzora* even if he were to be healed and his skin were perfect, because Hashem knows that he did not repent. The reason the *tzaraas* spread is in order that we should realize that a man who refuses to repent is worse than a *metzora,* and that based on this man's merits, he *is* an unmitigated *tzaraas*. We will therefore recognize the danger of refusing to repent.

❧ ❧ ❧

וּבָשָׂר כִּי־יִהְיֶה בוֹ־בְעֹרוֹ שְׁחִין . . . — *If flesh will have had an inflammation on its skin . . .* (13:18).

אוֹ בָשָׂר כִּי־יִהְיֶה בְעֹרוֹ מִכְוַת־אֵשׁ . . . — *If a person will have a burn from fire on his skin . . .* (13:24).

I n the *parashah* of *tzaraas,* the Torah lists as separate categories an inflammation of the skin and a fire burn on the skin. The rules concerning these two afflictions are identical. Still, if one would have a mark of inflammation half the size which would create *tzaraas* contiguous to a fire-burn mark of similar size, the two marks do not combine to create a state of *tzaraas.* For this reason, the Torah separates them into two categories.

The reason for this is that *tzaraas* comes as a result of a certain sin, and each type of affliction corresponds to a particular sin. We learn from here that a person must pay attention not only to the degree of his punishment through pain and suffering, but also to the means by which he is afflicted, for this, too, is related to his sin. Although the rules of these afflictions are the same, and so the degree of pain and suffering of the two are identical, they are separate punishments, each for a sin that resembles it, as indicated by the concept of "measure for measure." Bearing this in mind, a person will know how to repent. This is true with all suffering and punishment; all are meant to inspire repentance, and one must always meditate on the proximate cause of the pain and suffering, as this will awaken the ability to properly repent.

❧ ❧ ❧

פרשת מצרע
Parashas Metzora

וְהוּבָא אֶל־הַכֹּהֵן . . . וְיָצָא הַכֹּהֵן . . . — *He shall come to the* Kohen . . . *The Kohen shall go forth* (14:2-3).

First the Torah says, *He shall come to the Kohen,* and then it immediately says the opposite, *The Kohen shall go forth.* This can be interpreted homiletically to teach us about giving *mussar* — moral and ethical instruction. When a man sins and repents, like the *metzora* who has been healed, he should know to go to the teacher — the *Kohen* — to learn how to act from then on. But the *Kohen* should not wait for this to happen. The Kohen should go out and teach the sinner how to repent. Often, this benefits the other person, who would otherwise lack the impetus to repent. Every teacher or person who can influence others must keep this in mind and do so.

❧ ❧ ❧

וְצִוָּה הַכֹּהֵן וְלָקַח לַמִּטַּהֵר שְׁתֵּי־צִפֳּרִים חַיּוֹת טְהֹרוֹת — *The Kohen shall command; and for the person being purified there shall be taken two live, clean birds* (14:4).

At first glance, the need for the *Kohen* to "command" that the *metzora* purchase these birds is difficult to understand. We never find this requirement in the case of articles needed for other *mitzvos*. Instead, the Torah says that the person must do some act, and the person makes sure to have what he needs to do what is required. If he doesn't know what is needed, there are always people who can tell him. But here, it appears that he may not buy the birds unless commanded to do so by the *Kohen*!

The explanation is this: People often say that when it comes to matters about which they think the *halachah* is silent, they are wiser than Torah scholars, and they need not seek direction. This leads to their thinking that they are also expert in any *mitzvos* which are relevant to worldly things, such as priorities in charity distribution. People think that since it is their money, and their money cannot be taken without their willing agreement, this means that they can give to whomever they choose. In fact, not only are there laws which lay out the priorities for charitable giving, but in some cases it is actually forbidden for one to give. In all cases, there are laws governing how much and to whom to give, and the proper apportionment of funds. But almost nobody asks questions about this. Almost nobody asks about the proper relationship with their children, or how to educate them. If people realized that *halachah* does regulate and provide instruction for the vast majority of "worldly" matters, they certainly would come and ask.

A *metzora* must repent of this shortcoming before becoming pure. Many of the sins which cause *tzaraas* are those which people think are not regulated by *halachah* and are left up to them — such as lending utensils or money, or what we may or may not say about others. Therefore, the Torah says that for a *metzora* to repent, he must learn to consult Torah authorities in all matters — even the most mundane — until he knows what he needs to ask. To impress the lesson upon him, we require that he wait for the *Kohen* to tell him when and how to buy the birds for his purification.

❈ ❈ ❈

וְהִזַּרְתֶּם אֶת־בְּנֵי־יִשְׂרָאֵל מִטֻּמְאָתָם — *You shall separate the Bnei Yisrael from their contamination* (15:31).

Chazal explain that the separation, or barrier, the Torah requires here to distance us from impurity refers to the law that couples must abstain from marital relations within 12 hours of the expected onset of *niddah* impurity. This requires explanation, because this *parashah* deals with a *"zavah,"* who by definition cannot possibly become a *niddah,* and certainly is outside of any regular onset of *niddus*! Why was this prohibition, which concerns the 12 hours before *niddus,* stated where it has no relevance?

The lesson that the Torah comes to teach us is this: We must always see to it that we remain aware of all prohibitions which might be relevant — even if only to make the determination that they are not applicable. In other words, one should think about what he is doing, and not do things by rote. If there is nothing to worry about, he can think to himself, "Today there is no reason to consider the possibility of transgression." So, during those 11 days between *niddah* periods, or in any time he knows there is no real likelihood of the onset of *niddus,* he shouldn't act as if *niddus* was completely irrelevant. He should address the issue, and make the mental statement that today this prohibition has no practical application. By doing this, he is fulfilling the *mitzvah* of the *parashah* of *niddah* each day. Also, he will never forget it. This is why this *halachah* was stated in a *parashah* which discusses a period when the prohibition is not applied.

We should apply this lesson to every thing we do. For example: When we say the *tefillah* of *Shemoneh Esrei,* before each blessing we should establish in our minds that the next blessing is, for example, *Gevuros.* We should not just say it because our tongues are in the habit of doing so.

❈   ❈   ❈

פרשת אחרי מות
Parashas Acharei Mos

וַיְדַבֵּר ה' אֶל־מֹשֶׁה אַחֲרֵי מוֹת שְׁנֵי בְּנֵי אַהֲרֹן —
HASHEM spoke to Moshe after the death of
Aharon's two sons (16:1).

he Torah introduces the description of the service of Yom Kippur
with a verse mentioning the death of the two sons of Aharon,
righteous and holy men who died because of their error in
understanding the laws of the Temple. What is the connection of that
tragedy to Yom Kippur?

Most of the Yom Kippur service in the Temple involved the seeking of
forgiveness for the defilement of the Temple and other holy objects. Sins
that are caused by the base desires of the Evil Inclination, that occur
because a man is suddenly overpowered by his lust, are relatively easy to
repent when the lust evaporates. As soon as he has sinned, he knows
that he did wrong — indeed, sometimes he realizes his error even while
he is sinning. This is why *Chazal* say, "The wicked are filled with regret."
But sins involving the defilement of sanctified objects, which are sins
which concern holy things, are the result of a mistake concerning some
law or statement of *Chazal,* where the person's internal falsity moves him
to falsely interpret the Torah to support his lies and foolish beliefs. This
type of sinner is often far from repentance. This is especially true because
the sinner may provide some superficial basis for his position by
misinterpreting the holy Torah. Indeed, he will find it necessary to do so,
for even the simple masses would not sin unless shown some basis for
the spurious interpretations of sinners, because they have an innate
faith. Only because these subverters of the Torah claim a holy basis for
their statements do the people follow them.

This sin requires more forgiveness than one triggered by lust or greed; and this type of forgiveness can be inspired through the death of the righteous. Such tragedies arouse an emotional response, and inspire more vigilant attention to the words of the Torah. In reaction to their loss, people to seek out a *rebbi* that fears God, a great man that will teach them the truth. When they do this, they will not, Heaven forbid, stumble into the sin of the defilement of holy things.

❧ ❧ ❧

וַיְדַבֵּר ה' אֶל־מֹשֶׁה אַחֲרֵי מוֹת שְׁנֵי בְּנֵי אַהֲרֹן — *HASHEM spoke to Moshe after the death of Aharon's two sons* (16:1).

There are several different words the Torah uses for "speaking" or "saying." The word "*vayedaber*" denotes hard and forceful speech, as *Rashi* explains at the end of *Parashas Behaaloscha* (*Bamidbar* 12:2), where the Torah says, *and Miriam spoke*. It also implies love, as *Rashi* explains in *Parashas Devarim* (1:1). It is also used to describe a discussion of the laws of the Torah, as we find in the Gemara (*Makkos* 11), regarding the verse in *Yehoshua* (20:1) that says, *And Hashem spoke to* Yehoshua, concerning the designating of Cities of Refuge. It is used here although it is not directly dealing with discussion of laws (for on the contrary, the law of Yom Kippur is introduced with a different term, "*vayomer*"). The reason it is used here is because the Torah is discussing the death of the sons of Aharon. The Torah thereby teaches us that all men, even the greatest, need to be instructed and cautioned in a hard and powerful manner, but also with love. It is this manner of speech that will have the greatest influence on them. This is even more true where one is talking to and teaching children.

❧ ❧ ❧

וְאַל־יָבֹא בְכָל־עֵת אֶל הַקֹּדֶשׁ . . . — *he shall not come at all times into the Sanctuary . . .* (16:2).

The section dealing with the Temple service of Yom Kippur begins with the warning that even the *Kohen Gadol* (High Priest) may not enter the Holy of Holies at will. It would seem that the next verse should describe the circumstances that do allow entry. But in fact, those verses do not appear until much later in this section. This is because the awareness of the prohibition from going into the Holy of Holies is mandatory for the acceptability of the Yom Kippur service. Only if the *Kohen Gadol* knows that it is a supremely holy place — such that no one may enter other than to perform the Yom Kippur service — will he do the day's work in the elevated state of holiness that befits him, and thereby bring forgiveness.

In truth, once the law that the Holy of Holies may not be entered for other than the most important purposes was known, Aharon's high level of holiness could have allowed him to enter whenever he wanted to do service. But the Torah prohibited this by decree even for Aharon (see *Rashi*). Perhaps, despite his elevated spiritual level, the concept of "*hokar raglecha*" (see *Mishlei* 25:17; this term is understood in *Chagigah* 7a to mean that one should not excessively appear before Hashem with supplications) applied to him. Only Moshe, who merited a degree of prophecy unrivaled by any human, was allowed to enter at will, because the concept of "*hokar raglecha*" did not apply to him. Another possibility is that the Torah did not want to differentiate between Aharon and the High Priests that would follow him. This is the reason that the grant of entry on Yom Kippur is not mentioned in the beginning of the section; the main point is to let us know that entry is extremely limited due to the holiness of the place. Once that point is made clear, entry could have been permitted, but the Torah prohibited it all year and required it on Yom Kippur.

With this in mind, we can understand the statement "If someone tells you there is wisdom in Edom, you may believe him, but if he tells you there is Torah in Edom, do not believe him " (see *Eichah Rabbah* 2:17). For although we find that King Shavor was familiar with *halachah,* as *Tosafos* says in the end of Tractate *Bava Metzia* (119a), he knew it just as he knew natural sciences, as a field of study. Only in conjunction with the holiness of the nation of Israel can the true understanding of Torah exist, as the verse states: *judgments — they know them not (Psalms 147:20).*

We should learn from this *parashah* that whenever we do a *mitzvah,* we should take stock of its holiness and importance. This appreciation and awareness will elevate the performance of the *mitzvah.* Certainly, when a person has merited being a *rav* and leader and teacher, who influences the people to walk the path of the Torah, he must be constantly aware of the supreme importance of his position.

❧ ❧ ❧

בְּזֹאת יָבֹא אַהֲרֹן אֶל־הַקֹּדֶשׁ ... — **With this shall Aharon come into the Sanctuary ...** (16:3).

The Torah in this *parashah* begins by saying the *Kohen Gadol* may not enter the Holy of Holies at will, but only if he brings certain animal and incense sacrifices. The *parashah* then mentions that this is the procedure followed on Yom Kippur. This connection with Yom Kippur is not mentioned until the twenty-ninth verse of the *parashah,* several verses before the end of the discussion. The reason for this order is clear according to the Gaon, who holds that Aharon himself was allowed to follow this procedure at any time during the year, and enter once, and on Yom Kippur any *Kohen Gadol* follows the procedure and enters several times. But *Rashi* (16:34) indicates that even Aharon was only allowed to enter on Yom Kippur. If this *parashah* is only relevant to Yom Kippur, why isn't Yom Kippur mentioned in the beginning of the *parashah*?

The answer is that to enter the Holy of Holies, one must be on a very elevated spiritual level. To reach that level, one must prepare by studying how one acts in the Holy of Holies. This study itself is one of the elements necessary to create the lofty spiritual status needed to enter. We should learn from this that every holy endeavor, and particularly the education of children, must not be done extemporaneously. Instead, one must prepare an organized plan which focuses on how to act, how to teach, and how to best influence the children.

❧ ❧ ❧

וְכִפֶּר בַּעֲדוֹ וּבְעַד בֵּיתוֹ וּבְעַד כָּל־קְהַל יִשְׂרָאֵל — **he shall provide atonement for himself, for his household, and for the entire congregation of Israel** (16:17).

We find in this verse that the *Kohen Gadol* recited a confession in the name of his fellow *Kohanim,* and for the entire Jewish nation. One would think that confession and repentance are so intrinsically personal that one person cannot repent on behalf of another. The reason that the *Kohen Gadol* could confess on behalf of all of *Klal Yisrael* is because a leader must know and understand every member of *Klal Yisrael,* and influence each person to repent; also he must be able to perceive whether his efforts to influence the individuals is succeeding. Similarly, a teacher with his students, a *Rav* with his congregants, and certainly a *Rosh Yeshivah* or *Mashgiach* must constantly be sensitive to the success or failure of their efforts.

Along the same lines, we see that the *Kohen Gadol* was punished if during his tenure a man killed another man by not being as careful as he ought to have been, as the Gemara (*Makkos* 11a) explains. This is also why in *Malachi* (2:6) we find that the prophet praised Aharon for turning the people away from sin by dint of his own great righteousness.

I have heard a similar concept expressed in explaining the verse *injustice was not found on his lips. . . .* (*Malachi* 2:6) as meaning that Aharon never had to rebuke sinners or to bring up their sins to them, because "he is an angel of Hashem. . ." (ibid. v. 7), as I have explained in the verses describing David's flight to Shmuel.

❊ ❊ ❊

אִישׁ אִישׁ מִבֵּית יִשְׂרָאֵל אֲשֶׁר יִשְׁחַט שׁוֹר אוֹ־כֶשֶׂב אוֹ־עֵז בַּמַּחֲנֶה אוֹ אֲשֶׁר יִשְׁחָט מִחוּץ לַמַּחֲנֶה. וְאֶל־פֶּתַח אֹהֶל מוֹעֵד לֹא הֱבִיאוֹ . . . — *Any man from the House of Israel who will slaughter an ox, a sheep, or a goat in the camp, or who will slaughter outside the camp, and he has not brought it to the entrance of the Tent of Meeting . . .* (17:3-4).

Rashi explains that *in the camp* means outside of the Tabernacle courtyard. In the context of the Temple, this would mean in Yerushalayim or the Temple Mount, both being outside of the Temple proper. We must try to understand why the Torah gives two examples of places outside the Temple.

The answer is that people felt a great desire to bring sacrifices, because they understood the meaning of the Temple service and how it brings us to self-realization and the attainment of lofty levels of spirituality. But since the great majority of the nation lived far from Yerushalayim, many people transgressed the prohibition from bringing sacrifices outside of the Temple by erecting private altars. We see that even in the days of the righteous kings, such as Asa, Yehoshaphat, Yoash, Amatziah, Uziahu and Yosam, people sinned in this manner. Therefore the Torah had to tell us that this is prohibited, that Hashem wishes that we grow not by deciding for ourselves what path to take to greatness, but instead by following the path of the Torah by serving the wise men who have reached Torah greatness. When a person brings a sacrifice in order to grow, this may only be done in a place sanctified for that purpose, by way of the *Kohanim* that were sanctified for that purpose. When the person comes to such a place among such people, he will learn to fear Hashem when he sees all the people there busy in Hashem's service, as the Torah says concerning the second tithe (*Devarim* 14:23). But despite this warning, one might think that near the Courtyard, in Yerushalayim (which is a place that fosters fear of God), and certainly on the Temple Mount, where the most holy sacrifices may be eaten, it might be permissible to bring sacrifices. Moreover, one might think that since (during that long-ago time when a private altar was permissible) a private altar does not require a *Kohen,* perhaps he should build a private altar there so he could do the service himself. Therefore, the Torah had to warn us that this, too, is prohibited. Man must rule over his impulses, and subordinate his determinations of what is right or wrong to what he is told by the *Kohanim* in the Temple.

❀ ❀ ❀

וּשְׁמַרְתֶּם אֶת־חֻקֹּתַי וְאֶת־מִשְׁפָּטַי — *And you shall guard My decrees and My laws* (18:5).

I t is first written in verse 4, *My laws you shall do and My decrees you shall guard,* and then it is written, *And you shall guard My decrees and My laws, which man shall do.* Rashi explains that by this repetition the Torah adds "doing" in connection with decrees and "guarding" in connection with laws. But this is a perplexing interpretation. It would be understandable if the terms in the second verse were simply reversed; but instead, the second verse applies both terms equally to each of the the two types of laws. For what purpose, then, was the first verse written?

The answer appears to be that the first verse describes the way that things ought to be. Laws, which are understandable to human reason, should not require "guarding," which means special vigilance to avoid transgression, but simply "doing"; for a person that leads a just life and fears Heaven should naturally and automatically "guard" against such things. Unfortunately, we see that in reality this is not so, as the Gemara in *Bava Basra* (165a) says, "thievery is common," due to the strength of the Evil Inclination. Therefore, the second verse stresses "guarding" even in connection with laws whose logic is apparent to the human mind.

❧ ❧ ❧

וּשְׁמַרְתֶּם אֶת־חֻקֹתַי וְאֶת־מִשְׁפָּטַי — *And you shall guard My decrees and My laws* (18:5).

Elsewhere (*Devarim* 4:6) *Rashi* explains that the phrase *you shall observe* refers to the study of the Mishnah. This is because doing the *mitzvos* without study and understanding (characterized by study of the Mishnah) is akin to following a routine out of habit. Moreover, the Torah says *you shall observe* both in regard to laws (which an unbiased thinker can understand and appreciate) and decrees (which are not fathomable to the human intelligence). This is because we must learn and clearly know the parameters and rules of not only decrees, but even of the laws. Without study of the Torah, fulfillment of laws lacks the distinction that it ought to have. As it says in *Tehillim* (147:20), *judgments — they know them not;* this is because the nations do not have the Torah. Although they do have the seven Noachide *mitzvos,* they must fulfill them pursuant to the command of Hashem through Moshe in order to receive reward for observing them, as the *Rambam* states (*Hil. Melachim* 8:11).

❧ ❧ ❧

פרשת קדשים
Parashas Kedoshim

קְדֹשִׁים תִּהְיוּ . . . — *You shall be holy . . .* (19:2).

The *mitzvah* of *You shall be holy*, which is followed by a recitation of several of the fundamental *mitzvos*, is not of the same type as the *mitzvos* that follow it. This *mitzvah* means that every Jew should realize that he is sanctified with the holiness of the Jew, and it is only because of that holiness that we were given the Torah and obligated to do the *mitzvos*. As I have often written, *mitzvos* cannot be fulfilled properly unless the doer has the holiness of the Jew. The *Kohanim*, who have additional *mitzvos*, must have the particular holiness of *Kohanim*. This is why we make a blessing before *mitzvos* and say, "Who has sanctified us with His *mitzvos*"; and *Kohanim*, before doing *mitzvos* that are limited to *Kohanim*, say, "Who has sanctified us with the sanctity of Aharon." The expression "Who has sanctified us with His *mitzvos*" should not be misunderstood as meaning that the *mitzvos* are the source of the sanctity. It is self-understood that the sanctity the blessing refers to is the underlying sanctity of every Jew — that which enables us to fulfill the *mitzvos*.

❧ ❧ ❧

After the commandment that we must be holy, the Torah lists *mitzvos* of a very weighty and critical nature, and not the refined and elevated *mitzvos* we might think should follow such a commandment. This is because the proper fulfillment of the very serious *mitzvos*, even in the most basic way, requires holiness. This makes the fulfillment of such *mitzvos* an act of love and joy; and is the underlying reason for the high level of care necessary to properly do these *mitzvos* as Hashem *Yisbarach* wishes.

❧ ❧ ❧

The *Ramban,* explaining the admonition to be holy, says it is a warning that we should realize that without this admonition, it would be possible to be a degenerate despite fulfilling the letter of the law (נָבָל בִּרְשׁוּת הַתּוֹרָה). This commandment tells us that we must practice moderation and abstemiousness. One might wonder: Since the particulars of this concept are not provided for us, how can we know how to act in this fashion of holiness? The answer is, as I have written elsewhere, that a person must realize that he is holy, and this awareness should stem from the words of the end of the verse —*for holy am I, Hashem, your God.* We are all children of Hashem *Yisbarach,* and are therefore sons of holiness itself; it follows that our senses and intellect are attuned to an innate understanding of what holiness entails. There is no need to enumerate particulars for such a people. In addition, particulars are not enumerated because the practices of holiness which stem from this sensitivity must vary according to place and circumstance.

❧ ❧ ❧

קְדֹשִׁים תִּהְיוּ כִּי קָדוֹשׁ אֲנִי ה' אֱלֹקֵיכֶם — *You shall be holy, for holy am I, HASHEM, your God* (19:2).

Ramban explains that this verse generally includes all manner of things which are impossible to enumerate and prohibit individually. The admonition the Torah is making is that we may not be as "a degenerate with the permission of the Torah." But it would seem that *Ramban* has not explained the causal connection of this admonition to the words *for holy am I* at the end of the verse!

The explanation is that this verse commands us to change our nature, which tends to desire all sorts of barren and vain human pleasures. Instead, we should learn to desire holy things. This trait only comes when one has immersed himself in the study of the Torah. When one has diligently learned the Torah, his whole physical self and his attitudes and desires change. Only in this manner can the words of *Ramban* truly be fulfilled, so that the person will not be "a degenerate with the permission of the Torah."

We see, in this country, that there are wealthy people who heed the Torah, and also manage to seize all the worldly desires they can conceive of, but they ensure that this should be done without transgressing any prohibitions of the Torah. As Yalta said in *Chullin,* all those things which the Torah prohibits exist in a form which is not prohibited.

But this is not the way of the Torah. We must be holy and not desire superfluous things. Therefore the Torah says, *for holy am I.*

Although Hashem *Yisbarach* should have dealt with His creations with the attribute of Judgment, as it has been said that it was in this manner that the original intent to create the world occurred, He did not do so. He saw that the world could not survive if the attribute of Judgment was applied, and so He tempered Judgment with Mercy. Not only that, but the attribute of Mercy is the stronger of the two elements in Hashem's relationship with His creations. In a manner of speaking, Hashem acts, for the good of man, in a fashion that is different than He wishes to act. This is the command of *You shall be holy,* that you must habituate yourselves to desire holiness; do not do what your innate predilections lead you to desire, for, as the Torah says (*Bereishis* 8:21), *the imagery of man's heart is evil from his youth.* See that I, too, act contrary to My attribute of Judgment, which would have been My will, and I act with Mercy for the good of the world.

❧ ❧ ❧

קְדֹשִׁים תִּהְיוּ — You shall be holy (19:2).

You shall be holy commands us to be aware of the holiness we possess because we are Jews. It is because of this holiness that we are commanded to fulfill *mitzvos,* as indicated by the phrase "Who has sanctified us with His *mitzvos.*" Without this holiness, no *mitzvah* could be fulfilled. This concept serves to answer a question on a *Tosafos* (*Shabbos* 118b). The *Ri* says that he does not know of any prohibition for a non-*Kohen* to ascend to the platform and perform the priestly blessings, other than the wasted blessing he would pronounce. The question may be asked: How is this different from a woman who utters a blessing on one of those *mitzvos* which women are freed from performing? *Tosafos,* after all, does allow a woman to make those blessings.

The answer is that one needs the special holiness of Aharon to perform the Priestly Blessing. This is why the blessing made by the *Kohanim* states, "Who has sanctified us with the holiness of Aharon." A non-Kohen has no such holiness, and his blessing is said in vain. A woman, on the other hand, possesses the holiness of Israel, and can say, "Who has sanctified us."

Every Jew must remain aware of this holiness. Furthermore, this holiness is susceptible to profanation, as we find regarding the Temple, whose holiness was profaned through its destruction. Thus, we are commanded to maintain and increase the holiness we were granted, through the study of Torah and the fulfillment of *mitzvos*.

❦ ❦ ❦

לֹא תִּגְנֹבוּ — *You shall not steal* (19:11).

Y ou shall not steal is stated in the plural. This is because we interpret this verse to forbid us from stealing with the intention of allowing ourselves to be apprehended, and thereafter paying the owner the fine of *keifel* — double the value of the stolen object. The person that does this is motivated by a wish to benefit his friend, the owner, who is poor and refuses to accept charity. One might think that this is a fine and commendable way to help a friend without embarrassing him. In fact, the person who feels this way might even publicly advocate this as a new ideology, that one must love and help his neighbor even if this results in one's disgrace and being thought of as a thief. Similarly, one might steal and tell himself that he is doing so to teach the victim how painful the experience is, so that the victim himself will never steal. The Torah unmasks this as the doctrine of the wicked. This is why this is stated in the plural, because it refers to a type of stealing that a person might publicly boast about. On the other hand, robbery is invariably done for selfish motives so that one cannot even fool himself into believing that it is done to benefit the victim, because robbery does not carry with it the *keifel* penalty. Thus, its prohibition could not be stated in the plural, because the robber would never boast about it, knowing that it is a forbidden and disgraceful act.

We can apply the lesson learned from this verse to other prohibitions as well. There are wicked people who have made an ideology out of gently killing people who are suffering from painful diseases. This, too, is a doctrine of the wicked.

❦ ❦ ❦

הוֹכֵחַ תּוֹכִיחַ אֶת־עֲמִיתֶךָ וְלֹא־תִשָּׂא עָלָיו חֵטְא — *you shall reprove your fellow and do not bear a sin because of him* (19:17).

Another way of reading this verse is, *You shall reprove your friend, and you will not burden him with sin.* This means that you must reprove your friend while he is righteous and does all the *mitzvos,* in order to strengthen him in his faith and fear of Hashem and application to the *mitzvos.* Do not wait until after he sins; it is far better if you prevent his dissolution and help him to avoid ever sinning.

❧ ❧ ❧

וְכִי־תָבֹאוּ אֶל־הָאָרֶץ וּנְטַעְתֶּם כָּל־עֵץ מַאֲכָל וַעֲרַלְתֶּם
עָרְלָתוֹ אֶת־פִּרְיוֹ שָׁלֹשׁ שָׁנִים יִהְיֶה לָכֶם עֲרֵלִים לֹא יֵאָכֵל

— *When you shall come to the land and you shall plant any food tree, you shall treat its fruit as forbidden; for three years they shall be forbidden to you, they shall not be eaten* (19:23).

The Torah says that any fruit produced during the first three years of a tree's life, the *orlah* crops, are prohibited, and the fruit of the fourth year is allowed only within tightly defined conditions. Only from the fifth year and onward is the fruit freely available to us. The phrase used to describe this change that occurs in the fifth year is that you may eat its fruit *so that it will increase its crop for you. Rashi* explains that this phrase was only said to counter the usual subversions of the Evil Inclination, so that a man should not say that he wasted four good years of produce. The reason this is said in this *parashah* is because *orlah* does not provide any benefit to anyone, for the Torah commanded that we destroy those crops. Similarly, during the *shemittah* year we must leave our fields and orchards open to all men and even animals to depredate and ruin at will. These are *mitzvos* which a man might find very hard to fulfill, because what we are told to do is the opposite of the general rule which tells us that ruining a useful thing is sinful. Therefore, so that it should not be too difficult for a man to fulfill the *mitzvah* of *orlah* and let good things go to waste for no apparent reason, it was necessary to tell us that we must not second-guess Hashem, but instead do His will with faith and trust. If we do so, we will lack for nothing in this world, and this "waste" will not subtract a thing from what is destined for us. Similarly, the laws of *shemittah* should not cause anguish when one sees animals freely eating his crop, for this is the will of Hashem; and neither the owner nor the world as a whole will lose a thing by it, for Hashem will "command His blessing upon us." In the case of gifts to the poor or gifts to the *Kohen* and *Levi*, there are no similar verses guaranteeing that this will cause no loss, because *every* Jew knows that just as spending large sums on one's own needs is not wasteful, so too giving to the poor or giving the tithe to the Kohen or Levi is not wasteful. Indeed, doing so is also our own need. In the case of the tithes, we enjoy the chance to do this *mitzvah, and* it is not difficult at all. The only reason the Torah says, *Tithe, so that you may become wealthy* (see *Devarim* 14:22 and *Tanchuma* there §18; see also *Shabbos* 119b), is to inform us of the great reward for fulfilling *mitzvos*. In this *parashah,* however, the promise is necessary because of what might otherwise appear to be wasteful.

❧ ❧ ❧

וּבַשָּׁנָה הַחֲמִישָׁת תֹּאכְלוּ אֶת־פִּרְיוֹ לְהוֹסִיף לָכֶם תְּבוּאָתוֹ
— And in the fifth year you may eat its fruit — so that it will increase its crop for you (19:25).

Rashi quotes Rabbi Akiva's statement that the Torah says *it will increase its crop for you* (in the *parashah* which prohibits the use of the fruit of a tree less than three years old) to quiet the Evil Inclination. By promising to add to your harvest, Hashem anticipates and silences the Evil Inclination's argument that this *mitzvah* is too costly. This is hard to understand, because the Torah enunciates the promise of reward for *mitzvos* many times, even when the *mitzvah* costs nothing, such as in the case of *"shiluach haken"* — sending away the mother bird from its nest.

The answer to this question is that there are two payments for *mitzvos*: reimbursement and reward. The *Ribono Shel Olam* may choose to not give any reward in this world, and in any case the main reward is in the World to Come. As *Chazal* say, "Reward for *mitzvos* is not in this world' (*Kiddushin* 38b). But a person is always reimbursed for the expense of doing a *mitzvah* — quickly, if not immediately. This is what the verse means by saying "in the fifth year. . .it will increase its crop for you," which means that Hashem will certainly make sure that fulfilling the *mitzvah* will cause him no loss, and this is all beside the ultimate reward. This is a very novel explanation of this verse. Perhaps this verse is the source of the *Rambam's* statement (*Hilchos Tzedakah* 10:2), "no man ever becomes poor because he gives charity." *Rambam* is not referring to the reward for charity, in which Hashem promises wealth, because he only says that a person will not become poor from giving. Besides the verse which is expounded: *tithe, so that you may become wealthy* (see *Tanchuma* (§18) to *Devarim* 14:22), our verse tells us that whenever a *mitzvah* requires the incurring of expense, such as in the case of *orlah*, the expense will not result in any loss. This applies to charity just as well, which inevitably requires an outlay of money, and so the Torah guarantees that no loss will result.

This is what Rav Akiva meant. The evil inclination might say that although ultimately reward will come for charity, giving away one's money will cause him to have less for himself now. For this reason, the Torah tells us that Hashem very quickly makes good all the "losses" we need to incur in fulfilling *mitzvos*, and that this is above and beyond the great reward due in the World to Come; moreover, it is even besides the "fruit" of reward which one may receive for a *mitzvah* in this world. This interpretation is true.

❦ ❦ ❦

פרשת אמר
Parashas Emor

. . . וּמִן־הַמִּקְדָּשׁ לֹא יֵצֵא — *He shall not leave the Sanctuary . . . (21:12).*

T he Gemara in *Sanhedrin* (18a) says that the verse referring to a bereaved *Kohen Gadol* which states that *he shall not leave the Sanctuary* teaches us that the Torah creates an unusually strict barrier to prevent even a very small possibility of the impurification of the *Kohen Gadol.* According to Rav Yehudah, he may not accompany the funeral procession of a parent at all, and according to Rav Meir, he may accompany the procession, but only if he remains out of sight of the casket. This is all because of the highly unlikely possibility that he might, in his grief, touch the casket and become impure, as indicated by the fact that he may accompany the funeral procession of any other relative (see Gemara there).

The reason for this unusually strict barrier is his uniquely high level of holiness, for the verse continues: *he shall not desecrate the Sanctuary of his God.* This teaches us that anyone that is more holy must be more vigilant. Therefore, a Torah scholar, who also has a higher level of holiness, as the *Rambam* says (at the end of *Hilchos Shemittah*), "he is sanctified as the Holy of Holies," must be constantly alert to avoid even the slightest implication or suspicion of any impropriety, even if any such suspicion would be unfounded. This is why the Torah scholar that has stains on his garment — and most certainly on his soul — is punished severely. The reason for the strict punishment for a scholar who presents an improper appearance also is because it demeans the dignity of the Torah, as *Rashi* says in *Shabbos* (113a).

❈ ❈ ❈

כִּי כָל־אִישׁ אֲשֶׁר־בּוֹ מוּם לֹא יִקְרָב — *For any man in whom there is a blemish shall not approach* (21:18).

ashi explains that it would be improper for a person with a physical blemish to do the Temple service just as we find that the prophet said (*Malachi* 1:8), "*When you present a blind animal for sacrifice, is nothing wrong? Present it, if you please, to your governor. Would he be pleased with you or show you favor?*" We might have thought that since it says, ". . .*I look to the poor and broken-spirited person*" (*Yeshayahu* 66:2). *HaKadosh Baruch Hu* is different from flesh-and-blood kings, for He prefers to use "broken vessels" such as a broken-spirited person. If so, we might think that a person with a blemish would be fit for service. This is why the Torah explains that although this is indeed true from the perspective of Hashem, the blemished person should understand and feel that he is not fit to do the service. If he does not feel that way, then he suffers from haughtiness by thinking that despite his deficiency, his greatness outweighs his blemish. This is certainly despised, for *the haughty heart is the abomination of Hashem* (*Mishlei* 16:5).

Another explanation is that since these physical blemishes are considered shameful from the human perspective, as indicated in the verse "*Present it, if you please, to your governor,*" we have no right to say that Hashem does not mind such things, for in His eyes we are all equal. We must tender honor according to our own concepts of what is worthy.

There is another lesson here. Although Hashem despises haughtiness and loves humility, He does not want man to be humiliated. On the contrary, we find that a person that publicly disgraces himself is unfit to provide testimony to a court (*Kiddushin* 40b, regarding one who eats in the public market — see *Rashi* there), because this brings a lessening of one's sensitivity to shame, and this sensitivity is an important element in maintaining the fear of Hashem. Among the nations, there are also some who recognize that humility is a positive attribute. Some feel that since humility is a positive attribute, one should invite personal disgrace and humiliation. They made idols that represent this idea, called Pe'or and Markulis, and they worshiped them by heaping disgrace on them. This is not the way of the Torah. Although Hashem abominates the haughty, it is forbidden for us to disgrace ourselves. This has nothing to do with the humility the Torah commands.

🦋 🦋 🦋

וְלֹא תְחַלְּלוּ אֶת־שֵׁם קָדְשִׁי — *You shall not dese-crate My holy Name* (22:32).

After the Torah sets out various conditions which invalidate an animal sacrifice, we are told, *"You shall not desecrate My holy Name,"* which warns us to never do something that will dishonor the Name of God. This is a very strange juxtaposition. The laws discussed in the beginning of the section are the invalidation of a sacrifice which is younger than eight days old, the prohibition against slaughtering an animal and its offspring on the same day, and the prohibition to express an intention to do a part of the Temple service outside of its proper place or consume a sacrifice beyond the allotted time. These matters would seem to have nothing in common with the warning not to dishonor the Name of Hashem. We see from this that each and every *mitzvah* contains in its fulfillment the element of sanctification of Hashem's Name, and in its transgression the desecration of Hashem's Name — even if done in private, when no one will know. We cannot measure and compare *mitzvos*. All that matters is doing the will of our Creator, and doing so sanctifies His Name. Doing the opposite by disregarding His will desecrates His Name.

❧ ❧ ❧

וְלֹא תְחַלְּלוּ אֶת־שֵׁם קָדְשִׁי וְנִקְדַּשְׁתִּי בְּתוֹךְ בְּנֵי יִשְׂרָאֵל — *You shall not desecrate My holy Name, rather I should be sanctified among Bnei Yisrael* (22:32).

The verse first says *"You shall not desecrate,"* and then *"I should be sanctified."* *Rashi* begins his explanation by pointing out that if Torah would have only said *"You shall not desecrate,"* it would have been unnecessary to say *"I should be sanctified."* This is difficult to understand. There are many cases where one has not profaned, but where he has also not sanctified either! Certainly we would understand the need for a separate *mitzvah* to sanctify!

We must answer that a person profanes Hashem's Name whenever he acts below the level that he has established as appropriate for him. The Gemara in *Yoma* (86a) quotes various Amoraim as having said, "For me, not paying a bill immediately is a profanation. For me, walking four cubits without *tefillin* is a profanation." For Rav and Rav Yochanan, doing so would be profanation of Hashem's Name, although for others, who are not expected to behave in their elevated fashion, these things would not be profanations.

We can apply this lesson learned here to the average man: If he is capable of learning at a higher level, but is too lazy to do so, or if he is wealthy and capable of giving a large sum, but doesn't, this is a profanation of Hashem's Name. Thus, whoever does not sanctify, profanes. This is a very strong reminder of how carefully and diligently we should determine and carry out our duties.

❊   ❊   ❊

לֹא־תְכַלֶּה פְּאַת שָׂדְךָ בְּקֻצְרֶךָ . . . — *you shall not remove completely the corners of your field as you reap . . . (23:22).*

In this verse, the Torah brings up the *halachah* of *pe'ah* — the law that requires one to leave the edge of the field unharvested, so that the poor can come and share in our harvest. *Rashi* quotes *Chazal*: "Rabbi Avdimi ben Yitzchak says: For what reason did Scripture place the law of *pe'ah* in middle of the Festivals with Pesach and Shavuos on one side, and Rosh Hashanah and Yom Kippur on the other? To teach you that whoever properly provides the poor with *leket* (gleanings,) *shich'chah* (leavings), and *pe'ah*, the Torah credits him as if he built the Holy Temple and brought sacrifices in it."

We may ask: What connection does *pe'ah* have to the building of the Temple and the bringing of sacrifices? The answer is that in the merit of charity, we will be soon redeemed and the Holy Temple will be built. It follows that if a person gave charity properly, then as far as he is concerned, he has done his part to bring the redemption; if the majority of Israel would do as he did, *Mashiach* would come and the Holy Temple would be built, and sacrifices would be brought. Therefore, the Holy One, Blessed is He, considers that regarding this person the redemption has already occurred, and the Holy Temple was rebuilt, and sacrifices were brought. This righteous person does not have to suffer because of those that did not fulfill the *mitzvah* of charity and prevented the Holy Temple from being built. Thus, he receives reward as if he had actually brought sacrifices.

❊   ❊   ❊

בַּחֲמִשָּׁה עָשָׂר יוֹם לַחֹדֶשׁ הַשְּׁבִיעִי הַזֶּה חַג הַסֻּכּוֹת שִׁבְעַת יָמִים לַה' — *On the fifteenth day of this seventh month is the Festival of Succos, a seven-day period for* HASHEM (23:34).

The Torah introduces the law that we must dwell in temporary houses — *succos* — during the Festival of Succos. Obviously, the name of the holiday derives from this unique *mitzvah*. Why, then, is the holiday already referred to as the Festival of Succos in the immediate beginning of the *parashah,* even though the Torah only introduces the *mitzvah* of dwelling in the *succah* at the end of the *parashah* (in v. 42), after a lengthy discussion of other aspects of the holiday?

This is because the essence of the intent of Hashem *Yisbarach* in this *mitzvah* is to teach us that throughout our lives in this world, even if we live in beautiful mansions, we must remember that all of this life is merely a temporary dwelling, like a passageway leading to the true dwelling, as Rav Yaakov said in *Pirkei Avos* (4:16). The only goal in this life that has any substance is the pursuit of Torah and *mitzvos*. We must not struggle and suffer excessive anguish because of worldly events; and with this approach it will be easier to fulfill the commandments of Hashem with joy. We should not be so concerned with the high cost of some *mitzvos* or charity, as we should realize that the reward for the *mitzvah* is eternal, while the expense is temporary. The essence of this *mitzvah* thus applies equally wherever we happen to live. To reinforce this idea, the Torah gave us the *mitzvah* of *succah,* so that for seven days we actually dwell in a temporary home; this assists us in realizing the transitory nature of this world. It is for this reason that one who suffers due to adverse conditions in the *succah,* such as when it is raining or when it is excessively hot, is free from the obligation to dwell in the *succah.* As we have explained, the *mitzvah* is meant to teach us not to allow events of this life to cause us anguish, for this life is just a passageway and a temporary dwelling. Therefore, it is appropriate that we should not suffer in the fulfillment of the very *mitzvah* that is meant to teach us to approach all of this life without strife and suffering.

❧ ❧ ❧

עַל הַמְּנֹרָה הַטְּהֹרָה יַעֲרֹךְ אֶת־הַנֵּרוֹת — *On the pure Menorah shall he arrange the lamps* (24:4).

One explanation of this verse is that the Menorah must be made of pure gold. Another is that the lamps must be perfectly clean before they are refilled. This repetition of the requirement that the Menorah be made of pure gold teaches us that a person that enlightens others, a *rebbi,* must endeavor to explain himself in a perfectly clear and straightforward manner, and to act in a manner so upright that no observer could even momentarily question his deeds. Therefore, the Torah says that the Menorah should be of pure gold, with no admixture of any kind, and the oil should be so untainted that even oil that once contained dregs is invalid; also, the lamp must be perfectly clean — all to show us how clear and pure a *rebbi* must be in his understanding, his instruction, and his actions.

❀ ❀ ❀

This verse tells of the *mitzvah* of cleaning and preparing the lamps of the Menorah every morning. *Rashi* explains that the *Kohen* cleans and removes the ashes from the lamps. Clearly, as far as lighting the Menorah is concerned, there would be no difference whether or not he would remove whatever oil remained from the previous day. Even so, when *Rashi* says that the *Kohen* removes the ashes, he also means that the leftover oil is remove. [See *Menachos* 88 and *Rambam, Hilchos Temidin U'Mussafin* 3:14.] This may only be done by a *Kohen.* A reason for these requirements is because the Menorah represents our tradition of of teaching our students and children Torah, and providing the guidance for them to trust Hashem and fulfill His *mitzvos.* A teacher must perpetually be spotless of sin as well as any unpleasant trait. *Chazal* have said, "If a *rebbi* is like an angel of Hashem, seek Torah from his mouth" (*Moed Kattan* 17a). A teacher also must know how to explain things in a clear and understandable manner, so that his students should not misunderstand him. This is the "cleansing and preparation of the lamps" which a teacher must perform in his own soul, before he begins his work of teaching Torah.

❀ ❀ ❀

וַיִּקֹב בֶּן־הָאִשָּׁה הַיִּשְׂרְאֵלִית אֶת־הַשֵּׁם וַיְקַלֵּל — *The son of the Israelite woman pronounced the Name and blasphemed* (24:11).

The Torah relates here that a certain Jew blasphemed the Name of Hashem. Moshe asked Hashem what the appropriate punishment was, and Hashem answered that the man had incurred the death penalty. Only after listing certain other crimes and punishments, including murder, property damage, and personal injury, does the Torah relate that the sentence was carried out. There was no need to deliberate about this man's punishment, because Hashem Himself had made the judgment. But Hashem wanted Moshe to know that any person that does not love every Jewish person, no matter how lowly, to the degree that even property of a Jew is dear to him, is unfit to be a member of a court, and perhaps unfit even to carry out a death penalty. Only those people that have an exquisite appreciation for the inviolability of life and an abhorrence of injury or damage to other men are fit to sit in judgment or administer a penalty. This is the reason that a very elderly man, or a man rendered incapable of having children, or a childless man are unfit to be judges; as the *Rambam* explains (*Hil. Sanhedrin* 2:1), it is because their trait of mercifulness is not properly developed.

❁   ❁   ❁

פרשת בהר
Parashas Behar

וַיְדַבֵּר ה' אֶל־מֹשֶׁה בְּהַר סִינַי לֵאמֹר — *Hashem spoke to Moshe on Mount Sinai, saying* (25:1).

T
he *parashah* of *Behar*, "*On* Mount Sinai," begins by stating that Hashem gave the *mitzvos* to Moshe on Sinai, and goes on to relate the laws of *shemittah*, the Sabbatical Year, during which no agricultural work can be done and all crops that grow must be made available to any who wish to take them. *Rashi* offers several explanations for the juxtaposition of the laws of *shemittah* and the mention of the place where the Torah was given. An additional explanation is: We must remember that all the laws of the Torah and the *mitzvos* should be studied and fulfilled because they were commanded to Moshe at Mount Sinai. We, too, have received the *mitzvos* there, passed down to us, teacher to student, back to Moshe. We do not perform them because of reasons and logic we arrived at ourselves. Even if a person imagines that by imputing a pleasing rational basis to *mitzvos* he can influence others to appreciate and heed the Torah, he must not do so. Many groups of wicked people have come to impute to the Torah itself ideologies that are fundamentally contrary to the Torah. For example, some said that since the law of *shemittah* states that during the Sabbatical Year the owner and any stranger have equal rights, this shows that there is never any real legal ownership of crops; and since Hashem's will is that there should be no private ownership, theft cannot really be such a bad thing. Similarly, the Jubilee Year, the *Yovel*, wherein land and certain chattel returns to its original owner, has been misconstrued to mean that the ownership of land is of little significance. These *mitzvos* are particularly susceptible to misinterpretation and misapplication.

The true reason for these *mitzvos*, as stated in the Torah, and not simply thought of by people and ascribed to the Torah, is to teach that the land is Hashem's, and ours only to the degree that Hashem allows. All the *mitzvos* in this *parashah* lend themselves to similar misinterpretation. Another claim has been that the *mitzvah* of *shemittah* was meant to improve the land. All of these theories are just fabrications and lies. We must always remember that we fulfill the *mitzvos* as, and because, they were commanded at Mount Sinai.

❊ ❊ ❊

וּבַשָּׁנָה הַשְּׁבִיעָת . . . שָׂדְךָ לֹא תִזְרָע . . . יוֹבֵל הוּא לֹא תִזְרָעוּ . . . — *But on the seventh year . . . your field you shall not sow . . . It shall be a Jubilee Year . . . you shall not sow* (25:4,11).

The prohibition of agricultural field work during the Sabbatical Year is stated in the singular, while the prohibition of agricultural field work during the *Yovel* Year is stated in the plural. Perhaps this is because the Sabbatical year is self-actuating, and so every individual is obligated to ensure his own compliance. The *Yovel* Year, on the other hand, was addressed to the Sanhedrin, which was instructed to count the years of the cycle and sanctify the Yovel Year. Of course, *Yovel* also creates individual obligations, but it also is a communal *mitzvah* in the sense that this *mitzvah* in particular requires that we help and support each other in fulfilling it. This obligation goes beyond the *mitzvah* which requires that we rebuke transgressors of any *mitzvah*.

❊ ❊ ❊

אַל־תּוֹנוּ אִישׁ אֶת־אָחִיו — *do not aggrieve one another* (25:14).

The concepts of dealing unjustly in business and aggrieving others in personal relationships are inserted into the *parashah* of the *shemittah* (Sabbatical Year). The relation between these laws is this: Vigilance in avoiding unjust monetary practices comes from faith that Hashem *Yisbarach* gives us our sustenance, and the realization that if we would depend on our powers alone, we would be helpless. As the verse states: *It was He Who gave you strength to make wealth* (*Devarim*

18:8). Hashem does not allow any man to trespass into that which is destined for his friend, even by a hairsbreadth. Knowing this, no one would have any interest in dealing unjustly in business.

The proper fulfillment of the laws of the Sabbatical Year also requires great faith. When a man has the faith the Torah requires, he will find it easy to be completely honest in business affairs and to fulfill the laws of the Sabbatical Year.

❦ ❦ ❦

וְלֹא תוֹנוּ אִישׁ אֶת־עֲמִיתוֹ — *Each of you shall not aggrieve his fellow* (25:17).

During the discussion of the law of the Sabbatical Year and the reversion of land sales in the Jubilee Year, the Torah interjects the prohibition of using hurtful words in our personal relationships. This is because this section of the Torah is written in an order that describes the steps of Hashem's punishment of those that sin by doing business with Sabbatical Year crops. The Gemara in *Kiddushin* (20a) says that such a person will suffer a slow but inexorable decline of fortune, and will have to borrow money, then will have to sell his personal property, then his land, and so on, until he sells himself as a slave. We might think that if we see someone undergoing this misfortune, that we may confront him during these transactions and tell him that he is being punished for this sin. The Torah therefore says that this is hurtful speech and is prohibited. The same lesson is taught in the context of the *mitzvah* of rebuking a sinner (19:17: see *Rashi* there), where the Torah qualifies that *mitzvah* by saying that if this rebuke causes severe public humiliation, it is a sin and not a merit.

❦ ❦ ❦

פרשת בחקתי
Parashas Bechukosai

אִם־בְּחֻקֹּתַי תֵּלֵכוּ — *If you will follow My decrees* (26:3).

When the verse states, *If you will follow My decrees,* it means "that you will toil in the Torah" (*Toras Kohanim,* cited by *Rashi*). I have already explained that, as *Rashi* implies, if one does not toil, it is as if he did not learn at all. The reason for this is because even if one is the greatest genius, it is possible that with more studious analysis he would understand more. Also, one quickly forgets if he does not toil in a subject and learns only superficially. Furthermore, toil means that he must work on his character and realize that he cannot rely on his great intellect, and instead learn even from children, as we find in connection with the story of King David: David was punished for an error in interpreting the verse regarding the carrying of the Holy Ark which states, *they shall carry it on their shoulders.* He did not accept the interpretation of children's teachers, and thought he could depend on his great intellect, for after all, the *halachah* always followed his opinion, and he decided that the rule of carrying on the shoulders was not a requirement, but rather an option. This error is connected to the fact that David referred to the *Halachah* as "songs," which implied that they were as "light" (i.e. easily understood) as melodies. In a similar vein, we must all toil in every single *mitzvah,* and not view them as "light." For example, one might always give a small sum to charity simply to quiet someone's demands. This practice, while seemingly meritorious, might result in one's giving even to people collecting for places to whom it is not permissible to give at all. Instead, one must give with serious thought, and realize what he is giving and why; and, when he determines that the cause is worthy, he should give an amount which matches the worthiness and importance of the need.

We also see a similar concept from the *mitzvah* of *shich'chah* (which obligates us to leave for the poor whatever we forget after harvesting a field). *Rashi* quotes from *Chazal* that the reason the Torah mentions Hashem's blessing in the *parashah* of *shich'chah* is because the poor benefited from his forgetting. The fact that he does not go back and get the remainder when he realizes that he forgot is not a reason for blessing; for that, he is only rewarded as is anyone that withholds from theft. After all, after he walked away from the field, having forgotten some of the harvest, what he forgot is no longer his, but the property of the poor. Similarly, if one gives an amount of charity equal to his obligation, this really should not be considered true charitable giving, as we see from the various gifts to the *Kohanim,* in which they have a real ownership interest and so they are not really the giver's property at all.

This also gives us a new perspective of the rule of tithing income. Tithing income is not an absolute and enforceable monetary obligation, and more properly can be viewed as a personal obligation, since the money is completely his as far as the courts are concerned. However, one should view it as if the money is not his in a practical sense. If one's burden of debt exceeds his assets, although what he holds is legally his to the extent that if he uses those assets his property to effect a marriage the marriage is valid, in a sense what he owns is not his, because he is obligated to give it all to his creditor. If one withholds wages of a laborer, he transgresses the law of theft, although the money is legally his. We thus see that legal ownership is not the same as being the true owner of the money. This is the labor of the *mitzvah* of charity: Do not view what you give as charity, but rather as an obligation, although Hashem has promised a great reward for the charity; realize that what you have to give is not, in the truest sense, yours.

❁   ❁   ❁

אִם־בְּחֻקֹּתַי תֵּלֵכוּ — *If you will follow My decrees* (26:3).

The expression "follow My decrees," or, more literally, "walk in My decrees," is not paralleled elsewhere in the Torah. The Torah is teaching us that there is only one path, and that is to focus on actual fulfillment of the commandments by doing them. We may not seek illusory alternative approaches to bring us to perfection, as many sects that we have seen have done. Some have decided to negate some *mitzvos*, imagining that this will encourage the fulfillment of other *mitzvos*. All this is just the advice of the Evil Inclination. Only the path of the Torah, which tells us to diligently study, and to perfect our character traits, will bring us to fulfill the *mitzvos*.

This is the meaning of the verse in *Tehillim* (1:1), *Praiseworthy is the man who walked not in the counsel of the wicked.* The wicked do not attempt to seduce others by openly suggesting that they should sin and abandon the Torah, because they know that no one will pay attention to them. Instead, they give evil advice, which they claim will improve us. Following their advice, though, leads to the eventual abandonment of the Torah. For example, they might advise a person that spends his days in Torah study to learn secular wisdom while maintaining a religious lifestyle, and they say that this will lead to greater public appreciation of the Torah and sanctification of His Name. The real result of listening to them is that the student leaves the study of Torah to the point that he not only forgets what he learned, but may even abandon his fundamental beliefs entirely.

❧ ❧ ❧

וְנָתַתִּי גִשְׁמֵיכֶם בְּעִתָּם וְנָתְנָה הָאָרֶץ יְבוּלָהּ — *then I will provide your rains in their time, and the land will give its produce* (26:4).

The word *"gishmeichem,"* which means "your rains," is used here in place of the more commonly used word *"geshem."* which means rain. The reason the Torah uses this form of the word is to teach us about the different types of reward Hashem gives us.

A hired worker is certainly not entitled to ask for his wages until after he has done his work. At that time, the employer must compensate him for his efforts. This sort of reward would be called *"geshem."* Once we have followed Hashem's laws, it is His responsibility to give us the wages we have earned, and we are indeed assured that Hashem does reward those who do His will. But there is a type of payment which comes before any work is done. For example, in places where the accepted way of doing business is that one provides meals for his workers, then even before they have done any work the employer is obligated to give them their food, as the Gemara says in *Bava Metzia* (83a). This type of wage can be called the worker's, because it is an entitlement, not compensation. Since the employer must give it before he receives anything from the laborer, it is as if he is giving the worker something which is the worker's. Certainly if a person would buy a very young servant, he would have to support him until he earns his keep. This would be called *"gishmeichem."*

This is the idea alluded to in the ceremony of the *bris milah*. The father, a God-fearing and wise person, gives over to his son the status of being a servant of Hashem his whole life with this seal of the holy covenant. This is why the *mohel* says, "O Eliyahu, messenger of the covenant, behold yours is now before you"; because Eliyahu is the messenger of Hashem for the sealing of the covenant, and so Hashem gives the child his sustenance even before he earns it. This is akin to an obligation on the part of *HaKadosh Baruch Hu*. The word *"gishmeichem"* is used here to tell us that the reward for observing God's commandments is especially great.

❦   ❦   ❦

וְחֶרֶב לֹא־תַעֲבֹר בְּאַרְצְכֶם — *and a sword will not pass through your land* (26:6).

The story of King Yoshiahu and Pharaoh Necho is very difficult to understand (*Melachim II* 23). Yoshiahu went to war against Pharaoh Necho, who wanted only to cross the Land of Israel en route to Assyria, because Yoshiahu thought that his generation was righteous, and would be blessed by the fulfillment of the verse, *and a sword will not pass through your land.* But this is perplexing; for once he saw Pharaoh Necho coming, it should have been obvious, as was eventually shown, that they were not on that level of blessing.

We must say that the verse *and the sword. . .* is not meant as a blessing. What it means is that if the inhabitants of the Land of Israel will live a virtuous and peaceful life, all of the nations will perceive that war is a disgraceful and despicable thing. Even if the nations do go to war against each other, because of their wickedness and jealousy, they will be ashamed to pass through the Land of Israel. So when Yoshiahu decided that the nation was following the path of the Torah, he felt that if Pharaoh Necho was such an evil man that he was not ashamed at all to wage war, as was the case with Amalek in their time (which brazenly attacked Israel while all other nations trembled), then Pharaoh Necho deserved to be killed, just like Amalek was. Yoshiahu did not realize that his generation did not have the merit to cause that to happen.

❧ ❧ ❧

וְרָדְפוּ מִכֶּם חֲמִשָּׁה מֵאָה וּמֵאָה מִכֶּם רְבָבָה יִרְדֹּפוּ —
Five of you will pursue a hundred, and a hundred
of you will pursue ten thousand (26:8).

Rashi notes that if five people can pursue 100, 100 people should pursue 2,000, not 10,000 as the verse states. To resolve this, he quotes the *Sifra,* which says that the few that serve Hashem cannot be compared to large groups of people that serve Hashem. A question arises, however: We see that a righteous person surrounded by people that do not serve Hashem is praised for his singular dedication. This is illustrated in the story of Rivkah, where the Torah mentions her unenlightened family and society so as to praise her in that she was not influenced by what they did. It would seem, then, that the few who serve God also should merit a large degree of reward!

The explanation for the seemingly contrary *Sifra* is this: Sometimes, a person is called righteous because he is in a place where there are no real righteous people. Although he is not truly righteous, his actions acquire a luster because of the contrast between him and his fellows. We find an example of this in the case of the woman of Tzarfas and Eliyahu (*Melachim I* 17:8-18). The woman said that she had been visited with disaster when Eliyahu came, because although before Eliyahu visited her, she was considered righteous in comparison to the people that surrounded her, when Eliyahu visited her, she suffered by comparison to that great and holy man, and was punished. Such "righteousness" has a tinge of one who honors himself by embarrassing his friend. His special aura of righteousness comes only because of his superiority to his friends. Although such an accomplishment is a great thing, as long as one does not become proud of his superiority, it is less than true righteousness. Even if he is so great that he would stand out in the company of other righteous people, he is not rewarded for his humility, because perhaps there might be a little haughtiness of heart at his superior level of spirituality. But when many are serving Hashem, haughtiness would be impossible. So even though the righteous man would not be unique in his superiority to all those around him, he would have the great benefit of not being in a position of feeling superior. This would result in the great reward of being able to *pursue ten thousand.*

We find that Moshe said, *"Would that all Hashem's people could be prophets"* (Bamidbar 11:29). This means that he wanted not only that all should be prophets, but that they should be on his unequaled level of prophecy, so that no reason for haughtiness would exist. (This is why he was pained by the nation's request that he hear the word of God and relay it to them, because it meant that a gap would remain between his level and that of the nation.) If all would have been on the same level, this would mean that each individual righteous person would receive the highest possible reward.

❧ ❧ ❧

וְנָתַתִּי מִשְׁכָּנִי בְּתוֹכְכֶם וְלֹא־תִגְעַל נַפְשִׁי אֶתְכֶם — *I will place My Sanctuary among you; and My Spirit will not reject you* (26:11).

The phrase *I will not reject you* is stated in a very strong fashion, and can also be read as *I will not be revolted by you.* This verse, which follows a description of the blessings that Hashem will bestow on those that observe His Torah, is perplexing. Would we ever imagine that if we go in the path of the Torah to the degree that we merit such blessings, that we would be despicable in Hashem's eyes?

The inescapable answer is that if a person does the *mitzvos* only because he must, and because he feels bound by our covenant with Hashem, this is unacceptable to Hashem. Rabbi Eliezer once said, "One who makes his prayer a matter of rote, his prayer is not a real supplication" (Berachos 28b). This is interpreted by Rabbi Oshaya to refer to a person who feels that prayer is a burden (Berachos 29b), which shows that doing things by habit or rote really is the equivalent of viewing them as a burden, and this is unacceptable to Hashem. God forbid, Hashem might even consider such behavior despicable. As the verse states (Yeshayahu 1:11), *Why do I need your multitude of sacrifices?* Hashem wants us to fulfill His *mitzvos* with love and joy. It is true that *Chazal* have said, "Whoever says, 'Hashem, have mercy as You do on the nestlings,' should be silenced," because the laws should be seen as decrees, not channels for mercy. Similarly, when the Gemara in *Rosh Hashanah* (28a) says that *mitzvos* were not given to have pleasure from them, *Rashi* explains that they were not given so that their fulfillment bring us joy, but rather as a yoke on our shoulders. But this itself is an occasion for joy — for we merited to be trustworthy servants who serve with love and joy.

With this in mind, we can understand that there might be a person that fulfills the entire Torah, but is not in a state of grace before Hashem. Correspondingly, the Torah says that Noach found grace, despite an opinion that an adversarial examination would find flaws in his righteousness. How, then did he find grace? The answer is that whatever Noach did was with joy and love and in the best way possible. Therefore, he found grace. Once he had found this favor in the eyes of Hashem, no adversarial examination could take place — for Hashem was unwilling to hear or see anything negative about Noach.

Someone reminded me that this is the meaning of *Rambam's* interpretation of Rabbi Chanania ben Akashia's statement, "The Holy One, Blessed is He, wished to confer merit upon Israel; therefore He gave them Torah and mitzvos in abundance." *Rambam* (in his Commentary to the Mishnah, *Makkos* 23b) explains that Hashem wanted to afford everyone the opportunity to fulfill at least one *mitzvah* to the greatest possible degree. He did so by providing so many varieties of *mitzvos* for us to do, so that we could do at least one in the best way possible — which is without any ulterior motives, only motivated by the drive to serve Hashem with love.

※ ※ ※

אֵלֶּה הַחֻקִּים וְהַמִּשְׁפָּטִים וְהַתּוֹרֹת אֲשֶׁר נָתַן ה' בֵּינוֹ וּבֵין בְּנֵי יִשְׂרָאֵל בְּהַר סִינַי בְּיַד־מֹשֶׁה — *These are the decrees, the ordinances, and the teachings that* HASHEM *gave, between Himself and the Bnei Yisrael, at Mount Sinai, through Moshe* (26:46).

The verse near the end of *Parashas Bechukosai* uses an expression which reiterates the covenant between Hashem and our nation. The Covenant is hinted at in the words, *between Himself and the Bnei Yisrael.* This same verse mentions "decrees, ordinances, and teachings." This is because all the *mitzvos* mentioned, from the beginning of the *parashah* to the end, teach one important lesson. That is, that man does not really own what he possesses. Therefore, during the Sabbatical Year, agricultural land is left abandoned and open to the foot of any passerby, and even to the beasts of the field. We were not commanded to gather whatever grows and distribute it to the poor. This is because the intention is to reinforce this idea that we do not own wholly our land. Similarly, when a man sells family land, the sale is not permanent, because the land reverts to the family at the Jubilee. He cannot even put a condition into the contract in which he waives his right to reoccupy the land at the time of the Jubilee. The *Nimukei Yosef* (quoting the *Rashba*, in *Bava Metzia* 51b, in the pages of the *Rif* 31a) says this is because all the land is sanctified to Hashem's will, as the verse states (*Shemos* 19:5), *"for all the land is Mine,"* and so the "owner" has no right to make conditions as to the sale which interfere with Hashem's will that it revert at Jubilee. Also, the Torah says that when a man does sell agricultural land, he may redeem it by prorating the price over the years till the Jubilee, but he may not do so until two years have passed after the sale. If the two parties agree to allow the seller to redeem prior to that time, they have both transgressed a prohibition. This true understanding is contrary to those wicked people who misinterpret all of Hashem's laws, and impute to these laws the false ideology that Hashem disapproves of private ownership of land. This is the opposite of the truth: Hashem hates theft, and the fate of the generation of the Flood was sealed because of their disregard of the prohibition of theft. These laws are only between Hashem and his nation, and are not intended to teach us how to deal with our fellow's possession. When we fulfill these *mitzvos,* Hashem promised that He will give us blessings, and if, God forbid, the opposite, then the opposite will result. This is why the *parashah* ends with the words "between Himself and the *Bnei Yisrael."*

❈ ❈ ❈

לֹא יַחֲלִיפֶנּוּ וְלֹא־יָמִיר אֹתוֹ — *He shall not exchange it nor substitute it* (27:10).

An animal which a person attempted to substitute for a *korban* (*temurah*) is acceptable for sacrifice, although the act of attempted substitution is a transgression of two negative commandments, and thus the animal is somewhat similar to a accomplished by means of a transgression," which is generally unacceptable. This teaches us that the transgression of an *aveirah* does not always detract from the ultimate *mitzvah.* This brushes aside those claims of the *Yetzer Hara* which often hold people back from the study of Torah, by convincing them that if they learn, they will become haughty and transgress the *aveirah* of haughtiness, which is, indeed, very serious. Similarly, this reasoning can interfere with many other *mitzvos,* such as *tzedakah.* Therefore, the Torah gives one example, namely the rule of *temurah,* so that we may know that it is not always true that an accompanying *aveirah* detracts from the ultimate *mitzvah.* Instead, the *mitzvah* will remain meritorious and deserving of reward. A person must indeed be on guard to avoid the *aveirah,* but even if in the beginning he is haughty, he should not hold himself back from doing the *mitzvah* and learning the Torah.

❧ ❧ ❧

וְאִם כָּל־בְּהֵמָה טְמֵאָה אֲשֶׁר לֹא־יַקְרִיבוּ מִמֶּנָּה קָרְבָּן לַה׳
. . . — And if it is any disqualified animal from which they may not bring an offering to HASHEM . . . (27:11).

In discussing the ability to redeem a sacrifice so that its holiness is transferred to the proceeds of its sale, the Torah says that one may not redeem a blemishless animal. However, one may redeem an animal that was blemishless when sanctified which later became blemished. The term used in the verse to refer to such an animal is *beheimah temei'ah.* The word *temei'ah* usually means unclean. The use of this word is very surprising, because it is considered an unpleasant word, as the Gemara in *Pesachim* (3b) says.

The reason for the use of this word is to teach us that an animal that has now become blemished is just like an animal from an unclean species, such as donkeys or horses. Similarly, if a man has reached a level of holiness, if he then descends from his lofty attainment due to laziness, he is considered profane. Although others that never reached his previous level would be considered holy if they would attain his present level, he is considered *temei'ah.* A person must be very careful not to fall from the level of Torah and good deeds which he has reached through hard work and toil. Rather, he must strengthen himself to grow higher and higher. If he does so, then *HaKadosh Baruch Hu* will help him to avoid anything that would interfere with his continued growth, as the Torah implies in the blessings in the beginning of the *parashah.*

ספר במדבר

Sefer Bamidbar

פרשת במדבר
Parashas Bamidbar

שְׂאוּ אֶת־רֹאשׁ כָּל־עֲדַת בְּנֵי־יִשְׂרָאֵל . . . — *"Take a census of the entire assembly of the* Bnei Yisrael *. . ."* (1:2).

In the beginning of *Bamidbar* we find that each tribe is counted individually, and then the whole of the nation is counted as one. In every matter there is a difference between the individual and the group. In matters of holiness, it is imperative that the two numbers be equal; that is, we find a similar approach in the matter of the reckoning of the weights of the silver bowls and basins at the end of *Parashas Nasso,* where the Torah first listed the vessels individually and then tallies their weight as a whole. *Rashi* explains that the weights were exactly the same whether as a sum of the individual weighings and when weighed as a group, with no excess and no deficiency. The Torah intends to repeat there the lesson taught here.

❧ ❧ ❧

פְּקֹד אֶת־בְּנֵי לֵוִי לְבֵית אֲבֹתָם לְמִשְׁפְּחֹתָם — *Count the sons of Levi according to their fathers' household, according to their families* (3:15).

When Moshe was told to count the Levites, he was not told that the princes of Levi should accompany him, but Moshe did ask them to join him in order to honor them, as the *Medrash Rabbah* says. Of course, *HaKadosh Baruch Hu* agreed with him, for

Moshe did nothing of his own volition if not told to do so by Hashem. The explanation is this: The reason the princes of the other tribes needed to be present during the general census (1:4) was because the results of this census determined each tribe's proportional entitlement to the Land of Israel. Therefore, each tribe needed its prince to act as its advocate during the counting. The tribe of Levi did not receive land like the other tribes, and so the presence of princes was not necessary.

We should learn from here what is entailed in acting in a proper fashion: If one needed to join with others for some matter, for example where a quorum of three is required, and then another question arises which requires no quorum, the person to whom the second question is addressed should ask that the others join him in the decision. See *Sanhedrin* 8a, where in discussing a similar case, the Gemara says that according to the *Chachamim*, the larger quorum must be consulted in any other related matters that arise, even if those matters of themselves do not require the larger quorum, so as to maintain the honor of the whole group. We now find a source for this concept here, where Moshe requested the presence of the Levite princes for the counting of Levi.

❀ ❀ ❀

. . . וְנָתְנוּ עָלָיו כְּסוּי עוֹר תַּחַשׁ — They shall place upon it a tachash-hide covering . . . (4:6).

All the vessels of the Tabernacle had special covers to be used during travels. The sons of Kehas were to cover the *Aron* with the Partition-curtain, which was essentially part of the *Aron*. This was then covered with a *tachash* hide, which was in turn covered with a cloth of turquoise wool (*techeiles*). This is because it is only after penetrating all the veils that cover the Torah — those great and difficult subjects that require great toil to reach their depths with clarity and decisiveness as to the practical laws that derive from them — that one can come to the more hidden things. But these hidden truths can be grasped if the seeker has pure faith in Hashem, the Giver of the Torah, and truly understands that all the Torah is from Hashem, and that he must understand it in the terms that Hashem intended when He gave it to Moshe. The turquoise wool, which is symbolic of the highest level of the Torah, symbolizes and inspires pure faith, as Rav Meir explains with respect to the *techeiles* threads of the *tzitzis* (*Chullin* 89a).

❀ ❀ ❀

. . . וְעַל שֻׁלְחַן הַפָּנִים יִפְרְשׂוּ בֶּגֶד תְּכֵלֶת — *And upon the Table of the show-bread they shall spread a cloth of turquoise wool . . .* (4:7).

The *Shulchan* (the Table of the show-bread) was covered with a *tachash* hide, and then with both turquoise-colored and scarlet-colored cloths. This additional layer shows that a wealthy man, symbolized by the Table, should have deep internal faith that Hashem is the source of his wealth. If he has this faith, his wealth will have a shining beauty like that of a red rose, because he will certainly do with his wealth what Hashem wishes, in matters of charity to holy institutions and the poor.

❀ ❀ ❀

פרשת נשא
Parashas Naso

וְכָל־תְּרוּמָה לְכָל־קָדְשֵׁי בְנֵי־יִשְׂרָאֵל אֲשֶׁר־יַקְרִיבוּ לַכֹּהֵן לוֹ יִהְיֶה — *And every portion from any of the holies that the Children of Israel bring to the Kohen shall be his* (5:9).

The Torah mentions *terumah* in the *parashah* of theft, an association of two apparently unrelated laws. It appears that this is intended to teach that although no individual *Kohen* can demand that he be given *terumah*, because the owner can always say that he chooses to give it to some other *Kohen,* the real claimant is the law and obligation of *terumah* itself; and retention of the *temurah* is theft. After making this point, the Torah mentions the concept that the owner has the right to decide which *Kohen* will get his *terumah*. Although the owner has no right to use the *terumah* in any way, and it does belong exclusively to *Kohanim* as a group, this small right to determine the recipient is also meaningful. Accordingly, if some *Kohen* seizes the *terumah* by force, what he has done is also a form of robbery, since the owner prefers to give it to someone else.

❧ ❧ ❧

אַל־תַּכְרִיתוּ אֶת־שֵׁבֶט מִשְׁפְּחֹת הַקְּהָתִי מִתּוֹךְ הַלְוִיִּם — *"Do not let the tribe of the Kehasite families be cut off from among the Levites"* (4:18).

Rashi explains that this is a warning to the *Kohanim* that they must take care and see to it that the family of Kehas, whose work involved transporting the holiest vessels of the Tabernacle, should not be exposed to situations which might result in their death due to improper exposure to those vessels. In truth, the prohibition from touching those vessels, and its capital penalty, had already been stated. *Ohr HaChaim* says that the purpose of this verse is to tell us that "Aharon and his sons shall come and assign them," meaning that no Levite may enter and put his hand to carry the vessels until a *Kohen* tells each individual how and where to place his hand. But this is difficult — for then the Torah should have stated this explicitly!

The explanation of this verse is that this preparatory work that the *Kohanim* must do for the Levites could appear, to the *Kohanim*, to be a case of the *Kohanim*, possessors of great holiness, serving the Levites, whose holiness is lesser. This might appear to be an affront to the honor of the priesthood. Therefore, the Torah prefaces this command with the explanation that the *Kohanim* must take into account that the allure of the holy vessels might entice a Levite to touch a vessel where he is not allowed to do so. Therefore, only Aharon and his sons may prepare the vessels and direct the Levites in their work.

In a similar vein, we find that Moshe served Aharon and his sons in the most basic matters, such as washing their bodies and dressing them in the priestly vestments. Moshe did not need to be placated, because due to his great humility he did not feel superior to the Levites. He only was forced to accept honor in his role as teacher and prophet and messenger for the transmission of the Torah. Thus, when the law required that he serve Aharon and his sons, he did not feel this was inappropriate. But the Torah makes it clear that Aharon's sons, although they were great men, were not on the level of Moshe, and needed to be told that the reason they were to serve the Levites was in order to preserve their lives.

❧ ❧ ❧

נָשֹׂא אֶת־רֹאשׁ בְּנֵי גֵרְשׁוֹן גַּם־הֵם . . . — *"Take a census of the sons of Gershon, as well . . ."* (4:22).

The explanation of the expression "as well" is that there is no difference between the carrying task assigned to the sons of Kehas, who carried the Holy Ark, and the carrying task assigned to the sons of Gershon, who carried items of a lesser holiness, or the work of the sons of Merari, because between all those who carried the various items comprising the Tabernacle, the will of the Holy One,

Blessed is He, was fulfilled. Similarly, the *mitzvos* of those that teach little children, and those that teach students that are already great Torah scholars, are equal, so long as they each do their work to promote the glory of God.

❧ ❧ ❧

וְעָבַר עָלָיו רוּחַ־קִנְאָה וְקִנֵּא אֶת־אִשְׁתּוֹ — *and a spirit of jealousy had passed over him and he had warned his wife* (5:14).

In the *parashah* of *sotah,* the Torah says that if a man voices his jealousy of his wife's relationship with another man, and those two were seen to be alone, a doubt arises as to the woman's innocence — i.e. whether she was defiled or not. The Torah says, *a spirit of jealousy had passed over him,* and she was defiled, or *a spirit of jealousy had passed over him,* and she was not defiled; and so she is under suspicion until she proves her innocence. This repetition of *a spirit of jealousy had passed over him* appears to be unnecessary. Seemingly, the Torah could have written this phrase once, followed by the enunciation of the doubt as to whether she was defiled or not.

We may say that the reason for this repetition is to teach us that even if her husband does not suspect her of actual defilement, because he knows that her fear of sin would prevent actual defilement, the *parashah,* of *sotah* is still applicable. His voicing of his jealousy, and the status of *sotah* that results from her later indifference to the laws which forbid a man and woman to be in an isolated place, are laudable, because this is a jealousy that expresses resentment of her indifference to the laws of modesty, and a zealousness intended to ensure that henceforth she will be more conscientious and adhere to the proper standards. The intent of the repetition in the verse is to teach that no matter whether his jealousy stems from a possibility of defilement, or whether he knew from the beginning that even if she were to be alone with the other man, no defilement would result, both cases express a proper jealousy and zealousness to maintain and preserve the laws of Hashem.

❧ ❧ ❧

וּבְבֹא מֹשֶׁה אֶל־אֹהֶל מוֹעֵד לְדַבֵּר אִתּוֹ וַיִּשְׁמַע אֶת־הַקּוֹל
— **When Moshe arrived at the Tent of Meeting to speak with Him, he heard the Voice** (7:89).

The verse says, *When Moshe arrived at the Tent of Meeting, he heard the Voice speaking to him."* Rashi explains that this voice was not a small, still voice, but rather was the great voice that spoke to Moshe on *Har Sinai*. When the voice came to the walls of the Tabernacle, it stopped. We can wonder: What purpose did a great voice serve, when it ended at the walls of the Tabernacle, and no one but Moshe could hear it? For this purpose, a small and still voice would suffice!

Two possibilities can be suggested: 1) It was indeed a great and powerful voice, and it is audible by its very nature — everyone who fears God and is a *talmid chacham* can perceive the statements of Hashem through His acts and Torah, just as if His words could actually be heard. 2) The commandments were from *HaKadosh Baruch Hu* to all Israel directly, and therefore the volume of the voice was such that it could have reached the ears of every Jew — if they had merited this direct contact. The fault lay in them, and resulted in the voice stopping at the walls of the Tabernacle. This matter does, however, require more thought.

❧ ❧ ❧

וַיִּשְׁמַע אֶת־הַקּוֹל מִדַּבֵּר אֵלָיו — **he heard the Voice speaking to him** (7:89).

Rashi explains that "he heard the Voice speaking to him" means that Hashem spoke to Himself, and Moshe heard what was said. But later it says that Hashem spoke directly to Moshe. This is because when a person listens to what Hashem says to Himself (through His creations and His constant involvement with them), it is possible for him to understand what Hashem means when He speaks directly to him.

❧ ❧ ❧

פרשת בהעלתך
Parashas Beha'alosecha

בְּהַעֲלֹתְךָ אֶת־הַנֵּרֹת — **When you kindle the lamps** (8:2).

T he word *beha'aloscha* here means "*when you kindle.*" But this word, from the root *aloh*, also means raising, or lifting. *Rashi* uses this derivation to add two meanings. One is that the *Kohen* must hold the fire to the wick until the newly kindled flame is strong enough to rise up by itself. The other is that there were steps in front of the Menorah upon which the *Kohen* would stand when cleaning and filling the lamps.

In truth, the two explanations are closely related. The Menorah represents the enlightenment which comes from the study of Torah. Aharon and his sons are particularly delegated to learn and teach the Torah, as the verse states: *They will teach Your laws to Yaakov and Your Torah to Israel (Devarim 33:10).* When they teach, they must see to it that their teaching should "rise of itself" in their students — that is, that their understanding must grow to the point that they understand not only what they were told, but clearly understand all its applications and ramifications. We see this from the word *beha'aloscha*: Any *mitzvah* to light the Menorah would obviously demand that we see to it that the lamp remains lit, and that we may not stop lighting until we are sure it will stay lit. *Beha'aloscha* tells us more — that we cannot rely on our evaluations, and that we may assume nothing. We must know with absolute certainty that the flame is strong and increasing in strength. Exactly so is our responsibility when making halachic decisions and teaching and influencing others. We must keep our hand in the matter until it is absolutely clear that they understand and are growing in Torah and good deeds.

The same may be learned from the cleansing procedure. The cleaning could have been done without recourse to a set of steps, because the Menorah was only eighteen *tefachim* (approximately five and one-quarter feet) high. If we could rely on presumptions and evaluations, a cleaning done from ground level would allow us to confidently say the Menorah is perfectly clean and ready. But we may not rely on anything, and we must know absolutely, by looking *downwards into* the lamps, that they are perfectly clean and ready. Similarly, when we teach others to avoid sin and develop good character traits, we must do so fastidiously and with perfectionism.

Rashi explains the verse *Aharon did so* (8:3) to mean that Aharon did not alter from his instruction. This means that although we know that if Aharon was confident this would mean complete certainty, he did not rely on his confidence or his evaluations, and waited until he actually saw that the lamps were clean and that the flame grew. This is, indeed, a novel and thought-provoking explanation, because Aharon's certainty based on his confidence in his evaluation may be no less reliable than visual proof — and even so, he waited for visual proof.

❈ ❈ ❈

וְזֶה מַעֲשֵׂה הַמְּנוֹרָה — This is the workmanship of the Menorah (8:4).

The Torah tells us that the *Kohen* must light the Menorah each day so that it casts light in the Tabernacle. At the end of this instruction, the Torah describes the manner of the Menorah's construction. This is placed here to teach us that for the lighting of the lamps, we must first have a Menorah — that is, *yeshivos* should be built beautifully, with ample room for the *yeshivah*, and its teachers, and its students, so that nothing of what they need is missing. Only then can we properly light the flame, which means to teach the deep meanings of the Torah, so that the students will develop the ability to understand the laws and differentiate among them on their own. The Torah symbolizes this idea with the rule that the *Kohen* must hold the flame to the wick until the flame of the wick rises by itself.

❈ ❈ ❈

וּמִבֶּן חֲמִשִּׁים שָׁנָה יָשׁוּב מִצְּבָא הָעֲבֹדָה וְלֹא יַעֲבֹד עוֹד
*— From fifty years of age, he shall withdraw from
the legion of work and no longer work* (8:25).

We should learn from the Levites what it takes to reach
greatness in the Torah. *Rashi* says that each Levite had a
five-year apprenticeship period, which was necessary to
properly learn their one *mitzvah*. If so, the time needed to learn the
entire Torah is limitless. One must dedicate his entire life to studying. As
far as the obligation to teach others, there is never any time limitation.
This is why after the age of 50, when the Levite retires from active
service, the Torah says *He shall minister with his brethren* (8:26), which,
according to one explanation, means that he shall advise the younger
Levites.

❦ ❦ ❦

עֲשֵׂה לְךָ שְׁתֵּי חֲצוֹצְרֹת כֶּסֶף . . . *— "Make for
yourself two silver trumpets . . ."* (10:2).

Rashi says that these trumpets were to be used to provide a fanfare
for Moshe as for a king. *Rashi* also says that Moshe had to
provide the funds for the making of these trumpets. This last
requirement is very difficult to understand. Why would Moshe have to
pay for the trumpets? Inasmuch as he was to be treated as a king, why
shouldn't the people provide the money to make them?

The reason is that Moshe was not a king like other kings. Kings are
appointed, and they then have a royal status, for this is what the Torah
intended in the verse, *You shall surely place upon yourself a king*
(*Devarim* 17:15). Once appointed, the choice of how to enforce his
power over the nation is his to make. Moshe, on the other hand, was
never appointed by the people as king. He was the messenger of the
redemption, and the means of the receiving of the Torah and the
instruction of the Jewish nation. Through him Hashem provided for all
the needs of the people. Hashem wanted everyone to know that
Moshe's royalty was based on his primary purpose — that of being every
single person's teacher. It was proper that trumpets be blown before him
when he needed to gather the people, and they would each be obligated
to come to him. But since his royalty was an expression of the fact that
he was the Teacher of the Torah, he was not allowed to take anything

from the people. The Gemara in *Chagigah* (7a) says that a teacher of Torah may not be paid for his efforts, because Hashem says, "Just as I teach you and do not receive payment, you too must teach and not take payment." *HaRav Michel Barenbaum Shlita* pointed out that this also explains why the trumpets had to be hammered into shape, and not cast, just as the Menorah in the Tabernacle was made by hammering. The process of hammering symbolizes how Torah is learned. With this we can understand what *Chazal* mean when they say that our Torah scholars are our kings; although each one is not the teacher of the entire nation, certainly each is a king to his own students.

❧ ❧ ❧

וַתֹּאכַל בִּקְצֵה הַמַּחֲנֶה — *and it consumed at the edge of the camp* (11:1).

Rabbi Shimon ben Menassia says that the *edge of the camp* that was consumed in the episode of "Tav'erah" meant that leaders and great men died during the plague that followed the incident of complaining against Hashem. These are the people that, during the giving of the Torah, reached the level of *they gazed at God,* as *Rashi* explains in *Mishpatim* (*Shemos* 24:11). Why did they die when Hashem punished the complainers? Wouldn't this result in people thinking that they had been among the complainers?

The reason is that Hashem wants even the greatest men to know that there is no such thing as forging your own path based on personal philosophy. Everyone must listen to *HaKadosh Baruch Hu's* commandments, even if to their great minds it appears that some other path is better. This is why the travels in the Wilderness were sometimes many days, and sometimes only a few days, and even only one day. Time was not a factor in the travels. This was incomprehensible even to the greatest of the people, but they traveled by the word of God and camped by the word of God. This is how we must do all the *mitzvos* — not to change one iota of the *mitzvah,* as it often says about Aharon — he never wavered.

Sometimes, because of great love for Hashem *Yisbarach,* a man can dismiss some of the instruction of the Torah and strike out on his own path. To counter this, one needs fear of God. A man that fears will not dismiss the clearly laid out path of the Torah, as the *Yerushalmi* (cited in *Tosafos* to *Sotah* 22) says. Therefore, the Torah reveals that the great men of Israel, having gazed upon Hashem, had in their greatness itself the seed of committing the sin of the complainers by feeling frustration at the direction of Hashem to do things they did not understand. Although they did not sin by complaining, Hashem punished them at that time. Hashem was not concerned that some would attribute to them the sin of the complainers, because they were indeed susceptible to that same sin. It is possible that they actually did join the complainers, because although they certainly did not suffer physically during the travels, which were all directed by Hashem, they could not be involved in the study of the Torah in depth as they wished. But since this was the will of Hashem, they should have accepted their forced relinquishment of study as a necessary result of Hashem's will that they travel.

❦ ❦ ❦

וַתְּדַבֵּר מִרְיָם וְאַהֲרֹן בְּמֹשֶׁה — *Miriam and Aharon spoke against Moshe* (12:1).

Although Miriam and Aharon knew that Hashem agreed with Moshe's decision to end his marital relations with Tziporah, *Tosafos* in *Shabbos* writes that they were upset that Moshe had initially made the decision to do so, because having made a decision, "man is helped along the path he chooses to follow." But how could they have done so? Didn't they realize that if Moshe chose this path that it must have been better than any other option?

We must say that if a person, even a great man, wishes to do even the most laudatory thing, he may not do so if it conflicts with his responsibilities to his wife or to others. The *Chasam Sofer* was asked whether a man was allowed to follow a certain restrictive approach in matters which are clearly halachically permissible where this would interfere with his marital obligations. The *Chasam Sofer* answered that since his wife knew that the man she married was a Torah scholar, and that Torah scholars often do accept the more restrictive approach, she knew the likelihood of such changes and implicitly acquiesced. Miriam and Aharon's challenge of Moshe provides a strong basis for this concept. Despite this general limitation on unilateral acceptance of optional restrictions which interfere with a couple's way of life, or with any obligations to third parties, Moshe was different. He was the most trustworthy of those that dwell in the house of Hashem, and he knew with absolute clarity what Hashem desired. With this approach to the controversy in mind, we can understand what Miriam and Aharon meant when they said, *"Did [Hashem] not speak to us as well?"* For if all prophets separated from their wives, then this is the way of the prophets, and Tziporah would have known of this likelihood and implicitly acquiesced. But since Miriam and Aharon did not do so, then this reason did not apply. Moshe reasoned, however, that this was not optional in his case, but mandatory due to his exalted stature. This concept is also found in the case of Rabbah bar Bar Channah in *Bava Metzia* 83a. Rabbah bar Bar Channah had hired laborers to transport barrels of wine, and through a lack of diligence, they broke the barrels in transit. Rabbah bar Bar Chanah was told that not only could he not make a claim for damages from the laborers, but that he had to pay them their salaries. He asked, "Is this the law?" and he was told "Yes, for you [a renowned and righteous Torah scholar], this is the law." For Moshe, this was the law.

❀ ❀ ❀

פרשת שלח
Parashas Shelach

שְׁלַח־לְךָ אֲנָשִׁים . . . — *"Send forth men, if you please . . ."* (13:1).

It is possible that the sin of the *meraglim*, the spies, stemmed from their greatness. In the desert, every aspect of their sustenance was miraculous from beginning to end. They did not want to exchange that supernatural life for a mundane and temporal life. Indeed, perhaps the entire episode of the sending of the spies was predicated on this same potential change — because the people knew that in the Land of Israel they would live a natural and normal life, they reasoned that the natural and normal thing to do would be to prepare for the incursion by sending in spies.

The spies thought that Hashem would no longer perform miracles, and upon seeing the mighty people of Canaan, they said that those people were invincible. They therefore delivered the blasphemous report that Hashem was no longer concerned with the welfare of the Jewish people, and that they would die by the sword. They failed to realize that natural events only occur due to Hashem's unending involvement. In fact, having experienced so many miracles, they should have known that Hashem supervises and controls every aspect of life. Their sin was very great in that they did not learn this lesson from all the miracles that they themselves had experienced, and instead, depending on their own intellect, came to foolish and vacuous conclusions. Later, they realized how foolish they had been, and went to the opposite extreme of rushing into Canaan without waiting for permission. This too was a great sin. Our obligation is clear and specific — to listen, to trust, and to do what we are commanded.

❧ ❧ ❧

כֹּל נָשִׂיא בָהֶם — *every one a leader among them* (13:2).

Hashem told Moshe to choose twelve men, *every one a leader*. Of course, they were not actual kings or princes. But there is such a thing as innate royalty. When a person has the prominence and elevation of character that befits a king, so that he could serve in that position if chosen, he is a king even if in fact he is not chosen.

❧ ❧ ❧

עֲלוּ זֶה בַּנֶּגֶב . . . — *"Ascend here in the south . . ."* (13:17).

Moshe told the spies to *ascend here in the south*. *Rashi* explains that Hashem wanted the spies to enter Canaan through the Negev, the worst part of the land, just as merchants show the worst part first. It would seem that the real practice of merchants is to do the opposite, and show the best, in order to fool the buyer into thinking that all the merchandise is as good as what he was shown, and that there is no need to check whether all of the merchandise will satisfy his needs.

We must explain that what *Rashi* means is that God-fearing merchants show the worst merchandise first. Because they are scrupulously honest, they want to ensure that the buyer realizes the true quality of the merchandise, and so they show the worst and then the best of what they are offering.

❧ ❧ ❧

סָר צִלָּם מֵעֲלֵיהֶם — *Their protector has departed from them* (14:9).

Rashi explains that what Yehoshua and Calev meant when they said, regarding the Canaanites, *"Their protector has departed from them,"* was that Iyov, a righteous man whose merit could have protected the Canaanites (see *Bava Bara* 16b), had died. This is very difficult to understand. Why would we care whether their protector lived or not? Moshe had delivered to them the command he received directly from Hashem that they enter and conquer Canaan. Of course this would come to pass!

We must say that although they certainly would have conquered and inherited the land, the conquest would have come with difficulty, and Canaanites would also remain there with them even after the conquest. If so, the people's complaint that they would not wish to enter in those circumstances would have legitimacy. This is why Yehoshua and Calev said that the protector of the Canaanites had departed, and so the conquest would be fast and thorough. Accordingly, there could not be legitimate complaint or dispute.

❧ ❧ ❧

פרשת קרח
Parashas Korach

מַעֲשֵׂר מִן־הַמַּעֲשֵׂר — *a tithe from the tithe* (18:26).

The Torah says that when a Levi receives his tithe portion of the crop, he must give 10 percent of what he receives to the *Kohen* — a tithe on the tithe. Before he gives this second tithe, the Levi's portion is *tevel*, which means that it is forbidden. The Torah states this principle in the verse, *Your gift shall be reckoned for you like grain from the threshing-floor and like the ripeness of the vat* (18:27).

Although there are ways for one to legally circumvent the obligation to give the basic tithes to the *Kohen* and Levi, such as by bringing the produce into the storage house by way of the roof, or simply by selling it to a second party, there is absolutely no way for the Levi to free himself from his obligation to give a tithe on the tithe, and his portion remains *tevel* until he separates that which belongs to the *Kohen*. The reason for this difference is that since the Levi received his portion as a gift from Hashem *Yisbarach*, did not provide him with any option to avoid his obligation to give part of it away. There is a lesson to be learned from this. Every person should realize and understand that everything he has is solely a gift from Hashem *Yisbarach*, and that he cannot feel free to do with it whatever he wishes unless he fulfills the *mitzvos* that Hashem *Yisbarach* commanded. The Torah provided the option of avoiding the *mitzvah* for those that do not realize this. This is why the earlier generations did not want to avail themselves of the opportunities to circumvent the *mitzvos* of tithing. Only those of little faith will seek to avoid the *mitzvah* of giving away a part of what they have. These are the people who think that since Hashem did not give them what they have without their own hard labor and effort, it is not really a gift from Hashem *Yisbarach,* and Hashem only gave them a little help; or people who think that their strength and the might of their hands were the exclusive source of their accomplishments, and whose faith in Hashem *Yisbarach* is limited to believing that Hashem will not undermine their work, and will allow them to succeed on their own without interference. Later generations, indeed, did develop this corrupt attitude.

We must strengthen our faith in Hashem *Yisbarach,* and realize that He is the sole source of everything we have, and so we will not seek to avoid His *mitzvos* — even where we can find some permissible way to do so. Then, Hashem will help us in all that we do, and multiply our blessings.

❊ ❊ ❊

פרשת חקת
Parashas Chukas

זאת חֻקַּת הַתּוֹרָה — *This is the decree of the Torah*
(19:2).

I n the *parashah* of *parah adumah* (red heifer), the verse begins, "This
is the decree of the Torah." This implies that this is the decree of
the entire Torah! How can we understand this perplexing statement?

The explanation is this: Man must serve Hashem *Yisbarach* during all
times and periods, and with all the means available to him, including his
two inclinations, good and evil. However, one must know how to
properly apply each character trait only when it is appropriate. For
example: It is impossible to heed the Torah properly with the quality of
extravagance if it is always applied. Although an extravagant person will
fulfill the *mitzvah* of charity and kindness, he will come to theft and
cheating and similar dissolutions. If he is indifferent to what belongs to
him, because he is so profligate, certainly he will be indifferent to what
belongs to others, and what belongs to others will seem to him to be
ownerless. On the other hand, if he will be very parsimonious and
tightfisted so that if one penny of his is stolen he will feel as if his soul was
snatched away, he will not transgress theft, because he will view other's
property as sacrosanct, but he will not give charity. Even if he gives a
little, it will be with a miserly carefulness. So too with the quality of
humility. If he fulfills this to its extreme (as did Rabbi Levitas of Yavneh
[see *Avos* 4:4] according to the *Rambam*'s understanding), he will be
indifferent to the honor of others, and will shame them in public for
every trivial thing, despite this being a major transgression. If, on the
other hand, he will be possessed by arrogance, he will be arrogant in

everything and to everyone, and he will be an abomination in the eyes of Hashem, as the verse states (*Mishlei* 16:5), תּוֹעֲבַת ה׳ כָּל־גְּבַהּ־לֵב. This is true of each quality of one's personality. Therefore, one must know and experience each characteristic in combination — extravagance in charity and kindness, and parsimony in avoiding that which belongs to others. And with humility — total indifference to personal insults, but recognition that dignity and honor are very important, which results in the proper honoring of others, as required by the Torah. This is what is meant by serving Hashem with both inclinations. And this is the *mitzvah* of the red heifer, which has contradictory aspects to its *mitzvos,* in that it brings defilement to those that are pure, and purifies those that are defiled. This is indeed a decree that underlies the entire Torah.

With this concept I have also explained the Gemara's statement (*Berachos* 64a), "Torah scholars increase peace in the world, as it says, Great peace to your children (*banayich*)'; read not 'your children,' but rather your builders (*bonayich*) — the Torah scholars." This homiletical exegeses is stated as if it were an emendation necessary for proper understanding of the verse. But this is difficult — for seemingly there is no indication in the verse that such an emendation should be made. The explanation is that the basis for the exposition is the following verse, which says, "Establish yourselves in charity and distance yourselves from theft." What is meant is that if one follows these qualities to their extremes, the two qualities are opposite and contradictory, as is true with every character trait. But the Torah and the wise men of the Torah reconcile this contradiction. Concerning one's self, they serve Hashem with one trait, and regarding others, they serve Hashem with an opposite aspect of that trait. In this way, they can be true builders of peace.

❧ ❧ ❧

פרשת בלק
Parashas Balak

וַיָּבֹא אֱלֹקִים אֶל־בִּלְעָם לַיְלָה וַיֹּאמֶר לוֹ אִם־לִקְרֹא לְךָ בָּאוּ הָאֲנָשִׁים קוּם לֵךְ אִתָּם וְאַךְ אֶת־הַדָּבָר אֲשֶׁר־אֲדַבֵּר אֵלֶיךָ אֹתוֹ תַעֲשֶׂה — *And Hashem came to Bilam that night and said to him, "If the men came to summon you, arise and go with them; but only the thing that I shall speak to you — that shall you do"* (22:20).

The verse tells us that Hashem permitted Bilam to accompany the delegation that was sent to him by Balak; however, he did not grant him permission to curse the Jewish nation. The difficulty therefore presents itself: If Hashem wished to save the Jews from the curses of Bilam, why did He permit Bilam to embark on the journey, and thwart him once he had reached his destination? He could simply have refused to allow Bilam to go at all!

We may explain that Hashem allowed Bilam to travel to Balak in order to reveal to us the power that the Evil Inclination has while attempting to seduce a person into sin. Although Bilam was a prophet, and he certainly knew that Hashem did not want him to curse the Jewish nation, he went to great lengths and made many preparations to try to circumvent Hashem's will. Had his mission been disallowed at the outset, this would not have been revealed to us.

The lesson that we must derive from this is clear. One should not rely on his intellect, piety and belief in Hashem and his Torah to protect him from the wiles of his Evil Inclination. Unless a person is constantly vigilant, it is all too easy to be ensnared, and ultimately, to sin.

❧ ❧ ❧

וְאַהֲבַת חֶסֶד — *the love of kindness* (*Michah* 6:8 — *Haftaras Balak*).

The prophet Michah says that Hashem wants us to develop "the love of kindness." This is because Hashem wants our kindness to stem from total willingness and extraordinary love — a degree of love about which *Chazal* have said, "love goes beyond reason." This was the level of the kindness of Avraham. This is why he was so pained by not having the opportunity to do kindness after his circumcision, although even by the highest reasonable standards he could not have been expected to fulfill that *mitzvah* under the circumstances. Indeed, this is the reason that we symbolize Avraham with two bulls in the Temple service of Pesach — because the two bulls are symbolic of the two aspects of true *chesed* — duty and love.

❧ ❧ ❧

פרשת פנחס
Parashas Pinchas

הִנְנִי נֹתֵן לוֹ אֶת־בְּרִיתִי שָׁלוֹם — *Behold! I give him My covenant of peace* (25:12).

P inchas did not become a *Kohen* until he killed Zimri. For that status, one needs the special holiness of *kehunah,* and the ability to acquire that holiness was granted to Aharon and his descendants specifically. Outside of Aharon, it was impossible even for the greatest men to accede to that state. Aharon was given that holiness until the end of all generations. But this holiness was only automatically transferred to those generations born after his anointment. This is why even his adult sons needed a special anointment, and did not have *kehunah* as a matter of course. Pinchas, who was not anointed, did not become holy by the anointment of Elazar, his father, just as Elazar did not become holy through the anointment of Aharon, his father.

Now, while the gift given to Aharon that his descendants could be *Kohanim* did not *exclude* Pinchas from the ability to become a *Kohen,* he needed to merit the actual grant of that holiness. He merited that status with this act. The necessary merit was not the doing of many good deeds, but instead a specific type of deed that reflected Aharon's special qualities — lover of peace, pursuer of peace, lover of God's creatures, and drawer of men to the Torah, as taught in the Mishnah in *Avos* (1:2). The prophet Malachi also praises these special qualities in the verses of *Torah of pure truth* and continuing to *resembling an angel of God* (*Malachi* 2:6-7). Pinchas had these special qualities. He held no personal animus against Zimri, but was truly zealous for the honor of God. To clarify this, we need to look at the rules of *Beis Din* regarding corporal punishment. While generally it is proper to do a *mitzvah* even without the right intentions, this is not true when it comes to physical punishment. *Beis Din* has the right to strike and punish when required, but they may not do so if they do not have the right intentions. Similarly, the rule that "Those who hate You, God, I hate" (*Tehillim* 139:21) can only be applied when that feeling comes from the desire to serve Hashem, with no admixture of personal feelings. [This is also *Tosafos'* (to *Pesachim* 113b שראה ד״יה) explanation of the Gemara in *Bava Metzia* (32b). The Gemara there says that there is a preference for the *mitzvah* of helping someone you dislike to load his donkey over the *mitzvah* of helping a friend unload his overburdened donkey, because helping the person you hate adds the *mitzvah* of subordinating your Evil Inclination. *Tosafos* says that although the Gemara is referring to a person you are allowed to hate because of his enmity to Torah, perhaps you hate him more than his acts would justify.] The rule that under certain circumstances the zealot has free rein to strike down one who subverts the Torah is only valid when done with pure motivations. This is why if someone would come to the court and ask if he would be justified in acting as a zealot, the court cannot respond positively, because it is impossible to know whether this person is motivated exclusively by the proper reasons, or, perhaps, has slightly ulterior motives.[1] This is why the Torah testifies that his act was purely for the sake of the honor of Hashem. Thus, Pinchas actually had love for Zimri, in that Pinchas walked in the path of Aharon.

This explains how the act of Pinchas stopped the plague, and brought peace to the world, and between Israel and their heavenly Father. For this, Hashem gave Pinchas the covenant of peace and *kehunah,* for him and his children forever.

❀ ❀ ❀

וַיָּמָת נָדָב וַאֲבִיהוּא בְּהַקְרִיבָם אֵשׁ־זָרָה לִפְנֵי ה' —
Nadav and Avihu died when they brought an alien fire before HASHEM (26:61).

Whenever the sons of Aharon are mentioned, as in this verse (see also 3:4), Nadav and Avihu are counted and then described as having *died before Hashem.* The reason

---

1. Perhaps this was the reason the tribes scorned Pinchas, suspecting him of having some degree of ulterior motives. (see *Sanhedrin* 82b).

for this is that the great men of a generation, such as Nadav and Avihu, never lose their profound importance to their generation. Even if they are no longer among us, it is as if they are still here. We must learn from them, and feel honored by their relation to us, and to grasp and appreciate that they were part of of Israel, and to wish that there were more like them. We see from this the lofty station the Torah gives the great and righteous Torah scholar, and how much we should respect them.

❧ ❧ ❧

וְאָמַרְתָּ לָהֶם זֶה הָאִשֶּׁה אֲשֶׁר תַּקְרִיבוּ . . . שְׁנַיִם לַיּוֹם עֹלָה תָמִיד — *And you shall say to them: This is the fire-offering that you are to offer . . . two a day, as a continual elevation-offering* (28:3).

Hashem commanded *Bnei Yisrael* to bring a sacrifice called the *tamid*, meaning the "constant" or "continual" sacrifice, which was brought every morning and evening. This commandment is stated right after Moshe asked Hashem to appoint his successor, who would properly lead *Bnei Yisrael*. *Rashi* explains the connection between the two *parshios* by citing a Midrash which says: "Hashem said to Moshe: 'Instead of charging Me regarding My children, charge My children regarding Me.' " This Midrash seems perplexing. What connection does this *parashah* have to Moshe's request to appoint a worthy leader to guide *Bnei Yisrael*?

The answer appears to be this: The proper state of affairs is that *Bnei Yisrael* are so devoted to the Holy One, Blessed is He, that immediately upon arising they know that they must serve Hashem, and they feel the same way in the evening, and only between those times are they able to work to support themselves. The *tamid* sacrifices inspire these feelings in the properly receptive heart. The *tamid* sacrifices are brought on behalf of all the nation, and each person who shares in a *korban* must be present at the time of the offering, and so all of Israel ought to be present at the offering of the *tamid*. Instead, representatives called the "Anshei Ma'amad" stayed near the Tabernacle (and later the Temple), who were the agents of the nation as a whole, and this released everyone else to do their daily tasks. Their realization that they ought to have been present at the services generated a feeling in all the people that they were bound up with Hashem *Yisbarach,* and they were inspired to pray at that time (this is reflected in *Chazal's* formal institution of the daily prayers to correspond with those sacrifices). When the people acted and felt this way, they knew by themselves who their proper master, teacher, and leader should be, even without any nomination or announcement. [This is one of the reasons that Hashem *Yisbarach* found *Bnei Yisrael's* later request for a king to be vexatious.]

Thus, the commandment concerning the *tamid* was an answer to Moshe's request for the appointment of a leader: When you command *Bnei Yisrael* about the *tamid*, they will understand without being told that Yehoshua is to be their leader and mentor.

❦ ❦ ❦

וּשְׂעִיר עִזִּים אֶחָד לְחַטָּאת לַה' — *And one male of the goats for a sin-offering to* HASHEM (28:15).

In the *parashah* of *Rosh Chodesh*, the goat offering is described as a *chatas*-offering for Hashem. *Chazal* homiletically interpreted this verse (*Chullin*) to mean that Hashem is saying, "Bring a forgiveness *korban* on My behalf for My having diminished the moon." It appears that this is what is meant by this interpretation: The Gemara states that Hashem's diminishment of the moon was based on many reasons that showed the need for this diminishment and the benefits that would result therefrom. There were also good reasons not to do so, but on balance, *HaKadosh Baruch Hu* resolved the issue and followed the reasons that were more weighty.

HaKadosh Baruch Hu shows us through this verse that He did not nullify the arguments of the moon as if they were vacuous. Rather, although the moon's argument had justification, the resolution was to side against those arguments. Therefore, the Torah says that although Hashem is just in all his acts, and He is the rock Whose actions are without flaw, still, since some justifiable argument existed against the decision, Hashem wishes that we bring a forgiveness sacrifice for Him.

We can learn from this that whether one is a judge, or involved in any decision at all involving wisdom and deliberation, one must not disparage and belittle opinions contrary to his. Instead, one must consider those opinions, and agree that perhaps under certain circumstances they may be justified. If, then, when the time comes to make a decision, he decides against them because in the final balance, his approach is the more correct, that is a valid decision. Only if one takes this approach is his decision reliable. If a decisor disparages the arguments of those who disagree with him, and does not weigh the arguments against his opinion, his decisions are neither just nor true, and one cannot rely on such a decisor.

❦ ❦ ❦

וּשְׂעִיר חַטָּאת אֶחָד מִלְּבַד עֹלַת הַתָּמִיד וּמִנְחָתָהּ וּנְסָכֶיהָ
— One he-goat for a sin-offering; aside from the continual elevation-offering, its meal-offering, and its libations (29:31).

The ceremony that was performed on Succos is hinted at in the spelling of the word *unisacheha* which is found in the description of the Temple service for the sixth day of the holiday. There is an opinion in the beginning of Tractate *Taanis* that this ceremony is only performed on the sixth and seventh days of the holiday. What distinguishes these two days?

The answer is this: We find that the judgment which occurs on the High Holidays is a three-step process. On Rosh Hashanah we are judged, on Yom Kippur the judgment is sealed, and on the last day of Succos, the seventh day of the festival the judgment is sealed with finality. The judgment of Yom Kippur determines what events are destined to happen during the year, and the final seal of Hoshana Rabbah, the last day of Succos, determines how those events will be apportioned. For example, we find that Hashem may decide to bestow an abundance of rain. Even if the people's spiritual level later deteriorates, the judgments will not be revoked. But they will be re-examined. Therefore, Hashem will apportion the rains to places that do not benefit from it. If the judgment was for little rain, and the people improved, then Hashem will apportion the rain at exactly the right time to places that need it the most, and they will benefit from the rain just as they would have from greater amounts.

The same thing applies to the judgment of every individual. One of the ways which helps to ensure that the blessings will be applied in a beneficial manner is people's appreciation of the fact that everything they have is a special and important gift from Hashem. This not only applies to the fortunes of the wealthy, but applies equally to every thing we have, even if it is not a marketable or costly item. Every thing is a gift from Hashem, and we must properly appreciate the value of these gifts by recognizing that Hashem *Yisbarach* gave them to us, and thanking Him for them. This is the message of the drawing of the water. We must feel an appreciation even for water, which Hashem has granted to us in great abundance because of the great need for it. Although water is usually abundant and easily available, we cannot belittle the importance and value of water. Therefore we pour three *login* (approximately one and a half quarts) of water on the Altar with the greatest joy to remind of that the importance of water is not diminished because of its ready availability. Even three *login,* and indeed, even less, is very important and special to us. We find in Gemara *Taanis* (24b) that Rav Yehudah once saw two men that were handling bread with disrespect. He said, "It has become apparent that there is satiety in the world." He put his eye upon it, and famine began. We see that Rav Yehudah felt that the men had lost respect for bread due to their satiety and because of its easy availability. This upset him, because he knew that bread must be valued and respected for its utility to man, and no less respected because Hashem has blessed us by making it readily available.

The same applies to water. Therefore, before Hashem sends forth the fulfillment of the judgment of Rosh Hashanah and Yom Kippur on the day of Hoshana Rabbah, people must be warned to avoid the pitfall of those who are blessed — namely, loss of respect and appreciation for what they have. Instead, they must realize that even if Hashem has graced them with a vast number of blessings, they must appreciate every crumb and every drop. Even the most wealthy man in the world blesses Hashem for a piece of bread the size of an olive. This is the lesson of the drawing of water. To properly appreciate this lesson and fix it in our minds, we prepare for the final seal of the judgment by performing the ceremony the day before Hoshana Rabbah, the sixth day of Succos, and then perform the ceremony once again on Hoshana Rabbah itself.

❧ ❧ ❧

פרשת מטות
Parashas Matos

. . . וַיִּקְחוּ אֶת־כָּל־הַשָּׁלָל . . . וַיָּבִאוּ אֶל־מֹשֶׁה . . . — *And they took all the booty . . . and they brought to Moshe . . . (31:11-12).*

And they took all the booty. . .and they brought [it] to Moshe. Rashi explains that this verse teaches us that they were just and righteous, and not suspected of theft by putting their hands to the booty without permission. But this is a perplexing statement; for how can the concept of theft be applied to the spoils of war, which is by definition ownerless? Perhaps we can say that because the victory was won in a miraculous fashion, and not through the soldiers' merits, but instead through the merit of all of Israel, all of Israel deserved an equal share. Therefore, they brought it to Moshe to decide on the proper division. But one may still wonder: What novelty is there in the Torah's testimony as to their righteousness? The warriors of Israel were always just and righteous men, for anyone with a sin, even a minor transgression, left the ranks of soldiers before battle! The answer is that although the soldiers were allowed, even obligated, to kill and plunder, normally this behavior would naturally influence their personalities, so that killing and robbery would become less horrendous to them. This would possibly result in a lessening of their spiritual stature. Therefore, the Torah testifies that even the warriors remained fully righteous and just, to the degree that they were concerned about the possibility of theft if the booty would be divided inequitably.

Similarly, we see in *Parashas Re'eh* that after justice was meted out to the inhabitants of a subverted city, the Torah states, *And He will give you mercy (Devarim 13:18)*, meaning that the participants in that event will experience an increase in their trait of mercifulness, contrary to the natural course of events. Since all the killing and burning was done for the sake of Heaven and as commanded in the Torah, this will inculcate, and not diminish, the trait of mercifulness. See, also, the story of Shimshon, who, despite the great strength granted him by Hashem and his killing of the Philistines, was unable to kill even one Jew, even when they were pursuing and persecuting him. They had told him they would hand him over to the Philistines, and he simply requested of them not to harm him themselves, although he had nothing to fear from them. But due to his righteousness and highly developed sense of mercy, he could not bring himself to kill or even harm his fellow Jews.

There is another important thing to point out concerning theft. We must acknowledge that whatever good Hashem provides for us is given with the condition of using it as Hashem wishes; if we do not do Hashem's will, we are stealing from *HaKadosh Baruch Hu*. As *Chazal* have said, one who derives enjoyment from this world without blessing Hashem is tantamount to a thief of property consecrated to Hashem's use, and is no better than one who steals from his parents. We must recognize that even when we take possession of worldly things, they still inherently belong to Hashem. Our possessions are not given to us as absolute gifts; rather, Hashem allows us to choose to use those possessions properly, by doing the will of Hashem and fulfilling *mitzvos* and charity and blessing, or improperly. Man was given the ability to choose to do good or evil. The fact that we can use things without interference does not prove they are ours, for we may still be stealing from *HaKadosh Baruch Hu* with improper use. Even if one does bless Hashem prior to using something, he may be blaspheming, because there are many other obligations having to do with one's possessions, and disregarding those obligations is also theft. Perhaps this is why after *Ne'ilah* on Yom Kippur, after we have said all the confessions, we add "so that we may abstain from the unjust taking of property"; as there are many obligations which one may not have discharged in full.

❧ ❧ ❧

פרשת מסעי
Parashas Masei

אַךְ לְמִשְׁפַּחַת מַטֵּה אֲבִיהֶם תִּהְיֶינָה לְנָשִׁים — *only to the family of their father's tribe shall they become wives* (36:6).

T he Gemara notes (*Bava Basra* 120a) that with respect to whom the daughters of Tzelophchad were permitted to marry, the verse appears to contradict itself. On the one hand, the verse states, "*Let them be wives to whomever is good in their eyes.*" On the other hand, the verse continues by saying, "*only to the family of their father's tribe shall they become wives*"! In order to reconcile the two parts of this verse, the Gemara explains that the daughters of Tzelophchad were indeed permitted to marry whomever they desired. Hashem's direction that they marry within their own tribe should not be seen as a command, but rather as words of advice.

The above explanation brings to mind the following question: There is a Talmudic principle (*Kiddushin* 31a) that one who is commanded to fulfill a precept and does so (*metzuvah ve'oseh*) is greater than one who fulfills a precept without having been commanded to do so (*eino metzuvah ve'oseh*). While Hashem knew that the daughters of Tzelophchad would heed His words even without having received a direct command, why did He not command them — and thereby grant them the benefit of being *metzuvah ve'oseh*?

To answer our question, we must first understand why it is that the *metzuvah ve'oseh* is greater than the *eino metzuvah*. When a person sets out to fulfill a precept of the Torah, it is the task of the *yetzer hara*, the Evil Inclination, to try and sway him from acting on his noble intentions.

The reward that a person receives for adhering to the will of his Creator and performing His *mitzvos* is commensurate with the level of difficulty he had to face in order to do so. It therefore follows that the person with the stronger *yetzer hara,* who must constantly struggle to perform Hashem's *mitzvos,* and perseveres, will receive greater reward than the individual whom the *yetzer hara* has chosen not to battle. This is the difference between the *metzuvah ve'oseh* and the *eino metzuvah.* The *metzuvah ve'oseh* is obligated by the Torah to adhere to Hashem's will. This obligation brings with it the attention of the *yetzer hara,* who will constantly urge the person to flaunt these obligations and indulge his physical desires instead. The *eino metzuvah,* however, has no such problem. Since he is under no Divine obligation to perform Hashem's *mitzvos,* he is also freed from the influence of the *yetzer hara* that would normally try and dissuade him.

This logic, however, does not hold true concerning the daughters of Tzelophchad. Having received Divine advice that it would be best for them to marry within their own tribe, ignoring such advice would be tantamount to suggesting that they somehow were smarter than Hashem, and not in need of His advice. Obviously, taking such a stand would constitute heresy. For this reason, while it is true that the daughters of Tzelophchad were technically in the category of *eino metzuvah ve'oseh,* they still had to fight the *yetzer hara's* urging that they ignore Hashem's advice. Furthermore, in this instance the *yetzer hara* was actually able to make a stronger argument, attempting to convince them that they need not heed the words of Hashem since they were only words of advice — not a command that they were obligated to listen to! Thus, their reward was actually *greater* than it would have been had they received an actual command.

There is an additional valuable lesson to be learned here. The need to follow the advice of Hashem is not limited to the daughters of Tzelophchad, who merited receiving direct personal advice from Hashem Himself. Indeed, in every generation a person must take care to heed the advice of Torah sages. For a person must realize that it is their advice — not his own thinking — that represents the proper path that he must follow — for they are wiser than he. Just as we must adhere to the halachic decisions rendered by the Torah Sages of our day, so too we must heed their words of advice on any topic. As we find in *Avos* (6:1): *He who studies Torah for its own sake . . . will serve as a source of wise counsel.* Such a person is imbued by Hashem with the wisdom necessary to understand and advise people on questions regarding any topic — material as well as spiritual. Indeed, a person that does not believe in the truth of the advice of Torah scholars is seriously deficient. It is to this end that we ask Hashem in the *Shemoneh Esrei*, *"Restore our judges as in earliest times, and our counselors as at first."* We express our desire to Hashem that the Sages of the Torah should be our counselors, as they were at first; i.e. that all of the *Bnei Yisrael* should know and be aware that the Sages of the Torah have the knowledge and wisdom to serve in this capacity.

ספר דברים

Sefer Devarim

פרשת דברים
Parashas Devarim

אֵלֶּה הַדְּבָרִים אֲשֶׁר דִּבֶּר מֹשֶׁה אֶל־כָּל־יִשְׂרָאֵל — *These are the words that Moshe spoke to all Israel* (1:1).

Rashi explains: Moshe spoke to all Israel — for had he rebuked only some of them, the ones that had not been present would say, "If we had been there, we would have disproven him with this or that argument." It would seem that those who did attend would transmit all that was said, and those who were absent could have produced counterarguments in any case. Why, then, did they need to be present?

Perhaps we can explain this with an analysis of the content of Moshe's rebuke. This rebuke was given to the second generation in the Wilderness, who were not involved in all the sins listed here. Even the sin of Peor, which occurred in their lifetime, clearly involved none of those who were then living, as Moshe said, *"Every man that followed Baal-peor — Hashem, your God, destroyed him from your midst. But you who cling to Hashem, your God — you are all alive today"* (*Devarim* 4:4). Also, Baal Peor was not brought up as an admonishment, but rather to strengthen the faith of those that survived that event, as an example of how justice and mercy are meted out. Why, then, did Moshe bring up the sins of their fathers, which this generation had nothing to do with? The answer is that Moshe was warning this generation: "See and realize that your fathers sinned in these matters despite their recognition of the glory of Hashem. Do not think that you cannot possibly come to the same sins because of your understanding and greatness. You certainly are susceptible to the same temptations,

God forbid."

Sinning occurs due to the strength of the Evil Inclination. Even a person who is great in Torah and good deeds can stumble into the ugliest sins. Therefore, we must be very cautious to avoid sin, and to constantly be involved in the study of Torah and ethical teachings to gain the strength to stand up to the Evil Inclination without a moment of distraction, or false faith in our imperviousness to sin. That is what the previous generation did, and because of this they were susceptible to sin. Awareness of this weakness helps people to see themselves as they truly are, and enables them to develop safeguards against sin. Thus, if some had not attended, they might have said that they were well aware of their own character, and that they are not vulnerable to sin: They would assume that they required no special wariness of the Evil Inclination, rationalizing that Moshe did not have righteous people as them in mind. Therefore, Moshe gathered everyone together, and told them that he was speaking to every single one of them. This is why he did not rebuke them concerning Baal Peor; these people had been present at that time, and had not sinned, and so perhaps they could think that their defenses to that sort of sin were sufficient. Nevertheless, Moshe told them that they needed to strengthen themselves against all forms of sin; had they sinned at Baal Peor they would have been eradicated, and therefore all that did not sin ought to strengthen their resolve to fight the Evil Inclination constantly.

❈ ❈ ❈

טוֹב־הַדָּבָר אֲשֶׁר־דִּבַּרְתָּ לַעֲשׂוֹת — *"The thing that you have proposed to do is good"* (1:14).

When Moshe Rabbeinu proposed setting up a large judicial and educational system, which would replace a system wherein everyone came to him, the people answered, *"the thing you have proposed to do is good."* *Rashi* comments that Moshe was not pleased with this enthusiastic approval. Moshe said, "You should have said, 'From whom is it better to learn, from you or from your students? Isn't it better to learn from you, who has toiled and suffered in the study of the Torah?' " It would seem that *Rashi* should have said that they ought to have preferred Moshe as a teacher because he was the original teacher, as opposed to learning from Moshe's students. Why does *Rashi* mention the fact that Moshe suffered and toiled in his study?

The answer is that some people, who are not yet great scholars, might find it easier to learn from a student. But *Rashi* wanted to tell us that the best teacher, whom one should seek out and emulate, is one who has toiled and suffered in his acquisition of his learning in order to understand every subject with absolute clarity, as Hashem has commanded. Such a teacher does not depend on his sharp mind or wisdom, despite his greatness, but instead toils and labors constantly to reach the truth. Despite his having a great mind and memory, he does not trust his initial reactions, but works and labors to understand the truth of matters.

I have also used this explanation to interpret *Rashi* in the beginning of *Bechukosai*, where *Rashi* says that one who has not toiled in Torah is viewed as one who has not learned at all. Even a person with the greatest mind, who has not toiled, but depended on his genius and memory, cannot be considered a *talmid chacham* — a reliable and dispositive source of Torah. The wisdom of the Torah is greater than the wisdom of the human mind, no matter how great that mind may be. Only after a person invests great effort and toil does Hashem *Yisbarach* assist him to truly understand the words of the Torah.

❧ ❧ ❧

פרשת ואתחנן
Parashas Va'eschanan

ה' אֱלֹקִים אַתָּה הַחִלּוֹתָ לְהַרְאוֹת אֶת־עַבְדְּךָ . . .
"My Lord, HASHEM/ELOKIM, You have begun to show Your servant . . . (3:24).*

A s Moshe opened his request that he be allowed to enter the Land of Israel, he began with the words, *"My Lord, Hashem, You have begun to show Your servant Your greatness and Your strong hand."* Rav Simla'i (*Berachos* 32b) derives from this that one should begin with praise of Hashem before one asks that Hashem grant his needs (as we do in our daily *Shemoneh Esrei* prayers).

The reason for this is that when a person prays to Hashem, he should realize that what he is doing is not at all like asking for help from a fellow man, whose ability to help is limited. If he does not realize that, his prayer is not prayer at all. Only if it is manifestly apparent and clear to the supplicant that Hashem *Yisbarach* can do whatever He chooses to, and that He wants to help, is the prayer proper. We are to trust in Hashem's omnipotence and desire to help us, and ask that our words be acceptable before Him. This is why we must preface our prayers with praise. This reminds us that only Hashem has the ability to provide our needs, and that He certainly wishes to help, and therefore He certainly will help if we have some merit. Thus, this faith is the basis of prayer, and without this faith fixed and foremost in our minds, our prayers are empty words.

Another reason for Rav Simla'i's rule is that reaffirming our unlimited trust and belief in Hashem is in itself a great merit. This merit helps to make our prayers acceptable before Hashem.

❈ ❈ ❈

אָז יַבְדִּיל מֹשֶׁה שָׁלֹשׁ עָרִים — *Then Moshe set aside three cities* (4:41).

Moshe set aside these cities as places of refuge for those who killed without knowledge. *Rashi* explains that at that time Moshe took to heart the pressing need to designate these cities. We must try to understand: What does the word "then" refer to? What caused Moshe to take this to heart at that particular time? The answer is this: This act bespeaks Moshe's greatness. It is in connection with this that *Chazal* apply to Moshe the verse (*Koheles* 5:9), *A lover of money will never be satisfied with money*. We see how very wealthy men strive to increase their wealth, although they do not benefit at all from the extra riches they earn — indeed, the extra wealth benefits them even less than the pennies earned by a person that needs them. But they labor and exhaust themselves nevertheless, and lose sleep and go hungry, just for the love of money, which fulfills no real need. Just so was Moshe's love of the Torah and the *mitzvos*. He was never satisfied. Therefore, he designated the three cities even though he did not fulfill any *mitzvah* by doing so, because their protected status did not go into effect until Yehoshua designated the other three cities in the Land of Israel. Because of his great love for *mitzvos*, he yearned to contribute whatever he could toward the fulfillment of the *mitzvah*, even though no merit accrued to him for doing so. The verse tells us: At what point did he become so enamored of the *mitzvos* that he would do anything he could that would bring a *mitzvah* closer to realization? After he rebuked and chastened the *Bnei Yisrael*. Despite his great and exalted spiritual level, which he had reached many years before when his prophecy began, the rebuke he delivered to others generated even more love of *mitzvos* in him. Although such a statement concerning Moshe would seem inconceivable, the Torah still tells us that chastening others, and teaching them the supreme importance of discipline and moral responsibility, leaves a lasting impression even on the greatest of the great.

❧ ❧ ❧

אֲשֶׁר הִכָּה מֹשֶׁה וּבְנֵי יִשְׂרָאֵל בְּצֵאתָם מִמִּצְרָיִם — *whom Moshe and the Bnei Yisrael smote when they went out of Mitzrayim* (4:46).

T he verse here refers to the conquest of Sichon, *whom Moshe and the Bnei Yisrael smote when they went out of Mitzrayim.* Actually, this conquest took place 40 years after the Exodus. The reason for the association is that this event would have taken place immediately after the Exodus had they not sinned; and despite the 40-year delay caused by their sins, the eventual conquest was due to the merits of the *Bnei Yisrael* and the promise made by Hashem when they left Mitzrayim.

❦ ❦ ❦

וְאַתְּ תְּדַבֵּר אֵלֵינוּ — *and you should speak to us* (5:24).

A fter the *Bnei Yisrael* heard the first two Commandments from Hashem directly, they approached Moshe and asked that he speak to Hashem, and then tell them the *mitzvos.* The verse states: *vi'at tidaber eileinu*, and you will speak to us. The word *vi'at* is in the feminine grammatical form. *Rashi* explains that Moshe was not pleased with the request of *Bnei Yisrael,* and told them, "Would it not be better that you hear Hashem's word directly?" However, the Torah states in v. 25 that Hashem said, *"[t]hey did well in all that they spoke,"* which shows that Hashem approved of the request. We must seek to understand why Moshe Rabbeinu felt the request was improper, and what it was that Hashem pointed out to correct him.

Actually, the *Bnei Yisrael* made two statements that seem to be inherently contradictory. First they stated that they had seen that a person can survive God's speaking to him (v. 21), and then they immediately stated: *"If we continue to hear the voice of Hashem, our God, any longer, we will die!"* (v. 23). We must explain that they realized that two levels of "speaking with God" exist. Clearly, they understood that there is a level of prophecy which allows God to speak to man and which causes no injury at all. On the contrary, Hashem provides the recipient of the message with the strength to spread the prophecy and do Hashem's work. But they understood now, more than ever before, the awesome greatness of Hashem, which inspired greater fear in them. They realized that to accede to prophecy, and to hear the words of the Living God, requires long and laborious preparation. They also realized that Hashem was not speaking to them because they had reached any such level of prophecy. This shows us how great they were: Although they already saw that they had survived contact with Hashem, their fear did not diminish. In fact it increased, and they therefore wished to properly prepare themselves for such close contact with Hashem. This preparation would be possible only if Moshe would receive the Torah, and they would fulfill it and study it continuously until they would reach the level of prophecy. This is why Hashem approved of their request. Moshe, on the other hand, was the most humble of all men, and he felt that he, too, had not reached the level of prophecy, and that Hashem only spoke to him and rested the *Shechinah* on him because of Hashem's grace and kindness. Thus, he felt that there was no reason for the *Bnei Yisrael* to avoid this close contact. But Hashem told Moshe that the *Bnei Yisrael* were right, for they had indeed not reached the level of prophecy, whereas Moshe had reached the highest possible level of prophecy.

❧ ❧ ❧

וְאָהַבְתָּ אֵת ה' אֱלֹקֶיךָ בְּכָל־לְבָבְךָ — *You shall love* HASHEM, *your God, with all your heart* (6:5).

Chazal tell us that *all your heart* means with both your Good Inclination and your Evil Inclination. Why is it necessary to tell us to serve Hashem with the Good Inclination? The Good Inclination, after all, by its nature moves us to do only good things! The answer is very simple. When people follow the dictates of what their own philosophies tell them is "good," they often do bad things. For example, a person might give charity to institutions that he thinks are good, but actually, he is supporting activity which is not only not good, but sometimes even bad. One must ask a wise and experienced person how to give and to whom to give. Similarly, the trait of mercy can yield bad results.[1] Many merciful people in this country have mercy on murderers, and thus increase the shedding of innocent blood. Every good trait has this potential for bad. Therefore we have to be reminded and warned to love Hashem with our Good Inclination by seeking direction from Torah scholars, and not to do, God forbid, the opposite by misplaced reliance on our own notions.

❧ ❧ ❧

---

1. See comments to *Devarim* 7:12.

פרשת עקב
Parashas Eikev

וְהָיָה עֵקֶב תִּשְׁמְעוּן — *This shall be the reward when you hearken* (7:12).

Parashas Eikev begins with the words וְהָיָה עֵקֶב תִּשְׁמְעוּן, (7:12) *When (eikev) you will hearken.* The term *eikev* connotes a heel. Thus, in effect, the verse reads, "on the heels of your observance." *Rashi* explains, "This refers to 'light' *mitzvos* which a person treads with his heels."[1] It appears to me that *Rashi* does not mean that we are suspected of demeaning the *mitzvos,* God forbid. Rather, the idea is that a person should not trivialize the Torah by fulfilling the *mitzvos* while enjoying mundane pleasures, and merely avoiding transgressions. With this approach it is impossible to fulfill the Torah, for Torah can only be acquired by diminishing mundane pleasures, elevating personal characteristics such as contentment, patience, and the like, and by learning to ignore the Evil Inclination's powerful blandishments that one's acts are not transgressions. The Torah must be a yoke which presses a person to hard labor, whose results will ultimately be the greatest true pleasure and joy.

❧ ❧ ❧

Another possible interpretation of this *Rashi* is that this refers to the greatest *mitzvos,* such as the study of the Torah, and charity. These

---

1. See *Daas Zekeinim,* which discusses which mitzvos are meant here.

mitzvos are "tread upon" by people in the sense that they tend to follow their own counsel in determining how best to fulfill these *mitzvos*. To elaborate: I have previously explained the superiority of the Jews' statement at Mt. Sinai, "We shall do and we shall hear," over simply "We shall do." Only when the Jews said, "We shall do and we shall hear," did they merit the giving of the Torah. This is because "we shall do" means only that every person would do what he understands the will of Hashem to be, and this is worthless. People may believe they understand, and nonetheless be wrong. One can imagine that bad things are good, and good things are bad. People can err in the fundamentals of the Torah, and of Jewish faith itself. If the Torah was given to a people that said only, "We shall do," there would be a thousand Torahs, and perhaps not one of them would be true. If this were the case, we would not be worthy to receive the Torah. But when the Jews said, "We shall do and we shall hear," this meant they would do what they heard from the wise men of the Torah as transmitted in the chain of tradition, from the mouth of the teacher to student, all hewing to the true wisdom. In this way, the Torah would always remain one and true. Then, the nation was worthy to receive the Torah.

Now, generally the majority of the Jews that have faith in God and his Torah fulfill the *mitzvos* as instructed by the wise men of the generation. When they do not know what to do, they ask, and then they follow the decision rendered. But when it comes to the study of the Torah, and the *mitzvah* of charity, very few ask the Rabbis or halachic decisors. Instead, everyone makes decisions and determines his path for himself — how much to learn, whether to learn in the first place, what to learn; when it comes to charity, most people do not ask how much they ought to give, and to whom to give, but instead make their own decisions. Because of this, these *mitzvos* are often not properly fulfilled. This is what *"mitzvos that are tread upon with the heel"* means. People walk along in their own footsteps, choosing their own path and deciding for themselves what is right or wrong, and not in the footsteps of the wise men who have established and taught us how to fulfill the *mitzvos* of Torah and charity.

When this is the case, we do not merit blessing. But when the instruction of the wise men of the Torah is sought even with regard to these *mitzvos* (a path indicated by the word "hearken" or "hear"), then you will merit the blessings enumerated in this *parashah*.

❄ ❄ ❄

וְשָׁמַר ה' אֱלֹקֶיךָ לְךָ אֶת־הַבְּרִית וְאֶת־הַחֶסֶד —
*HASHEM, your God, will safeguard for you the
covenant and the kindness* (7:12).

This can be understood by applying the verse, *Love Hashem with
all your heart,* which *Chazal* explain to mean that one must love
God with both Good and Evil Inclinations. It would seem that
there is no need to command us to love God with our Good Inclination,
because by its nature it seeks to do only good! In fact, though, the trait of
goodness which Hashem graced us with (as *Chazal* said, *And Hashem
will safeguard the kindness* means that we are by nature sympathetic,
sensitive to embarrassment, and kind) can be used against Hashem's will
and in a self-contradictory manner. That is, in the case of wicked
murderers, who ought to be punished, and whose punishment benefits
the whole community and literally saves lives, sympathy is contrary to
Hashem's will and conflicts with the trait of sympathy itself. As King
Solomon said (*Mishlei* 12:10), *"the mercy of the wicked is cruel."* The
same can be true of deeds of kindness. When one is kind to violent and
depraved criminals, his kindness is cruelty to the world as a whole. We
see this in the episode of Achav's kindness to Ben-hadad, which resulted
in the greatest cruelties to Achav and to all the Jewish people (see
Melachim I 20:26). Achav was criminally negligent in that he failed to ask
the prophet whether or not to be kind to Ben-hadad. Ultimately,
Ben-hadad declared war on Israel, and forgot all the kindness Achav had
shown him.

This is why we have been commanded that although we are innately
good natured and kind, we may not act on those traits on our own
initiative; doing so might be contrary to the will of God and contrary to the
concept of mercy itself. This is why the Torah instructs us to guard the
attribute of kindness, which will ensure that what we perceive as kindness
will in fact truly be kindness in the fullest sense of the word.

❀ ❀ ❀

וְאָכַלְתָּ וְשָׂבָעְתָּ וּבֵרַכְתָּ אֶת ה' — *You will eat and you
will be satisfied, and bless Hashem* (8:10).

The Gemara (*Berachos* 48b) says that if the Torah requires a
blessing after we eat, when we are sated, we can derive via a *kal
vachomer* (an *a fortiori* argument) that we should bless Hashem

before we eat, when we are hungry. *Tosafos* (to *Yoma* 79a ד"ה לא) say that this *kal vachomer* is not meant to elicit a Biblical requirement for a blessing before eating, and the prior blessing is actually of Rabbinical origin. We are, in any case, forced to agree that the *kal vachomer* is not meant as a true halachic exegesis. We know that the Gemara intends to provide a basis for our blessing both before and after eating. If this were a true *kal vachomer*, it would be sufficient to make a blessing *only* before eating, based on the rule of *dayo*, which states that a *kal vachomer* cannot create a higher level of obligation than exists at the source of the *kal vachomer;* here, the source law of blessing after eating only requires one blessing. [The *kal vachomer* would thus teach us that a blessing is acceptable either before eating or after eating.]

With this in mind, we can understand the true explanation of this Gemara. The *kal vachomer* would indeed show that one blessing is sufficient, and that blessing should be said before eating, when the person is hungry. In truth, however, a blessing before eating is completely different in purpose from a blessing after eating. Even if Hashem has given us the wealth and ability to acquire what we desire, and it is before us on the table, it is not really in our hands at all. We cannot say that we have, or have benefited from, anything. We still need Hashem's assistance to use what we have. If we were to thank Hashem for our enjoyment of the food we have before us, we would be risking a wasted blessing. Furthermore, if one were to thank Hashem for the benefit we have from things we have not yet used, it would be a sort of lack of faith in Hashem's intimate and constant involvement in our lives; for it would show that the person thinks that what he has is in his power, and that he no longer needs Hashem's assistance to sustain and nourish him, because he already has what he needs. But this is untrue as can be seen from the Priestly Blessing, *May Hashem bless you and safeguard you* (*Bamidbar* 6:24), which indicates that even after we are blessed, we need Hashem to safeguard us so that we can enjoy the blessing. This is why the Torah said that we should thank Hashem after we have eaten. However, the Sages instituted an additional blessing before eating, because, as the *kal vachomer* indicates, we appreciate the food even more when we are hungry and the food is ready for our immediate use. Since we also bless Hashem after eating, this prior blessing no longer appears to be a fault in our faith, since this blessing is for the *availability* of the food, while the second blessing is for the benefit we derived from it.

In any case, the Sages can resolve that a blessing on the availability of food would not be a wasted blessing even if we were subsequently not able to eat it or benefit from it. Thus, we see that although the *kal vachomer* could not teach that a blessing would be equally appropriate before eating, it still provides a very good reason for the sages to institute that blessing.

❊ ❊ ❊

וְאָכַלְתָּ וְשָׂבָעְתָּ וּבֵרַכְתָּ — *You will eat and you will be satisfied, and bless* (8:10).

God says: "How can I not favor the Jewish people? I said in My Torah, 'You will eat and you will be satisfied, and bless Hashem,' but they bless Hashem on food the size of an olive or a fig" (*Berachos* 20b). What is meant here is that even the most wealthy person should perceive and feel that every piece of food he eats is a gift from Hashem *Yisbarach* which was granted him at the moment he ate it. The fact that he had so much wealth, and even the fact that the food had been on the table and ready to eat, did not guarantee that he would benefit from it. It is not his with any certainty until he actually eats and benefits from it. Therefore, he must bless Hashem on even a little bit of food just as he would for a great feast. Everything we enjoy is a gift granted anew by Hashem every day and every moment. This approach also explains *Chazal's* statement concerning Yitzchak's blessing of Yaakov (*Bereishis* 27:28), "And may God give you," that Hashem will give and give again.

❊ ❊ ❊

וְהָיָה אִם־שָׁכֹחַ תִּשְׁכַּח אֶת־ה' אֱלֹקֶיךָ — *It shall be that if you forget HASHEM, your God* (8:19).

The word *vehayah* which means "and it shall be" in the verse *and it shall be if you forget Hashem* is very difficult to understand. *Vehayah* denotes a joyous event — the opposite of what this verse refers to! We can explain it thus: There are wicked people who do some good things. Others see the good they do, and think that those acts show that the person is worthy of emulation. People are then influenced by the wicked acts of those people. If so, it is, God forbid, like a joyous occasion if the wicked would not perform those good acts. This verse thus refers to the previous *parashah* which talked of a person that has faith in Hashem's Torah, but believes that his material success is due to his own skill and effort. The good that such people do would be better forgotten.

The Gemara in *Sanhedrin* (107a) tells us a similar idea. The Gemara there describes how David Hamelech considered working for a house of idolatry while he was pursued by Avshalom. Chushai the Arkite found him, and said, "Do you want people to say that a righteous king such as yourself serves idols?" David answered, "Shall people say that the righteous king was killed by his own son (and, God forbid, question the justice of Hashem)?" We see that David Hamelech wanted people to forget all the good he had done so that they would not be badly influenced by what might happen to him.

❈ ❈ ❈

וָאֵשֵׁב בָּהָר אַרְבָּעִים יוֹם וְאַרְבָּעִים לַיְלָה — *and I remained on the mountain for forty days and forty nights* (9:9).

Rashi explains that *va'eisheiv* means "I tarried." But this is very hard to understand. Why was it necessary to use a word that connotes long delay? After all, the verse states explicitly the length of his stay, and no nuance is added by saying that the forty-day period was a lengthy stay. It is because of this question that other *Tannaim* (in *Megillah* 21a) explain *va'eisheiv* in the literal sense of being seated, from which we derive certain *halachos*.

We may explain that the special significance of the interpretation "I tarried" is that it does not refer to the period of forty days, but rather it means "to tarry forever." In other words, although Moshe knew that he would be on Mount Sinai for only forty days, he settled in to learn the Torah as if he would be there forever. This teaches that all of us, even if we only have a few minutes to learn, should sit down to learn as if we will have all the time in the world. This way, we will spend whatever time is available well, delving deeply into our study, without the lazy excuse that since we only have a short time to study, we will study superficially. Of course, this would not have occurred in any case when Moshe learned from Hashem, but the Torah chose these words to teach *us* how to succeed in our studies.

וְאֶת־חַטַּאתְכֶם אֲשֶׁר־עֲשִׂיתֶם אֶת־הָעֵגֶל לָקַחְתִּי וָאֶשְׂרֹף
אֹתוֹ בָּאֵשׁ וָאֶכֹּת אֹתוֹ טָחוֹן הֵיטֵב — *Your sin that you*
committed — the calf — I took and burned it in
fire, and I pounded it, grinding it well. . . (9:21).

This verse means that not only did Moshe Rabbeinu burn the calf,
but he also burned the sin of idolatry, thereby allowing the
people to repent their sin. The grammatical term "grinding,"
which can be read "I grind it," is thus more understandable, because it
refers to a constant and ongoing result, that the sins themselves remain
"ground down," which enables easier *teshuvah*.

I have seen that one commentator interprets this verse to mean that
Moshe Rabbeinu burned whatever remained of the animals that had been
designated as sacrifices to the calf. However, one must carefully examine
this interpretation: Such an act ought to be impermissible, in that burning
the sacrifices was itself the means by which the calf was to have been
worshiped. Although the usual means of disposing of objects designated
for service of idolatry is by burning, here this should not be permissible.
Perhaps, however, if the burning is done in a demeaning fashion it would
be allowed. Although the halachic determination of this question remains
unclear, the interpretation offered here is more reasonable and likely.

※ ※ ※

מָה ה' אֱלֹקֶיךָ שֹׁאֵל מֵעִמָּךְ כִּי אִם־לְיִרְאָה אֶת־ה' אֱלֹהֶיךָ
— *what does* HASHEM, *your God, ask of you? Only*
to fear Hashem, your God. . .. (10:12).

The Gemara in *Berachos* (33b) asks: "Is fear of God a small thing,
that the verse should state that this is 'only' what Hashem asks"?
The Gemara answers, "Yes. For Moshe it was a small thing." The
question that follows is: Wasn't this request made of the entire nation, for
whom this fear is not at all a small thing?

The answer is that there are two aspects of fear of God: awe of
Hashem's grandeur, and fear of punishment, since Hashem punishes not
only for transgressions, but also for any improper behavior. Awareness of
each of these ideas motivates fear of Hashem. The fear of punishment is
one of the fundamental tenets of faith. If one does not believe, God
forbid, in reward and punishment, he is an absolute *apikorus*, completely

cut off from the Jewish faith. Now, when a verse mentions the fear of God, it includes both types. For example, when the verse later in this *parashah* (10:20) says, "Hashem, your God, you shall fear," this means both fear of punishment and awe of grandeur. [When *Chazal* derive from there that we must also fear Torah scholars, the word "fear" only concerns awe of greatness, as it does concerning our obligation to fear our parents. Perhaps this is why Shimon the Amsonite (*Pesachim* 22b) was unwilling to derive the fear of the Torah scholar from the verse, because the word "fear" could not be applied to the scholar as it is meant in the literal meaning of the verse, referring to both types of fear of Hashem. Rabbi Akiva, however, held that the rules of exegesis allow a partial application.]

Now, the fear of punishment, which is the more fundamental of the two, should be a matter of course among the people, because they know that they have many sins, and ought to fear punishment for the past and be vigilant about the future. For Moshe, this fear should have been a major undertaking, because he never sinned, and considering his level of sanctity, he could be virtually certain that he would never sin. Therefore, Moshe charged the Jews saying that they must fear God, reasoning that for them, fear of punishment should be self-evident.

The truth is, though, that the reality is the opposite. Even this elementary fear, which every man should have due to his sins, is not complete or tangible to people. If it were, they would never sin. And to Moshe, the fear of punishment was elementary, because despite all his righteousness and good deeds, he still feared the strict justice of Hashem.

❀ ❀ ❀

הִשָּׁמְרוּ לָכֶם פֶּן־יִפְתֶּה לְבַבְכֶם וְסַרְתֶּם וַעֲבַדְתֶּם אֱלֹהִים אֲחֵרִים — *Beware for yourselves, lest your heart be seduced and you turn astray and serve gods of others* (11:16).

It would seem that the verse ought to go directly to the description of the sin it warns against, and not begin with the words *lest your heart be seduced*. We may explain that the reason for this introductory phrase is to teach us that no man goes from faith to idolatry in one step. There is always a threshold sin involving some other matter. After doing the first sin, the sinner moves on to a loss of faith and ultimately to idolatry. Therefore, the verse warns us to be extremely careful to avoid the threshold seduction, for while the first sin may not seem deadly, it is the true cause of the ultimate blasphemy that follows.

❧ ❧ ❧

— כָּל־הַמָּקוֹם אֲשֶׁר תִּדְרֹךְ כַּף־רַגְלְכֶם בּוֹ לָכֶם יִהְיֶה
Every place where the soul of your foot will tread shall be yours (11:24).

This verse is a reference to the Baraisa that states that whatever land the *Bnei Yisrael* conquer after they have conquered all of Eretz Yisrael will have the same holiness and laws as *Eretz Yisrael*, but not if the land is conquered before the conquest of all of *Eretz Yisrael* proper — the secondary is only possible after the primary is in place. Because the *Bnei Yisrael* want their dwelling places to be holy, they are granted this *kedushah* in whatever places they conquer. But if they have not yet conquered the primary *Eretz Yisrael* which is inherently holy and which they were commanded to conquer and inherit, their assertions that they are motivated by a desire for *kedushah* cannot be accepted, and so those prematurely conquered areas are not granted *kedushah*. We can apply the lesson learned here to the marital union. First, the couple must see to it that they sanctify their union, which they are commanded to maintain in a state of holiness, by observing all those laws which the state of marriage invokes, and by developing a relationship with harmony, mutual honor, and respect. After accomplishing this, Hashem will grant that all their external endeavors will be graced by holiness and purity, leading to ever greater blessing and success.

❧ ❧ ❧

פרשת ראה
Parashas Re'eh

רְאֵה אָנֹכִי נֹתֵן לִפְנֵיכֶם הַיּוֹם בְּרָכָה וּקְלָלָה — *See* (stated in the singular), *I present before you* (stated in the plural) *today a blessing and a curse* (11:26).

W e must think about the change from singular to plural in this verse. Also noteworthy is the next verse, which says, *The blessing: that you hearken,* which does not begin with a conditional word, such as "if," but simply *that you hearken.* The reason for this is that the hearkening to Hashem is in itself a blessing. It produces the true bliss of spiritual calmness and emotional satisfaction which cannot exist in one who who does not hearken to Hashem's words. After all, one who has 100 wants 200, and anguishes over the fact that he does not possess the greater amount as much as if he would be lacking something necessary to his basic well-being. Those that do not understand this in the beginning, understand it in the end, as Shlomo said in *Mishlei* (5:11), *You will groan at your [life's] end.* It is in itself a curse, for understanding comes at one's penultimate moment. This state of blessing and curse stand alone, unrelated to punishment and reward, which may not even take place during one's lifetime. Since this is what the verse means, we understand why the verse, which is addressed to the individual, uses the plural for the word "see." This means that the person should contemplate the lives of the righteous and the wicked, and realize how one is a life of calmness and satisfaction, and the other is a life of unrequited seeking and spiritual frustration, and then the person will choose the life of the just.

This explanation is sound concerning sins of passion, even idolatry, for Jews that choose idolatry only do so to rationalize erotic promiscuity. But there are sins, such as performing the Temple service outside of the Temple, which are even harder to stop than sins of passion, because people do such things mistakenly, thinking that doing so will bring them to spiritual perfection, and so they do feel spiritual fulfillment. Of course, such sins are extremely serious and carry the punishment of *kares*. How does this verse address these sins? The answer appears to be that since people who do such sins are attempting to ascend to spiritual elevation by following the dictates of their own rationality, they will not find satisfaction from doing so. Only when one follows the path of the Torah, and rises step by step on that path, will he reach the spiritual fulfillment and satisfaction promised here.

❀ ❀ ❀

לֹא תִתְגֹּדְדוּ — *you shall not cut yourselves* (14:1).

The phrase *lo sisgodedu* has two meanings. One is that we may not injure ourselves as a sign of mourning. The other is that we must not polarize the members of our communities by forming partisan groups. These two meanings actually mirror each other. Polarized groups wound the ability of the community to function, and injure the spirituality of the community. Thus, they make the community repulsive, just as self-mutilation injures a person and makes him hideous.

We, the children of Hashem, must strive to remain physically wholesome, and certainly must guard our spiritual status and our interpersonal behavior.

❀ ❀ ❀

לֹא תְאַמֵּץ אֶת־לְבָבְךָ . . . וְלֹא־יֵרַע לְבָבְךָ — *you shall not harden your heart . . . and let your heart not feel bad* (15:7,10).

In the *parashah* of *tzedakah*, the Torah says, *you shall not harden your heart* and *let your heart not feel bad when you give*. This shows that even after a person has given charity, if he later regrets his charity he transgresses these commandments. This can be understood in the light of my interpretation of the *mitzvah* of charity, and all the *mitzvos* between man and fellow man; All these *mitzvos* have a special added requirement, which is that they be done with full accord and fellowship. This also explains why the Torah uses the expression, *If you will lend to My people* (*Shemos* 22:24), even though this is not an option but rather an obligation; for the *mitzvah* must be done willingly, without regrets. Here, not only does the Torah enforce this teaching with a positive commandment, but also warns that transgression carries with it the punishment of an explicit negative commandment.

❈ ❈ ❈

פָּתֹחַ תִּפְתַּח אֶת־יָדְךָ — *you shall open your hand* (15:8).

The expression *open your hand* to your poor brethren teaches that one should give charity as if he has renounced ownership in the money, so that the poor person can take it, instead of receiving it as a gift from the donor. Although the donor must agree to give it, the poor person may not take it without permission, even if he is taking only what the donor is obligated to give; indeed, even if the donor has already promised to give this amount to the poor, and even if the donor said that he would give this specific coin to the poor, still and all the donor should feel that he has renounced ownership in this amount, and that the poor has the right to take it just like anyone else. We find this concept in the case of Yoav, the chief officer of King David, whose home was described as being *in the desert* (*Melachim I* 2:34). The Gemara (*Sanhedrin* 49a) interprets this as meaning that he did not give charity with a formal handing over, but rather he left provisions available to the poor, so that they could come and take what they needed as if it had no owner. We also find this reflected in the story of Rav Abba, who would toss money behind him as he walked so that the poor could come and take it (*Kesubos* 67b).

❈ ❈ ❈

. . . לֹא תְאַמֵּץ אֶת־לְבָבְךָ וְלֹא תִקְפֹּץ אֶת־יָדְךָ מֵאָחִיךָ הָאֶבְיוֹן. כִּי־פָתֹחַ תִּפְתַּח אֶת־יָדְךָ לוֹ . . . — *you shall not harden your heart or close your hand against your destitute brother. Rather, you shall open you hand to him . . .* (15:7-8).

I n teaching the *mitzvah* of charity, the Torah says, *you shall not harden your heart or close your hand,* and then says, *you shall open your hand to him* and provide whatever the poor person needs. What the giver feels, and whether he gives from hand to hand, is seemingly not the essence of the *mitzvah.* The *mitzvah* is to ensure that the poor person receives what he needs. It does not matter whether the money is in the hand of the benefactor, or whether it is locked up somewhere, or buried in the ground, or whether the benefactor tells the poor person to go and get the money from wherever it happens to be. All that has to do with the manner of fulfilling the *mitzvah,* and usually the Torah does not concern itself with such things. For example, the Torah says we must dwell in the *succah,* and take the *lulav* in our hand, but nothing is said about building the *succah,* or cutting the *lulav.* We are expected to know by ourselves how to enable ourselves to do the *mitzvah.* Similarly, the Torah could have said we must give charity, and we would know how to do so. Why, then, does the Torah speak of the giver's feelings?

The answer is that there is a separate *mitzvah* that the poor person should not have to convince one to give, and wait for him to find the money. Instead, one's heart and hand must be ready for the *mitzvah,* so that as soon as asked he is ready and able to give. Thus, the *mitzvah* is to prepare oneself to be *willing* to give. Then the Torah states further that even if one cannot convince himself that he wants to give, he must give anyway. Even if he did not feel the *mitzvah* in his heart, one should not regret having given and think of it as lost money, for Hashem will not only make up what he gave, but also will bless him far beyond the amount that he gave.

This is similar to the explanation that I have given in the verse *If you will lend money to My nation* (Shemos 22:24), where I explained there is *one* mitzvah to lend, and a separate *mitzvah* to wish to lend. The same thing applies here to the *mitzvah* of charity.

❧ ❧ ❧

וְאַף לַאֲמָתְךָ תַּעֲשֶׂה־כֵּן — *even to your maidservant shall you do the same* (15:17).

T his *parashah* describes several laws concerning Jewish slaves. One is that upon their leaving, the master must provide the former slave with a generous gift (*ha'anakah*). Another law

DARASH MOSHE ON THE TORAH

described in the *parashah,* is that if a Jewish slave refuses to go free at the end of the maximum initial period of slavery (that is, at the end of six years), then the master can take him to the door of the court, and drive an awl through the slave's ear into the doorpost (*retziyah*). If this is done, the slave may remain in slavery until the Jubilee. At the end of the verse describing the *retziyah,* it is stated: *even to your maidservant you shall do the same.* *Rashi* points out that this last statement only refers to the law of the gift at the end of the term of slavery. The law of the awl does not apply to a maidservant. This is difficult to see in the verse, since the maidservant reference is made immediately after the law of *retziyah* and much later than the law of the gift.

The reason that *Rashi's* application must be true is this: The procedure of *retziyah* is similar to a new sale of one's self. A woman may never sell herself. Only a father may sell his daughter, and that right of sale is limited to the time before the daughter reaches the age of twelve and one half. Thus, neither the father nor the daughter can possibly allow the procedure of *retziyah.* On the other hand, the law of the gift certainly can apply to a maidservant, because a girl sold by her father is in a status similar to that of a man sold involuntarily by the court, in whose case the rule of the gift is explicitly applied. Therefore, it applies equally to a maidservant.

❧ ❧ ❧

כָּל־הַבְּכוֹר אֲשֶׁר יִוָּלֵד בִּבְקָרְךָ וּבְצֹאנְךָ הַזָּכָר תַּקְדִּישׁ לַה׳
אֱלֹקֶיךָ — *Every firstborn male that is born in your cattle and in your flock, you shall sanctify to* HASHEM, *your God* (15:19).

In the *parashah* of the firstborn animal, the *bechor* (15:19), the Torah uses the term *takdish* — you shall sanctify — the *bechor.* This teaches that there is a *mitzvah* to sanctify the firstborn, despite the fact that the animal is no less holy if the owner does not sanctify it. This innate holiness is such, that according to one opinion, a firstborn animal is included in the category of *"davar ha'assur"* — things that are holy or proscribed by definition, with no component of human intent or will. Similarly, the *mitzvah* of the nullification of *chametz* before Pesach requires that we nullify and abandon ownership of our *chametz,* although even without that act the *chametz* automatically becomes ownerless as Pesach begins. Still, one is personally obligated to nullify his *chametz.* Only if one has personally nullified his *chametz* will he avoid the *issur* of *"baal yeiro'eh"* — "no *chametz* of yours shall be seen." If he has not, then despite the fact that the *chametz* is automatically rendered ownerless with the advent of *Yom Tov,* he will transgress the *issur* of *baal yeiro'eh.*

We see from this that we ourselves must accept and reaffirm these *mitzvos,* and not do them only as a result of our oath to follow the Torah which we swore at *Har Sinai.* Even now, each person must consciously accept these *mitzvos.* He benefits thereby by fulfilling the *mitzvah* of sanctifying the *bechor,* and he avoids the *issur* of *baal yeiro'eh.*

This lesson applies to all the *mitzvos.* Hashem wishes that we accept them anew and reaffirm them, even though no practical difference in *halachah* results from the failure to consciously reaffirm them. This is what *Chazal* mean when they said, "Approach the *mitzvos* as if they were given to you on this very day."

פרשת שופטים
Parashas Shoftim

שֹׁפְטִים וְשֹׁטְרִים תִּתֶּן־לְךָ — *Judges and offi-
cers shall you appoint* (16:18).

The Torah phrases the *mitzvah* of appointing judges by saying,
titein lecha — you shall appoint. Another way to understand this
verse is to read it as saying, "appoint yourselves (as judges)."
This means that every man is obligated to study the entire Torah to the
point that his opinions on all matters are reliable and that he is worthy of
being a judge and a teacher of the Torah. The obligation to give charity
does not mean that we are required to attain wealth in order to
completely fulfill the *mitzvah* of charity; only if we do become wealthy do
we have the greater obligations of the wealthy. No one is obligated to
learn the science of medicine in order to heal the sick; but if one does
attain that knowledge, he does become obligated to do so. But the
obligation to appoint judges makes it incumbent on everyone to study
Torah from his early youth, from the age of six till the end of our days.
Although of 1,000 who make the attempt, only one does become
qualified to decide *halachah,* each person must work to the extent of his
ability. We are not required to reach the ultimate goal of the *mitzvah,* but
only to do as much as we can with what we are given. If a person tries his
best, and is not lazy, what he fails to attain is not his fault. But in truth, if
a person does try his hardest, Hashem *Yisbarach* will help him to
become a judge and leader of the nation, and he will truly merit to
perform this *mitzvah* in the fullest sense.

❀ ❀ ❀

וְשָׁפְטוּ אֶת־הָעָם מִשְׁפַּט־צֶדֶק . . . וְלֹא־תִקַּח שֹׁחַד —
and they shall judge the people with righteous judgment . . . and you shall not accept a bribe (16:18-19).

It would seen that once the Torah says, *they shall judge the people with righteous judgment* (in verse 18), obviously we are prohibited from taking bribes! The answer is that the perversion of justice mentioned here refers to what happens when a person relies on himself too readily. He may be a great man, well versed in the law and intellectually keen, but if he does not ponder the matter at hand carefully, he perverts the law. If he is a scholar, this type of negligent error is the equivalent of an intentional perversion of the law. As Rav Yehudah says (*Avos* 4:13 and *Bava Metzia* 33b), a scholar's error is considered willful.

Along the same lines, the prohibition from taking bribes refers to a different sort of problem. Once a person has stated an opinion, he tends to expend great effort to defend that opinion. This is included in the prohibition from taking a bribe, because his self-interest blinds him to the truth. Instead, he must re-examine his earlier decision with all his ability — just as if he had never made any decisions in this matter. Only then will he be able to make just and true determinations of *halachah*.

❧ ❧ ❧

וְשָׁפְטוּ אֶת־הָעָם מִשְׁפַּט־צֶדֶק — *and they shall judge the people with righteous judgment* (16:18).

The first verse in this *parashah* tells us to appoint judges that *shall judge the people with righteous judgment.* It seems clear that as far as the actual judgments rendered, there is no need to say that the judges must provide *righteous judgment,* because it is only righteous judgment that is any judgment at all. Perhaps this caution is addressed to the people who are responsible for appointing the judges, telling them that they should find experienced and righteous judges.

We can also understand this to refer to the judge himself: In certain matters, a judge can appoint himself to a position; namely, by choosing to teach Torah to students, to influence their behavior, and to help them find their path. A judge may, and indeed is obligated, to seek students, and even to establish *yeshivos,* to spread the Torah. But he must evaluate himself. If he has the character and spiritual magnitude necessary to be a teacher, he must seek the opportunity to teach. If he does not, he must recognize that fact and refrain.

❧ ❧ ❧

וְשָׁפְטוּ אֶת־הָעָם מִשְׁפַּט־צֶדֶק — *and they shall judge the people with righteous judgment* (16:18).

T hey shall judge the people with righteous judgment is not stated as a command intended to warn the nation to choose judges that will be righteous, for this is implicit in the basic concept of choosing people to do justice. Even so, the Torah needed to warn the judges, *You shall not pervert justice.* This is because with the passage of time, a judge will find that many people so strongly want a judge to do as they wish that they will apply tremendous pressure to him. Even if he is a great Torah scholar and extremely righteous, he needs to be warned not to listen to them, and to withstand all trials and tribulations in the name of justice.

❧ ❧ ❧

לֹא־תַטֶּה מִשְׁפָּט — *You shall not pervert judgment* (16:19).

Y ou shall not pervert judgment means that one may not make a judgment on the basis of first impressions, but must put all his ability and intelligence to the task. If a person does not investigate properly, and errs in judgment, the inadvertent error is considered intentional, as the Gemara says in Tractate *Bava Metiza* (33b).

The literal meaning of the verse, referring to actual perversion of justice, is very difficult to understand, because if one intentionally perverts justice, then he is not a judge at all; and such a warning would not be addressed to judges. On the other hand, *you shall not accept a bribe* is properly addressed to judges, because this refers to a judge that accepts not an actual bribe, but accepts payment from one party which simply covers the wages he lost from his usual employment due to time spent sitting in judgment, as is evident from the Gemara in Tractate

Kesubos (105a). Even if he undertakes to judge the case honestly, he will actually be incapable of seeing fault in the party that paid for his time. A possible explanation of *You shall not pervert judgment* is that when a judge is forced by the exigencies of the times to make a temporary extraordinary ruling, he must be absolutely certain that he is doing so exclusively for Hashem, without any ulterior motive.

❦ ❦ ❦

צֶדֶק צֶדֶק תִּרְדֹּף — *Righteousness, righteousness shall you pursue* (16:20).

Chazal comment (*Sanhedrin* 32b), "Journey to find the outstanding courts; to Rabbi Eliezer in Lod, to Rabbi Akiva in Beror Chayil, etc." This seems to be contrary to the rule that *Chazal* were lenient in defining the qualifications of judges, and do not even require special certification for the individuals comprising the court. How, then, can *Chazal* say one should journey to the most famous and outstanding courts?

The underlying message here is this: When a judge errs, his negligence is not limited to the moment he sat down in judgment, but extends back to all the time that he did not devote the proper diligence to his studies from his youth to that day. Had he taken the proper approach to his studies, he would not have erred. Therefore, *Chazal* say, "follow Rabbi Eliezer and Rabbi Akiva," i.e. that the judges should learn from the greatest and most outstanding courts and thereby avoid error and do justice.

Indeed, this lesson can be applied to each and every one of us. Although not every man is a judge, the fact is that one cannot ask others every question that arises, and so each of us decides the majority of our halachic questions for ourselves. Also, one must at least know what needs to be asked of a judge. Therefore the Torah tells all of us to pursue justice by seeking out the outstanding court — the best teachers we can find.

❦ ❦ ❦

עַל־פִּי שְׁנַיִם עֵדִים . . . — *By the testimony of two witnesses* . . . (17:6).

In laying out the death penalty for an idolater, the Torah says, *By the testimony of two witnesses or three witnesses shall the condemned person be put to death; he shall not be put to death by the testimony of a single witness.* The testimony of one witness is actually never sufficient in cases involving any sort of determination of liability, even one of much lower severity than liability to capital punishment. Why, then, does the Torah have to restate this rule here?

We may explain that this is in order to teach us that if a solitary witness comes before a judge, even though he may be generally considered honest, and even though the sin he accuses the other person of is of the greatest severity and a deprecation of Hashem, the judge must be careful not to let his zealousness for Hashem's honor convince him to accept the testimony. The judge's zealousness may make him believe the words of the witness, and, outraged, he might be tempted to act on those words in order to eradicate such vile behavior from the community. But this behavior is incorrect. Even when the sin of idolatry is involved, Hashem does not desire zealotry which is contrary to the rules of the Torah. If a court takes a life on the basis of a single witness' testimony, they are not acting as a court, but rather as murderers.

We see this idea in the story mentioned in the Gemara in Tractate *Pesachim* (113b). The Gemara says that Tuvia sinned, and he was seen by Zigud. Zigud, knowing that he was the only witness, nevertheless testified against Tuvia. The court not only did not punish Tuvia, but instead punished Zigud with lashes for his talebearing. Zigud was astonished, and asked, "Tuvia sins and Zigud is lashed?" And the court responded, "Yes. You knew you were the only witness, and that your words would not be accepted. All you have done is spread tales about a man not shown to be guilty, and the Torah says, 'You shall not be a bearer of tales.' " It appears from that story that Zigud was honest, for the Gemara uses the expression "Tuvia sinned," indicating that we can fairly assume that he did indeed sin. Even so, Zigud transgressed the sin of talebearing, and he was punished for that. Even involving the worst sins, we can only follow the rules of the Torah. Not only did Zigud not accomplish what he set out to do, he actually transgressed the very serious sin of talebearing. There is another point to be made here; although Zigud knew for a fact that he was bearing tales about a wicked person, having witnessed Tuvia's sin himself, this did not absolve him from the sin of talebearing, since the world at large did not know what Zigud knew about Tuvia's character.

I have already written about this concept in discussing the rights of a blood-redeemer — a relative given the right to exact justice from his relative's murderer who was freed on a technicality. Although in some cases he is granted immunity if he avenges his relative, the law is that if he saw the actual murder, he may not kill the murderer. Only the court can investigate and interrogate the witnesses and grant leave to the relative to mete out justice. Now, what is the reason for this law? Certainly, it is not logical to say that a relative that witnesses a murder is allowed to kill the murderer, yet might later be killed himself for this act since he cannot prove that he had the right to do what he did. Rather, we must say that since the facts of the case are not known through properly admitted and examined witnesses, even if this person saw the act himself, he may not act on his knowledge. This is exactly the same as the story of Zigud and the lesson taught here in the *parashah* of idolatry.

※ ※ ※

תָּמִים תִּהְיֶה עִם ה' אֱלֹקֶיךָ — *You shall be whole-hearted with HASHEM, your God* (18:13).

Rashi explains that the word *tamim*, which is translated as "wholehearted," also refers to a flawless faith in Hashem. The verse thus means that one should walk in flawless faith with Hashem, and not try to divine the future.

There are two very different aspects to this instruction. One is that we must overcome our natural curiosity to know what the future holds. Not only may we not query diviners, sorcerers, or astrologers, but we actually do not have any permission to know what will happen. Indeed, a prophet is prohibited from revealing his knowledge of what is to come unless Hashem explicitly commands him to do so.

The second aspect is a very important instruction as to how we should form our hopes and expectations. A person may not hold back from attempting an urgent and important task, such as founding a *yeshivah,* just because his common sense tells him that he cannot possibly raise enough money that such a task requires, and he may not despair from doing anything. If it is an urgent and important need, he must do it, even though he knows that in the natural course of events there is no future in it. Be of flawless faith, and look to Hashem. He will assuredly help you, and will place the desire to help you and finance your work into the hearts of many people. If not for righteous men who lived by the ideal of this verse, no *yeshivos* would have been built in America. *Chazal* have said that one who has just enough for today, and asks, "What will I have to eat tomorrow?" is of little faith. So too, those who have the vision to found *yeshivos* and spread Torah should not worry about how they will have the strength to maintain those *yeshivos*. Hashem will certainly help them.

Similarly, all Torah scholars must fulfill the instruction of this verse. They should not worry about how they will earn a living until they actually must support a wife and children. They should not study in their youth the fields of knowledge or skill which are used in earning a living. Those concerns should be left for the time that they actually become obligatory. Leave the affairs of the future in Hashem's hands.

❧ ❧ ❧

תָּמִים תִּהְיֶה עִם ה' אֱלֹקֶיךָ — *You shall be whole-hearted with HASHEM, your God* (18:13).

From *Rashi's* explanation of the *mitzvah, You shall be whole-hearted with Hashem,* we see that *Rashi* means that people should not even want to try to uncover the secrets of the future, even through a prophet. Instead, we must go in faith and trust that whatever Hashem does will be for the best, as long as we do what we are obligated to do by going in Hashem's path, fulfilling *mitzvos,* and studying the Torah. The primary duty of the prophet is to rebuke the people, and only occasionally to reveal the future when Hashem so wishes. Although we find that the *Urim VeTumim* worn by the *Kohen Gadol* was consulted when a declaration of war was being considered, this is only because it was absolutely necessary to do so. When a war which was not mandated by the need to conquer the Land of Israel was being considered, the obvious threat to life would automatically prohibit the war unless the *Urim VeTumim* was consulted.

Perhaps the fact that that prophets were occasionally consulted for mundane matters, such as the episode when Shaul was asked as to the whereabouts of certain lost mules, can be explained by saying that a long and tedious search would result in time lost from study. All cases where we find that a prophet was asked to reveal hidden things must have a valid explanation for the departure from the general rule of *You shall be wholehearted with Hashem.*

❀ ❀ ❀

יָדֵינוּ לֹא שָׁפְכוּ אֶת־הַדָּם הַזֶּה וְעֵינֵינוּ לֹא רָאוּ — *"Our hands have not spilled this blood, and our eyes did not see"* (21:7).

If a murdered man is found near a city, and there are no witnesses to his death, the Torah says that the *eglah arufah* procedure must be followed. A heifer is killed, and then the elders of the city say the verse, *"Our hands have not spilled this blood, and our eyes did not see."* The next verse in the *parashah* says, *"Atone for Your people Israel. . . ."* The Torah does not say who it is that says the second verse beginning with *"Atone."* The Mishnah in *Sotah* (46a) and *Targum Onkelos* say that the *Kohanim* respond to the elders by saying this verse. But why doesn't the Torah make this clear?

The answer is that the identity of the speakers is really evident from the content of the verse. The words *"Our hands have not spilled"* must be said by the members of the court, who descend to the depths of the law. They should realize that if a murder occurs even in a distant city they should be worried that perhaps they, too, are guilty to a degree. They should have taught the Torah properly, and had they done so, human life would not be so little valued by some individual. We see that the members of the court carry this responsibility from the story of the concubine of Giv'ah (*Shoftim* ch. 19-20), where the members of the court shared the blame. They also should have taught the laws of accompanying travelers and the laws of charity, as *Chazal* have explained here. The *Kohanim,* on the other hand, are more concerned with the need for forgiveness. They have to realize that they can never despair, God forbid, and that even if there is such a terrible sin, forgiveness is possible if the heifer is brought and the people repent. Therefore there is no need for the Torah to clarify who says this second verse.

A general lesson to learn from this *parashah* is that one must be very meticulous even in his choice of words, because if people recognize that a person is a Torah scholar, they will observe not only the way he acts, but also what he says and the manner in which he expresses himself.

❀ ❀ ❀

פרשת כי תצא
Parashas Ki Seitzei

וּמָכֹר לֹא־תִמְכְּרֶנָּה בַּכָּסֶף — *but you may not sell her for money* (21:14).

I f a soldier sees a woman of the enemy nation during battle, the Torah allows him to take her back with him and force her into conversion with the understanding that he will ultimately marry her. If the marriage ultimately does not take place, he must allow her to go where she chooses, and he *may not sell her for money*. This is not out of respect for any virtue on her part. On the contrary; he would normally be allowed to take her as a servant or to sell her. But since he enjoyed a marital relationship with her for a time, the Torah forbids him from dealing with her as a slave. This freedom may result in her returning to idolatry as before, for although he does not send her home, nothing prevents her from returning there, while if he could sell her as a servant she could not do so.

We see from this how highly the Torah values good character traits. Here, the concept of gratefulness is so overriding that we encourage its development and do not take into consideration the real possibility that she might fall into sin. Similarly, the Torah says that we may not despise the Mitzri or the Edomi. Although they certainly deserve disdain, our need to nurture our good character traits overrides any other consideration, and so we focus on our debt of gratitude to them and disregard the many reasons we have for scorning them. Similarly, although *"those who hate You, O Hashem, I hate them"* (*Tehillim* 139:21), it is very clear that this hatred is permissible only when the person is motivated by the desire to serve Hashem. If there is any other motive, it is forbidden to hate. This is not at all like other *mitzvos*, where other motives do not preclude the fulfillment of the *mitzvah*.

❀ ❀ ❀

לֹא־יִהְיֶה כְלִי־גֶבֶר עַל־אִשָּׁה וְלֹא־יִלְבַּשׁ גֶּבֶר שִׂמְלַת אִשָּׁה כִּי תוֹעֲבַת ה' אֱלֹקֶיךָ כָּל־עֹשֵׂה אֵלֶּה — *Male garb shall not be on a woman, and a man shall not wear a feminine garment, for anyone who does so is an abomination of* HASHEM (22:5).

We find the description *an abomination of Hashem* applied to the prohibition against men wearing feminine clothing and vice versa, and exactly the same expression concerning false weights and measures. It is also found in the invalidation for Temple use of an animal used to purchase the services of a harlot, or used in barter for a dog. It is also found in the Torah's prohibition of remarriage of a divorced couple if the woman had been married to someone else in the interim. The usual and expected use of this description would be concerning incestuous relationships. Why is it used in these cases?

The reason why this term does apply equally well to these cases is this: A person might put himself in a position where sinning would be easier, and tell himself that by tantalizing himself and withstanding temptation he will be doubly rewarded. For example, a man might put on women's clothing, knowing that by masquerading as a woman, sinning would be easy and hard to detect, and think that he does so in order to overcome the greater temptation and thereby earn great merit. The Torah tells us that such thoughts are an abomination of Hashem. Man must flee temptation out of fear of the possibility of sinning. Perhaps he will not be able to overcome his Evil Inclination, and he will fall into sin. *Chazal* instituted that every morning we pray, "bring us not to temptation." [The fact that *Chazal* say that the greatest level of penitence is when the penitent is faced with the same opportunity to sin that he faced before, and overcomes it, does not, God forbid, mean that he should orchestrate such an event. This would be an abomination to Hashem. It only means that if such an opportunity arose inadvertently, and he fled the sin, this proves the genuineness of his repentance. He should try to reach such a level of purity that Hashem, Who sees to the depths of the soul, can testify that he would withstand such a test. But the penitent cannot possibly know this, and must fear that he would not withstand the test, and must therefore constantly try to reach higher and higher levels of purity through repentance.]

This is exactly the concept of false weights and measures; it is prohibited to keep such tools of deception in one's possession even if one has no intention to ever use them, as is made clear in the Gemara in *Bava Basra* (89b). If one keeps such measures because he is confident he would never use them, this is an abomination of Hashem.

In the case of an animal used as wages of a harlot, she might think that bringing the animal as a sacrifice, and thereby ridding herself of the benefit of the sin, cleanses her. Similarly, one who acquires a sheep in trade for a dog, which is considered a threat to public safety, might wish to be forgiven by bringing the sheep as a sacrifice. This is also an abomination of Hashem, because repentance only comes through *teshuvah*. There is no such thing as washing away even a minor sin by doing a big *mitzvah*. Certainly one cannot depend on this concept of buying his way into forgiveness, for Hashem does not take bribes. A person is rewarded for the *mitzvah,* and remains liable for the sin. *Ramban* and others also explain that this is the reason the Torah invalidates such animals for sacrificial use. I add here that this also explains why the Torah uses the term *abomination.*

We also find that certain people wish to fulfill all their wicked desires, and search out means of doing so which are technically legitimate. The Torah says that this, too, is an abomination. Instead, one must learn to distance himself as far as possible from such lust. So, if some wicked persons desire each other's wives, they might think of a way to satisfy that abominable desire by divorcing their wives, marrying each other's divorced wife, and then divorcing again and remarrying their own wives. The Torah prohibits this, and tells us that this is an abomination. This is equally true in any case where a person attempts to satisfy an illicit desire by arranging some circumstance which would enable him to do so within the letter of the law. The Torah tells us that this, too, is an abomination.

❦ ❦ ❦

פֶּן־תִּקְדַּשׁ הַמְלֵאָה ... — *lest the growth* ... *become forbidden* (22:9).

The Torah says that we may not plant *kil'ei hakerem* — grapevines and grain growing in close proximity — *lest the ... become forbidden.* This implies that the prohibition of planting such a mixture is tied to the fact that the resulting growth is prohibited. This, however, is difficult; for we cannot interpret the verse as saying that the fact that the growth is forbidden is the reason for the *basic* prohibition to plant them together, because in the case of *kil'ei zeraim* — any different species of food crops planted together — planting them together is forbidden even though we *may* eat the growth! Therefore, we must say that the fact that the growth of a *kil'ei hakerem* field is forbidden is the basis for a *new and separate* prohibition to plant them together. This separate prohibition teaches us that the Torah forbids us from causing any permitted thing to become forbidden. Perhaps this is why Hashem commanded Yehoshua that although the spoils of Jericho were forbidden, the spoils of the conquests that followed should be given to the people (see *Yehoshua* 8:2, and *Sanhedrin* 44a).

❀ ❀ ❀

עַל־דְּבַר אֲשֶׁר לֹא־קִדְּמוּ אֶתְכֶם בַּלֶּחֶם וּבַמַּיִם ... —
because of the fact that they did not greet you
with bread and water . . . (23:5).

The *Ramban* says that the nation of Ammon sinned by hiring Bilam to curse the Jews, and the nation of Moab sinned by refusing to sell the Jews bread and water as they traversed the Wilderness. Although the sin of Ammon is certainly more egregious, the punishments of each nation are the same: We may not seek peace with either nation, and neither Ammonite nor Moabite males may join the *Bnei Yisrael* by marriage, even if they become proselytes. The reason for this equivalence of punishment is because the sin of Moab expressed very wicked character traits. If they could have, they would have hired Bilam, or even killed the Jews with their own hands. After their actual sin, the next step would have been to come to the greater sins of deciding to and attempting to kill. Therefore, they and Ammon are considered equally sinful. Although *HaKadosh Baruch Hu* did not allow them to carry out their plans, the nations are punished for wicked intent as if they had acted on their decisions, even if in fact they were prevented from doing so by external conditions.

❀ ❀ ❀

לֹא־תַשִּׁיךְ לְאָחִיךְ — *You shall not cause your brother to take interest* (23:20).

W e are prohibited from any participation in loans between Jews in which the borrower is obligated to pay interest. Here, this law is addressed to the borrower, who is warned not to agree to such a loan. In *Vayikra* 25:37, it is addressed to the lender, who is warned not to make an interest-bearing loan. Here, the Torah says that we may pay interest to a non-Jewish lender. Certainly, we also may make an interest-bearing loan to a non-Jewish borrower. The reason the Torah only explicitly states that we may pay interest to a non-Jew is because the Torah desires peace in the world, and by stating that we may pay interest to a non-Jewish lender, it provides a reason for the allowance to take interest from a non-Jewish borrower. It only stands to reason that if we may pay interest, we ought to be able to request interest. Therefore, the nations have no basis for a complaint against the Torah. Of course, according to the *Rambam* who holds that such taking is a *mitzvah,* certainly that is the reason to mention this aspect.

❊ ❊ ❊

אֵיפָה שְׁלֵמָה וָצֶדֶק יִהְיֶה־לָּךְ — *a full fect and honest measure shall you have . . .* (25:15).

R ashi explains the verse to be saying that if you keep a full and honest measure, you will have — i.e. you will be blessed with plenty. This seems to contradict the lesson of *Chazal* that only the giving of tithes invokes the promise of wealth. We must say that honesty in business dealings provides a receptacle for receiving Hashem's blessings. After all, what benefit would one derive from wealth and blessing if he cannot receive and contain those blessings? Thus, while tithing may cause one to *merit* wealth, dealing honestly will enable him to receive it.

Similarly, one must provide an appropriate receptacle for success in the study of the Torah, for only then can he succeed in the many aspects of his studies.

❊ ❊ ❊

פרשת כי תבא
Parashas Ki Savo

"I — הִגַּדְתִּי הַיּוֹם לַה' אֱלֹקֶיךָ כִּי־בָאתִי אֶל־הָאָרֶץ
declare today to HASHEM, your God, that I have
come to the land . . ." (26:3).

In the *parashah* of *bikkurim,* the Torah says that we must bring the new fruit to the *Kohen* in the *Beis Hamikdash,* and recite the following to the *Kohen:* "I declare today to Hashem, your God, that I have come to the land that Hashem swore to our forefathers. . . .," although this person's ancestors already came to the land and he was born there, and did not *come* there himself. What is meant is that since each day is newly born, in that every day is a renewal of the act of Creation of the universe, each day must be evaluated independently. If one has done a meritorious act on that day, he can say that that one day has meaning, and he can make a good accounting of his life and presence on earth for that day. If one day passes wherein a person has done nothing important, he must recognize it as a wasted day, with nothing of lasting value having been accomplished. This is true of every day of one's life, in or out of *Eretz Yisrael.*

❧ ❧ ❧

הִגַּדְתִּי הַיּוֹם לַה' אֱלֹקֶיךָ . . . — *"I declare today to*
HASHEM, your God . . ." (26:3).

When we bring the first of the harvest, the *bikkurim,* to the *Kohen* in the Holy Temple, we say, "I declare today to Hashem, your G-d, that I have come to the land that Hashem

---

swore to our forefathers to give us." This is said even by a person that was born on land that was owned by his ancestors, who did not come to the land at all. This is because by his act of bringing the *bikkurim* — which are precious to the one that raised the crop, while to the *Kohen* that receives them they are no different than any other fruits — he proclaims that he has come to the land which Hashem promised. That is, he recognizes that this land is not just one place among many to live in, but a place wherein we can acquire perfection. Even by observing material things in this land, we learn that everything is His. So only after giving away the first fruits, by which he recognizes through an overt act Who the true Master of the land is, can he say that he knows that all that he has was given to him by Hashem, including his home and all he owns, as a blessing, and that his ownership is defined by the will of Hashem. Thus, it is through his act of bringing the *bikkurim* that he demonstrates and evidences this understanding, and so it is his act of bringing that declares this fundamental idea to the world and proves his faith.

❦ ❦ ❦

— וְאָמַרְתָּ לִפְנֵי ה' אֱלֹקֶיךָ בִּעַרְתִּי הַקֹּדֶשׁ מִן־הַבַּיִת . . .
Then you shall say before HASHEM, your God, "I have removed the holy things from the house . . ." (26:13).

The Torah prescribes a formal declaration which every person that has given tithes must make every fourth and seventh year of the tithe cycle. This is called the "Confession of the *Maaser* Tithes." This appellation is unusual for two reasons. Firstly, because this declaration states that the person fulfilled his obligations concerning these special portions, and so the term "confession" requires explanation. Secondly, this declaration refers to the *terumah* portion of the *Kohen*, the *maaser* portion of the *Levi*, and the second *maaser*, which must be brought to Jerusalem and consumed there. Despite the generality of its theme, this declaration is generally referred to as "the confession of the *second maaser* tithe." Why do we focus on the second tithe?

We can explain as follows. If a person knows that the time will come when he will have to stand and say that he properly fulfilled all his obligations regarding the various tithes, he will be very motivated to repent for his lapses, and to make sure to fulfill his obligations as completely as possible. It is a stronger motivator than the usual oral confession, wherein he admits his sins and states his regret. Here, he has to stand before Hashem, Who knows our deepest secrets, and say, "I have done all that You commanded me." People will be frightened of this prospect, and therefore will be very diligent in fulfilling their obligations, so that they can honestly make this declaration. Accordingly, the declaration can properly be referred to as a "confession."

This would be true in the case of a person that recognizes that our personal responsibilities have not changed from the time of the giving of the Torah till today. Even in a generation when many people do not act as they should, he would still be afraid to say he has done Hashem's will if he has not. But some people look at the people around them, and they think, "These people are not living as they ought to, and compared to them, the little that I am doing is enough to satisfy my responsibilities to Hashem." Such a person will find it easy to make the confession even if he has not really complied. Only if he has sanctified himself and studied diligently will he understand that even if he compares favorably to the people of his generation, he has not necessarily fulfilled his obligations. The function of the second tithe is to teach this very lesson. The second tithe requires that a person take a significant portion of his produce (10 percent), and use it only in Jerusalem. This means that he will have to set aside a considerate amount of his time to remain in Jerusalem, where he will be in an atmosphere of Torah study, and will witness the *Kohanim* doing the Temple service. This is why the Torah says concerning the second *maaser, in order that you learn to fear* (14:23). Proper observance of this obligation thus requires the dedication of a large part of a man's life. Through this dedication, he will come to understand that there is no difference in the degree of our responsibilities and obligations, whether we live in an elevated or lowly generation or place. We must always remember that we must fulfill all the *mitzvos* just as the early generations fulfilled them. Only then can we truly say, "I have done as You commanded me."

❈ ❈ ❈

אֶת־ה' הֶאֱמַרְתָּ הַיּוֹם לִהְיוֹת לְךָ לֵאלֹקִים וְלָלֶכֶת בִּדְרָכָיו וְלִשְׁמֹר חֻקָּיו וּמִצְוֹתָיו וּמִשְׁפָּטָיו וְלִשְׁמֹעַ בְּקֹלוֹ — *You have distinguished HASHEM today to be a God for you, and to walk in His ways, and to observe His decrees, His commandments, and His statutes, and to hearken to His voice* (26:17).

Why does the verse state *and to hearken to His voice,* after already having said *to walk in His ways, and to observe His decrees, His commandments, and His statutes?* Certainly one who observes all of these laws has already hearkened to God's voice!

The answer is that we must do the *mitzvos* in a manner that will be pleasing and acceptable before Hashem. We cannot do them as one would pay a debt, but instead with love, joy, and graciousness. *Chazal* have said this by saying that one who prays by rote, his prayer is not a supplication (*Berachos* 28b). We see this concept demonstrated when we examine the difference between one who pays off a loan and one who gives a gift. When a lender awaits repayment of a loan, he only hopes and wishes that he will be paid back on time. When the borrower does pay, he does so under pressure from the lender, and with a jaundiced eye. When one gives a gift he is also, in a sense, repaying a debt, for clearly he feels a debt of gratitude to the recipient of the gift for some past favor or kindness. But when he gives the gift, he does so with a joyful eye. This is because a debt of gratitude cannot be enforced, but instead the giver presses himself to give, and so he gives with joy and love. A loan, on the other hand, is a binding obligation, and so it is fulfilled only to the extent of the lender's ability to enforce it. Logic would dictate that the opposite should be the case, but this is the nature of man. We need to feel that our indebtedness stems from our recognition of a favor bestowed upon us, and not from an obligation. If we think about all of Hashem's kindnesses to us, we certainly should develop a tangible sense of gratitude, and do the *mitzvos* with joy and love. This is why it says *to hearken to His voice,* which means to do so out of love so that He will find our actions pleasing.

With this in mind, we can understand all the various terms used in the verse to describe the path to holiness. 1) *To be a God for you* refers to faith. 2) *To walk in His ways* means to endeavor to emulate His traits. 3) *To observe His decrees, His commandments, and His statutes* means we should do meritorious acts as we were commanded, and not fashion philosophies about other paths to fulfilling His will. 4) *To hearken to His voice* means to do with love and joy and a full heart. Corresponding to these are the four things by which *Hashem has distinguished you.* 1) *To be for Him a treasured people* refers to the precious treasure which comes on the heels of understanding what faith in Hashem means. 2) *And to observe all His commandments* means that once a person understands that he must go in the path of Hashem and emulate His traits, Hashem will grace him with the ability to fulfill all His *mitzvos* without hindrance. 3) *To make you supreme* means that you will not feel lowly and worthless, for if one fulfills the will of Hashem, he knows that he is the most important creature in the universe. 4) *So that you will be a holy people* teaches that once we hearken to the voice of Hashem, and do His will with love, joy, and a full heart, we will have achieved the holiness of the righteous.

❈ ❈ ❈

אֶת־ה' הֶאֱמַרְתָּ הַיּוֹם. . . וַה' הֶאֱמִירְךָ הַיּוֹם. . . — *You have distinguished* HASHEM *today. . . And* HASHEM *has distinguished you today. . .* (26:17-18).

The words *he'emarta* and *he'emircha* are unusual, and *Rashi* says that no clear evidence of their meaning is found elsewhere in the Torah. But *Rashi* then says that he has found a similar use of the term in *Tehillim* (94:4), where the word is used to mean "glorify." *Rashi's* phrasing implies however, that he does not find that this meaning fits the verse here.

We can explain it, however, thusly: We see that what one person finds beautiful is not necessarily beautiful to others, neither in terms of actual beauty or in what is considered a beautiful act. Here, the verse tells us that *Bnei Yisrael* defines the concepts of beauty and glory only by what *HaKadosh Baruch Hu* considers fit and beautiful. In this merit, *HaKadosh Baruch Hu* finds whatever we do to honor Him to be beautiful and glorious.

❈ ❈ ❈

וּבָנִיתָ שָּׁם מִזְבֵּחַ. . . — *There you shall build an altar. . .* (27:5).

The Torah tells us that upon crossing the Jordan, *Bnei Yisrael* were commanded to erect altars on Mt. Eival and bring sacrifices, and rejoice before Hashem. This joy was specifically expressed on Mt. Eival, where the curses against the transgressors of the Torah were recited, because the essential making of the covenant was based on the pronouncement of punishments that would befall those who, G-d forbid, transgress the Torah. The promised reward to those who fulfill the Torah, which took place on Mt. Grizim, left open the possibility of the erroneous claim that one who is willing to waive the potential rewards may choose to not fulfill the Torah, as we find many claimed in the days of Yechezkel. It follows, then, that the threat of punishment is the inescapable fact which provides a basis for a covenant. [The rewards, in truth, are automatic and not tied to any covenant, since the Holy One, Blessed is He, does not withhold the reward of any creature, and even the nations of the world are rewarded appropriately.]

This also explains why the Torah recites the statements of curses but not the statements of blessings, despite the fact that it would seemingly be more appropriate to write the blessings and despite the fact that the blessings were recited first. The explanation is that only punishment can form the basis of a covenant. This also explains why the word *olos* (burnt offerings) in verse 6 is written out in full vocalization (*malei*);[1] it is written so to convey the fact that the accepting of the covenant by accepting responsibility and liability for punishment provides a good basis for a covenant, which in turn enables us to fully and completely fulfill the words of the Torah.

❦ ❦ ❦

> וַתָּבֹאוּ אֶל־הַמָּקוֹם הַזֶּה וַיֵּצֵא סִיחֹן מֶלֶךְ־חֶשְׁבּוֹן וְעוֹג
> . . . וַנַּכֵּם . . . וּשְׁמַרְתֶּם אֶת־דִּבְרֵי הַבְּרִית הַזֹּאת . . .
> — *Then you arrived at this place, and Sichon, king of Cheshbon, and Og . . . went out and we smote them . . . You shall observe the words of this covenant . . .* (29:6-8).

Hashem told the *Bnei Yisrael* that he miraculously brought them through the Wilderness, *"Then you arrived at this place. . . ."* and slew kings and giants. The *parashah* ends by saying, *"you shall observe the words of this covenant. . . ."* Rashi explains, "Now that you see yourselves in greatness and glory, do not 'kick out' against Hashem." This requires explanation, because the nation still had not come to greatness and glory, for they still had to battle the kings of Canaan.

We must say that since they had a strong trust in Hashem's word through Moshe, and so truly believed that they would soon destroy their enemies and inherit the land, they felt that those events were, for all practical purposes, accomplished. This was so true that Moshe felt that

---

1. I.e. with a *vav* following the *ayin;* see *Minchas Shai* to the verse.

the time had already come when he would have to worry about the haughtiness and spiritual deterioration that usually accompany wealth and honor, and so he warned them about that. Perhaps this is what Moshe meant to say when he said earlier (v.3), *"But Hashem did not give you a heart to know, or eyes to see, or ears to hear until this day."* In other words, until now their trust was not so strong that they would feel that whatever Hashem had promised was as real as things that had happened already. But now that their faith had strengthened and had reached a level of near-perfection, there was no difference between promise and fulfillment.

[*Rashi's* explanation of the earlier verse is that a man does not understand his master's deepest teachings until he reaches the age of 40, and so Hashem had been less than strict until this point. This is very difficult to understand, because if so, no one at the age of 13 should be liable for sinning; but in fact we know that after one reaches the age of 13 and physical maturity, he is responsible for his acts and punished for transgressions.]

❈ ❈ ❈

פרשת נצבים
Parashas Nitzavim

אַתֶּם נִצָּבִים הַיּוֹם כֻּלְּכֶם . . . רָאשֵׁיכֶם שִׁבְטֵיכֶם . . .
— *You are standing today, all of you . . . the*
heads of your tribes . . . (29:9).

Yਂou all standing today before Hashem, your God: the heads
of your tribes. The literal translation of the words רָאשֵׁיכֶם
שִׁבְטֵיכֶם is *your heads, your tribes. Rashi* explains that this is the
equivalent of "the heads of your tribes." The explanation for the unusual
wording is this: The Torah teaches that it is forbidden for any person to
denigrate himself by saying that because his talents are so minor, he
cannot be a great man or a leader; such humility actually is the counsel
of the Evil Inclination. Rather, every man must develop the self-esteem
to realize that he, too, can be a leader of his generation, and so he must
learn the Torah in its entirety and in great depth with all his ability, and
Hashem will aid him to reach greatness in the Torah. If he belittles
himself, saying that he will never reach greatness in Torah or good
deeds, he will never learn and never attempt to fulfill the obligation to
study the Torah properly, and nothing that he does will ever be suitable.
Therefore the Torah writes *your heads, your tribes* instead of writing *of*
your tribes, to tell us that everyone must hold himself capable of
leadership; as a result, each person will learn a great deal and do many
great deeds. As Moshe Rabbeinu said, "If only all of God's people would
be prophets!" (*Bamidbar* 11:29). Moshe Rabbeinu would not wish for
the impossible; it follows, then, that such a condition is, indeed, possible.

❧ ❧ ❧

אַתֶּם נִצָּבִים הַיּוֹם כֻּלְּכֶם לִפְנֵי ה' אֱלֹקֵיכֶם ... — *You are standing today, all of you, before HASHEM, your God ...* (29:9).

Rashi's second explanation states that at this time, when Moshe was transferring the *Bnei Yisrael* over to a new leader, Yehoshua, he made them stand up straight as a monolith. [The word for monolith, *matzeivah*, is related to the word for standing up, *nitzav*.] However, *Rashi* does not explain the meaning of this symbolism.

We can understand what *Rashi* means with what I have explained concerning the prohibition the Torah states, *You shall not erect for yourself a monolith, which Hashem hates* (16:22), which refers to an altar made of one stone. I have explained that this prohibition derives from the fact that such an altar cannot increase in size; this prohibition teaches us that man must grow from day to day in Torah and good deeds for his entire life. One can never say that since he has spent so many years doing good deeds, he needs not spend the few years he has left doing more good deeds, because in any case he has amassed so many merits. As the verse states (*Yechezkel* 18:24), *all his righteousness that he had done will not be remembered.*

We see that a monolith symbolizes a fixed spiritual state. Here, the Torah states that when Moshe handed over the *Bnei Yisrael* to Yehoshua, he made them into a monolith, in the sense that he portrayed to Yehoshua the exact state of spiritual growth they were at at that moment, and told him that it was his responsibility to see to it that they grew further.

We learn from here that every person must occasionally stand himself up as a monolith — that is, to assess his spiritual status in fear of Hashem and good deeds and Torah, in order to know how to continue growing.

❧ ❧ ❧

אַתֶּם נִצָּבִים הַיּוֹם ... — *You are standing today* ... (29:9).

Rashi explains that the curses listed in the previous *parashah* stand one up and maintain him before Hashem. What *Rashi* means is that Hashem was telling the Jews that they should not fear the Admonition which described the punishments that await a sinful generation, because those punishments need only concern those that will not listen to Hashem's Torah. It is true that certain grievous sins are punished by death, such as the transgression of the laws of the Sabbath which invokes the punishment of stoning. But those that observe the Sabbath are not stoned, and to the contrary, receive great reward. The punishment helps us to realize the severity of the transgression of the laws of Sabbath, and this helps us to be very careful to properly observe those laws. In a sense, then, the punishment "stands us up" and maintains us in the observance of Sabbath, and ensures that we are rewarded for doing so.

Similarly, the Admonition, which was addressed to whoever does not observe the Torah, inspires greater observance of the Torah, and this will lead us to merit the multitudinous blessings that come to those that do observe. This is why the Torah instructed us that upon crossing the Jordan we are to erect altars and rejoice on Mount Eival, the place where the curses were pronounced.

❧ ❧ ❧

פֶּן־יֵשׁ בָּכֶם שֹׁרֶשׁ פֹּרֶה רֹאשׁ וְלַעֲנָה — *perhaps there is among you a root flourishing with gall and wormwood* (29:17).

What does the phrase *a root flourishing with gall and wormwood* mean? If the person is wicked and a blasphemer, he could not possibly *bless himself in his heart, saying, "peace will be with me,"* for he clearly is among those who are cursed. It is also unlikely that he denies the truth of the curses entirely, for all he says is *"Peace will be with me,"* which implies that he agrees that other wicked people will be cursed, but not him.

The answer is that the verse refers to a person who heeds the Torah and the *mitzvos*, but thinks that doing so is very hard, and that he does so despite all the difficulty it causes, and so deserves great reward for withstanding such a hard test. This is the root of evil, for it is possible that with the passage of time he will become wicked when the *mitzvos* become too burdensome to him. Even if he remains righteous, his children will leave the Torah, for not everyone can be so disciplined as to overpower the natural inclination to avoid such a heavy burden. It is extremely important for people to realize that the observance of the Torah is the greatest joy. It is the easiest thing to do, for there is no free man but one who heeds the Torah. If it appears to a person that observing the Shabbos causes him a loss of potential profit, he should realize that what he gains by observing the Shabbos is much greater than what he loses. Just as people do not anguish over the cost of their new houses, and on the contrary are proud of what they have created for themselves, as is the case with all the physical things people purchase for themselves, so too, people should be joyful when the observance of the Shabbos costs them a great sum of money. If a person feels this way, there is no doubt that his children and grandchildren will fulfill the *mitzvos* of the Torah with the same joy and ease, and will never think that doing so tries the strength of their resolve.

❅ ❅ ❅

HASHEM, — וּמָל ה' אֱלֹקֶיךָ אֶת־לְבָבְךָ וְאֶת־לְבַב זַרְעֶךָ
your God, will circumcise your heart and the heart of your offspring (30:6).

Hashem, your God, will circumcise your heart and the heart of your offspring. This verse seems perplexing — whose hearts are being referred to here? Moshe knew that his generation was not going to sin, because Hashem had told him that only after his death would the nation rise and go astray. In fact, this only occurred after the death of Yehoshua and the Elders, as *Rashi* says, and even that later generation did not go into exile!

The Torah means to teach us a great lesson about the education of children. If a child knows that his parent was evil as a youth and later repented, it will be difficult to properly educate that child, even if the child wishes to emulate his parent. We see that Amon, who was born 11 years after his father Menashe already had repented, and who was certainly educated to observe the Torah of Hashem, was an evil man who worshiped idols because his father, too, had done so, as the text of *Melachim II* clearly states. This is also stated in the verse (ibid. 21:21): *He went the same way as his father had gone; he worshiped the idols that his father had worshiped.* This is because he was seduced by the Evil Inclination to believe that his father's actions as a child were the correct ones, and not his later path. Therefore the prophets say, regarding Amon, that he did not bend himself before Hashem as did Menashe his father, which means to say that although he should have followed the righteous path taken by his father after his repentance, he instead followed his father's youthful, sinful path. So the verse here teaches us a general rule; even if Hashem "circumcises the heart of the fathers," this is not enough to ensure that the children will follow in his just path, although he certainly educates them to do so. This might not help, and all the education might have no effect, and so he needs Hashem's help in "circumcising the heart of the children" too. From here we learn that such parents must exercise the greatest diligence to ensure that their children are educated in a place of Torah among teachers and friends that will be a good influence. This is true not only when the parent is totally wicked, but even if the parent was at one time wicked in one matter. Merely educating the child as to what is correct will not help, unless the parents exercise the greatest diligence to ensure an environment of Torah.

❧ ❧ ❧

וּמָל ה' אֱלֹקֶיךָ אֶת־לְבָבְךָ וְאֶת־לְבַב זַרְעֶךָ — *HASHEM, your God, will circumcise your heart and the heart of your offspring* (30:6).

The month of Elul is hinted at in the words *es livavcha v'es livav —* your heart and the heart," whose initials form the word Elul. Why were these words chosen to allude to that month? This is in order to teach us that even if a person has repented and improved himself, this is not considered to be the betterment one should accomplish in preparation for the Days of Awe if he has not seen to it that his children also will follow the path of the Torah.

❧ ❧ ❧

פרשת וילך
Parashas Vayeilech

. . . כִּי אַתָּה תָּבוֹא אֶת־הָעָם הַזֶּה . . . — . . . *for you*
shall come with this people . . . (31:7).

In this verse, Moshe told Yehoshua, *"for you shall come with this*
people to the land. . .," without according to Yehoshua the leading
role. In verse 23, however, Hashem told Yehoshua, *"for you*
shall bring *the Bnei Yisrael to the land. . .,"* implying that he
would be the sole leader. This is no contradiction, for Moshe said
nothing of his own volition. Certainly, one leader ought to seek advice in
every matter from other leaders of the generation, the elders and the
Sanhedrin. Indeed, *HaKadosh Baruch Hu* himself taught us this lesson
by saying (*Bereishis* 1:26), *"Let us make man,"* as *Rashi* explains there.
But this seeking of advice is only to help decide what to do, which is not
to say that he will do as advised by those whose counsel he sought even
when he does not agree with the advice. This is why Hashem later told
Yehoshua: That which Moshe told you meant only that you must seek
advice, to engage others in dialogue and to determine their opinions and
to consider their words, but not that you should do as they say if after
consideration you have a different viewpoint. Only one man can speak
with authority in a generation, not two. The final responsibility for all
actions taken is yours.

❁　❁　❁

וְעַתָּה כִּתְבוּ לָכֶם אֶת־הַשִּׁירָה הַזֹּאת . . . — *So now, write this song for yourselves. . . .* (31:19).

According to *Rambam*, this *mitzvah* only obligates us to write the *parashah* that follows, *Ha'azinu*. But since we are not allowed to write one *parashah* by itself, we perforce must write the entire Torah. This teaching of *Rambam* presents a difficulty: We do, after all, find that we are allowed to write individual *parshiyos* for *tefillin* and *mezuzos*. Apparently, we may write whatever *parashah* the Torah tells us is necessary for the fulfillment of a particular *mitzvah*. If the essential *mitzvah* of writing "this song" is the *parashah* of Ha'azinu, why would we be constrained from writing that *parashah* alone?

The answer is that to perceive all that is said in *Ha'azinu*, so that it influences us to repent and attain holiness, we must understand the entire Torah and become Torah scholars, each to his ability. Only then can one truly perceive what is meant in *Ha'azinu*. Thus, although the purpose of the *mitzvah* is to write and understand that one *parashah*, it is necessary to write and understand the entire Torah to do so.

❀ ❀ ❀

הַקְהִילוּ אֵלַי אֶת־כָּל־זִקְנֵי שִׁבְטֵיכֶם . . . — *Gather to me all the elders of your tribes . . .* (31:28).

Rashi explains that "on that day (the day Moshe was to die) the trumpets were not used to gather the people, because Yehoshua had no authority over them. Even during the life of Moshe (on the last day of his life) they were permanently hidden away, because there is no authority on the day of death." The statement of *Rashi* that Yehoshua had no authority over the trumpets seems superfluous, in that Yehoshua was not yet the leader of Israel, and whether or not he would later have authority over the trumpets is irrelevant. Seemingly, *Rashi* needed only to say that Moshe lost his authority to use them on the day of his death.

It appears that the reason that Yehoshua never obtained authority over the trumpets is that even Moshe had no right to them on the last day of his life, and so Yehoshua, the heir, could not inherit what his master did not have at the time of his death. Similarly, in the case of the inheritance of property, the sons do not inherit what the father gave away or sanctified or abandoned before his death, even though he owned it all of his life.

The same applies to the inheritance of Torah and spiritual matters. We learn from this that the proper teacher one should seek out as a mentor and master is one who will retain his greatness in Torah and fear of Hashem his whole life. Even if during his old age he loses some of his earlier greatness, his stature is not diminished, as the Gemara says (*Berachos* 8b), "Be careful with the honor of an elderly scholar who has involuntarily forgotten his Torah learning, for we say [that the second set of] Tablets and the broken pieces of the first Tablets both rest in the Ark." But if he shows inconsistency in his dedication to Torah learning — for example, if he thinks there are other worthy topics to study (if his interest is not motivated by a desire to serve Hashem as was the case with *Rambam* and other Rishonim who did study natural sciences) — then there is no guarantee that he will remain as he is now for his whole life, and one should not choose him as a mentor.

❦ ❦ ❦

וַאֲדַבְּרָה בְאָזְנֵיהֶם־וְאָעִידָה בָּם אֶת־הַשָּׁמַיִם וְאֶת־הָאָרֶץ
— *and I shall speak these words into their ears, and call heaven and earth to bear witness against them* (31:28).

Rashi writes that although Hashem had already called heaven and earth to testify (see 30:19), the difference is that the previous verse was said to Israel, and now He came to say, "Give ear, O heavens." What *Rashi* means is that the earlier verse, which was said to Israel, instructed them to learn from the constancy of the heaven and the earth, which have never changed their characteristics. Although they have no free will, and are incapable of making choices, we are told to look at them and see that the command of Hashem is what created the universe, which stands forever as Hashem wills. As the verse states, *He issued a decree that will not change* (*Tehillim* 148:6), regarding the reliable constancy of the laws of nature. Therefore, we certainly should be as constant as they are, notwithstanding the added gift Hashem granted us of free will to disobey, because that was only given in order to increase our reward. The directive to the heavens and the earth is that they stand witness, because since they exist through the ages they have seen how the early generations fulfilled the

Torah, and they see how our spiritually orphaned generation fulfills the Torah. They saw what rebuke was necessary for the previous generations, and they see what rebuke we need today. When we consider these age-old witnesses, who weigh us against our predecessors, we too must compare ourselves with those that came before, and be inspired to turn our path to heed the Torah and *mitzvos* as our forefathers did.

❧ ❧ ❧

וַיְדַבֵּר מֹשֶׁה בְּאָזְנֵי כָּל־קְהַל יִשְׂרָאֵל אֶת־דִּבְרֵי הַשִּׁירָה הַזֹּאת עַד תֻּמָּם — *Moshe spoke the words of this song into the ears of the entire congregation of Israel, until their conclusion* (31:30).

The phrase *until their conclusion* is difficult to understand. How could one err and think that Moshe did not recite the entire song? What the verse means is not that he recited just the words alone, but that he provided an in-depth scrutiny of all the levels of meaning within it, for the Holy One, Blessed is He, instructed him to *teach it to the Bnei Yisrael, place it in their mouths.* This means to inculcate the deepest meanings of the Torah in their mouths, hearts, and intellects. Thus, the words *until their conclusion* refer not to a verbatim indoctrination, but instead to the deepest understanding of their meaning.

❧ ❧ ❧

פרשת האזינו
Parashas Ha'azinu

***HASHEM* — וַיְדַבֵּר ה' אֶל־מֹשֶׁה בְּעֶצֶם הַיּוֹם הַזֶּה לֵאמֹר**
spoke to Moshe on that very day, saying (32:48).

Rashi explains that the words used to describe the death of Moshe as having taken place *on that very day* imply that the event was intended to take place in broad daylight and in full view of all, despite threatened interference. *Rashi* notes two other places where this expression is used. One is in *Bereishis* (7:13), regarding Noach. The people of his generation said, "If he tries to go into the Ark, we will stop him and destroy the Ark." Hashem said, 'I will take him into the Ark in broad daylight and in full view, and no one will be able to stop him." The other is in *Shemos* (12:51), regarding the Exodus. The Egyptians said, "If they try to leave, we will stop them, and even take weapons and kill them." Hashem said, "I will take them out in broad daylight and in full view, and you will be powerless to stop them." Here too, *Bnei Yisrael* said, "If Moshe is taken away, we will stop him, for how can we lose our great leader?" Hashem said, "He will go in broad daylight and in full view, and no one will stop him." *Rashi,* however, does not cite the same phrase from *Bereishis* (17:26), where the Torah talks of the circumcision of Avraham! The reason is this: In the case of Avraham, there was no fear of interference, for why would anyone care what Avraham did to himself? The issue there, which Avraham discussed with Mamre (see *Bereishis Rabbah* 42:8 and 58:4), was whether Avraham should publicize his *mitzvah* of circumcision. If Avraham was known to be circumcised, while no one else had this *mitzvah,* logic would tell us that his ability to influence others to do their *mitzvos* and have faith in

Hashem would diminish. People would say that Avraham is fit to do *mitzvos*, because he was singled out for his greatness. "This," they would say, 'is why he must observe all the *mitzvos*, while common people like us can do as we please." The final decision made by Avraham and Mamre was to do the circumcision openly, for it is not for men to try to be wiser than the *mitzvos* of Hashem, but instead to fulfill them openly. They should not worry about any untoward effect, but instead should trust that their influence would not diminish. Even without these rationalizations, the main thing is not to try to be wiser than the *mitzvos*, but just to do them.

This is what *Chazal* meant when they say that Avraham did not fear those that ridiculed and criticized him. If meant literally, this would not be a great praise of Avraham, for even in our poor, spiritually orphaned generation there are people that disregard such cynics and critics. What they mean is that here, the cynics and critics came with a sanctimonious criticism, saying that Avraham will no longer be able to do as he did before, in drawing people away from idolatry and to Hashem, and so he would be ruining himself. Still, Avraham paid no attention to them, and did not hesitate to fulfill his *mitzvah* "in broad daylight," in a manner of speaking, with everyone's awareness.

This is meant to have halachic implications as well. We find that the *Rama* (*Orach Chaim* §1) states that "one should pay no attention to those that ridicule him" only in connection with the first *halachah* in *Orach Chaim,* which states that one should rise in the morning to go to prayers. This is because a person's critics could come forward with the sanctimonious claim that getting up so early will interfere with his concentration in learning during the day. Thus, the *Rama* states that one should ignore such criticism; if he feels that this will not harm him in his doing *mitzvos* and learning Torah, he should not be ashamed to do what he knows is right, even if his critics think they have pure motivations.

❈ ❈ ❈

עַל אֲשֶׁר מְעַלְתֶּם בִּי בְּתוֹךְ בְּנֵי יִשְׂרָאֵל . . . — *because you (Moshe) trespassed against Me among the Bnei Yisrael . . .* (32:51).

The word *trespassed* is the translation of the word *mi'altem,* from the word *me'ilah,* which means misuse, as the Gemara in *Me'ilah* states (18a). This indicates that Hashem considered what

Moshe had done to be an actual flaw or offense. Afterward, the Torah says that Moshe's error was that he *did not sanctify* Hashem, which means that he did not do as much as he could have. This is understandable, for the fact that striking the stone brought forth water was actually a great miracle that sanctifies Hashem's Name, and really it is difficult to understand what superiority speaking would have over striking. As far as the stone is concerned, it is all the same — speak or strike, water will not come out unless a miracle occurs. But the Torah says that by striking the rock, Moshe would have caused a greater sanctification. This is indeed a very small sin. How, then, can the Torah call this *me'ilah*?

We see from here that if a man is lazy, and does not do the good that he could have done, this is *me'ilah,* an active offense. We learn from here that every *ben Torah* who has the ability to learn more, either quantitatively or qualitatively, and is lazy and does not learn as he ought to, not only sins by not being what he could have been, but is also considered to have committed the active offense of *me'ilah*.

The same applies to developing positive character traits and learning to fear Hashem. Every person must grow every day. If he sees that he is not growing, he must feel as if he has sinned and has committed *me'ilah* against Hashem, since every person was created to honor Him. All a man's talents and abilities were given to him to enable him to become great in Torah and good deeds. If he does not grow because he is lazy, he has committed *me'ilah,* and abused the talents given him for the purposes of serving Hashem.

❦ ❦ ❦

פרשת וזאת הברכה
Parashas Vezos Haberachah

וַיִּקְבֹּר אֹתוֹ בַגַּי בְּאֶרֶץ מוֹאָב מוּל בֵּית פְּעוֹר ... — *And He buried him [Moshe] in the depression, in the land of Moav, opposite Beis-peor . . .* (34:6).

Rashi (based on *Sotah* 14a) explains that Moshe's grave was prepared in this particular location from the time of Creation in order to atone for the sin of *Peor*. [1]

What was so fundamentally unique about this sin that its atonement had to be arranged at the world's Creation? In what way did this sin differ from the Golden Calf and the sin of the spies?

At Peor the Jews practiced idolatry — which they knew to be a grievous sin — for the sole purpose of allowing them to fulfill their lustful desires. In certain respects, such behavior is even more reprehensible than sinning spitefully because of one's lack of belief in Hashem. In the latter case, the sinner is not violating any of his principles by sinning; in the former he is willing, for a small amount of pleasure or money, to forgo his beliefs, and we must thus question whether such a person has any integrity at all (see *Sanhedrin* 27a).

The existence of such sinners, whose desires can lead them to ignore the very truths they accept, poses a more serious challenge to the fulfillment of the Torah (which is the very purpose of Creation) than the existence of disbelievers. For while there will be those who worship idols and deny Hashem's existence, there will also be righteous men who believe in Him and observe His commandments. But if even those who

---

1. At Peor, the Jews worshiped the idol of Baal-peor to facilitate their engaging in immorality (see *Bamidbar* 25:1-9 and *Rashi* there).

are steadfast in their beliefs can be led to sin by their desires, there is never any guarantee that the Torah will always be fulfilled — for even explaining the error of their ways to such people will not necessarily prevent them from succumbing to their desires yet again.

It is for this reason that it was necessary for Hashem to agree, as it were, even as He was creating the universe [which was created predicated upon the Jews' accepting Torah and *mitzvos*], that even believers will sin; and He requires of such sinners that they involve themselves in the study of Torah, as an avenue for true atonement and repentance.

Thus, at Creation, when Hashem recognized that the universe could not exist if it were to be ruled by the Divine Attribute of Strict Justice, He created the grave of Moshe, to assist in the atonement and rehabilitation for those who believe in Him, yet sin because of their desires.